# SENECA: THE TRAGEDIES

# Complete Roman Drama in Translation

*David R. Slavitt and Palmer Bovie, Series Editors*

# SENECA:
# THE TRAGEDIES
## Volume II

EDITED BY

DAVID R. SLAVITT

THE JOHNS HOPKINS UNIVERSITY PRESS
Baltimore and London

*For Sonja and William Jay Smith*

The Johns Hopkins University Press
2715 North Charles Street
Baltimore, Maryland 21218-4319
The Johns Hopkins Press Ltd., London

Library of Congress Cataloging-in-Publication Data

Seneca, Lucius Annaeus, 4 B.C.–65 A.D.
    Seneca.

    (Complete Roman drama in translation)
    Contents: v. 1–2 The tragedies.
    1. Seneca, Lucius Annaeus, ca. 4 B.C.–65 A.D.—Translations into English.
2. Latin drama (Tragedy)—Translations into English.   3. Mythology, Classical—
Drama.   I. Slavitt, David R. 1935–      .   II. Title.   III. Series.
PA6666.A1    1992        882'.01          91-36347
ISBN 0-8018-4931-4 (alk. paper) (vol. 2)
ISBN 0-8018-4932-2 (pbk.) (vol. 2)

A catalog record for this book is available from the British Library.

# CONTENTS

v

# INTRODUCTION

## I

In 1543 Giambattista Giraldi Cinthio, the influential Italian play-wright, critic, and writer of *novelle* (from whom Shakespeare bor-rowed the plots of *Othello* and *Measure for Measure*), judiciously summarized the Renaissance view of Seneca's dramas: "In almost all his tragedies he surpassed (in as far as I can judge) all the Greeks who ever wrote—in wisdom, in gravity, in decorum, in majesty, and in memorable aphorism."

Renaissance criticism often employs vague and platitudinous language, but Cinthio's terms of praise are refreshingly exact. He asserts Seneca's preeminence among classical tragedians in five spe-cific areas: *wisdom* (the moral truth and importance of what is pre-sented), *gravity* (the integrity of tragic tone and vision), *decorum* (the appropriate consistency of language, character, action, and idea), *majesty* (the ability to create the imposing and sublime), and *memorable aphorism* (Cinthio's Italian term is *sentenze*, in the Eliz-abethan sense of *sententiae*, insightful and quotable maxims). Need-less to say, none of Cinthio's evaluative categories enjoys much criti-cal currency today (though whether their absence represents our age's gain remains an open question). Indeed, Cinthio himself has been largely forgotten except by Renaissance scholars, and yet his perspective on Seneca remains illuminating, because he was no academic antiquarian. He was a visionary artist-intellectual engaged in an imaginative enterprise beyond the scope and ambition of most writers—to recreate one of the central European literary genres, tragic theater, after a hiatus of nearly fifteen hundred years. Though Cinthio and his Italian contemporaries failed to compose enduring masterpieces, they decisively shaped the renascence of European

tragedy that culminated in Shakespeare, Corneille, and Racine, a
tradition they consciously grounded in Seneca.

Today Cinthio's high opinion appears perverse and ill-informed.
Seneca the tragedian is a forgotten author. The plays are never performed, rarely discussed, and hardly read, except by specialists. To
ascertain how low Seneca now stands in critical esteem requires no
great scholarly effort. A cursory examination of a few dozen histories
of theater or comprehensive dramatic anthologies will reveal the
little there is to know. If Seneca is mentioned at all in these general
surveys, he is never presented as an author whose plays have enduring intrinsic worth. He usually appears in a few sentences about his
historical influence on Renaissance tragedy. Among the many critical volumes that discuss the history or theory of tragedy, I have yet to
find one that affords Seneca serious, extended coverage. Nor have I
found a general anthology of drama that reprints one of Seneca's
tragedies. Even collections of classical drama or poetry rarely represent him. In part, Seneca's decline reflects the broader devaluation
of Roman literature over the past two centuries, but contemporary
critics and scholars have seemed especially eager to jettison him
wholesale from the classical canon. Bernard Knox's *Norton Book of
Classical Literature* (1993), for example, finds no space in its 864
pages for a single line of Seneca's verse or prose. (Knox also excludes
Seneca's eminent fellow Iberians, Martial and Lucan—crypto-
Hispanaphobia?) Although Seneca has had some champions among
modern classicists—notably Moses Hadas, John Fitch, and Frederick Ahl—he remains a marginal figure, even among specialists.
Elsewhere Seneca *tragicus* is less a dramatist than a footnote.

On those rare occasions when Seneca's plays are discussed outside of the classics department, one finds a standard set of indict-
ments. Herbert J. Muller's *The Spirit of Tragedy* (1956) presents the
conventional view of his dramatic *oeuvre:* "Almost all readers today
are struck by how crude his drama is, and how invincibly abominable his taste. It is hard to understand why for centuries Western
critics and poets had so high an admiration of Seneca, installing his
plays among the classics."

Muller's study, which is exceptional in affording Seneca a few
pages (and unique in devoting an entire paragraph to discussing an
actual text, the *Oedipus*), presents the material in a chapter entitled

"Greek Tragedy" under the subtitle "Epilogue: The Decline to
Seneca." Subtitle tells all. The Roman dramatist, he asserts, is "an
unconscious caricature of Greek tragedy." Muller gets so excited in
condemning Seneca that the complaints come out pell-mell. If one
liberally paraphrases and organizes his objections, we can list the
standard legal charges leveled against the ancient Iberian:

1.  Seneca is derivative and decadent. He borrows the formal conven-
    tions of Greek tragedy without capturing its essential spirit. His use of
    devices like the chorus no longer has dramatic meaning. He repre-
    sents aesthetic decline rather than meaningful innovation or renewal.
2.  Seneca is rhetorical rather than dramatic. His plays are full of oratori-
    cal declamation and aphoristic repartee rather than the economic
    unfolding of dramatic action. His verse is marred, to quote another
    critic, by "aphoristic obscurities and far-fetched allusions."
3.  Seneca's sensibility is lurid and violent. Seneca's chief innovation on
    his Greek models was to make them more graphic in their violence.
    Killings occur onstage. Characters describe gruesome and terrifying
    offstage events in dramatic set pieces.
4.  Seneca is technically incompetent as a dramatist. His plays lack "econ-
    omy, purity, symmetry, appropriateness of any sort." He is "in-
    different to form." The plays are shapeless displays of rhetoric and
    horror.
5.  Seneca's vision is ultimately not tragic, only terrifying. Seneca (and,
    according to Muller, all Romans) lacked "a tragic sense of life." There
    is no catharsis in Seneca, no pity and awe—just horror.

Muller's charges may sound excessive to anyone familiar with
Seneca's longstanding (if now long-vanished) popularity and influence on European literature. But to the average student of literature
the condemnation probably comes as good news. As David Slavitt
has remarked, "we live in a busy time with many distractions and
pressures, and it is a relief to be told that we may skip these plays."
Muller's charges, moreover, merely echo the Romantic assessment
of Seneca. In his lectures on drama, August Wilhelm von Schlegel
declared Seneca's tragedies "beyond all description bombastic and
frigid, utterly devoid of nature in character and action, full of the
most revolting violations of propriety." G. W. F. Hegel referred to
Seneca's plays as "dramatic failures." Friedrich Nietzsche, a classicist by training, mentioned him not at all in his many discussions of

tragedy. By the beginning of the twentieth century Seneca had ceased to exist for both critics and readers as a living presence in the tradition of European tragedy. Meanwhile, for classical scholars he became more interesting as a set of textual problems to unravel than as an artist deserving advocacy. Discriminating literary critics were properly concerned, to use George Steiner's terms from *The Death of Tragedy,* with "the genius of Greek tragedy" and not "its inferior Latin version."

## II

Giraldi Cinthio was not alone in admiring Seneca. For over fifteen hundred years no classical author except Virgil enjoyed more esteem than Seneca. (Virgil had the unbeatable advantage, in the view of medieval readers, of divine inspiration: in his fourth *Eclogue* he was generally believed to have predicted Christ's birth.) Along with Cicero, Horace, and Ovid, as well as Aristotle and Homer in Latin translation, Seneca was an indispensable author. The early Church Fathers, anxious to save the best classical literature, found him greatly to their liking, largely for the same reasons Cinthio celebrated a millennium later—his moral seriousness, decorous style, imaginative sweep, and exceptionally quotable *sententiae.* The Iberian's Stoic philosophy neatly corresponded to the austere puritanism of early Christianity. Stern Tertullian affectionately called him "our Seneca." Saint Jerome went even further. He suggested that Seneca deserved sainthood, an unusual honor, to say the least, for the pagan who had tutored the Emperor Nero. (Jerome's enthusiasm had been fanned by reading inspirational correspondence between Seneca and Saint Paul, which was later revealed to be a pious forgery.) Seneca's work, especially his essays and epistles, became part of medieval Catholic culture.

As long as Latin remained the central language in European learning, Seneca occupied an eminent position in literature. Erasmus produced the first critical edition of his work. Calvin's first publication was a commentary on *De Clementia.* Montaigne listed Seneca and Plutarch as his favorite reading, and he quotes the Iberian more than any author except Plato. Scaliger preferred him to Euripides. Dante and Chaucer praised his skillful rhetoric and stoic morality. Petrarch wrote him an epistle as an ideal spiritual companion. Queen Elizabeth I admired his "wholesome advisings." Meanwhile her subject Ben Jonson inscribed Seneca's motto *"tanquam explorator"* ("as an explorer") on the title page of his books. Jonson was not the only explorer inspired by the philosopher poet. In the margins of the family copy of Seneca's tragedies Christopher Columbus's son Ferdinand wrote that his father had fulfilled the poet's prophesy that a later age would find a land beyond Thule, the boundary of the Roman known world.

If the Middle Ages prized Seneca the philosopher, the Renaissance found transforming inspiration in the dramatist. Seneca stands, without any serious rival, as the most important influence on Renaissance tragedy, not only in English, but also in Italian, French, and Spanish. He was, first of all, the only classical tragedian whom most writers could savor in the original. The early Renaissance barely knew Greek literature and even then mainly in Latin translation. Seneca, however, was avidly studied and performed in grammar schools, seminaries, legal academies, and universities. Latin remained Western Europe's spoken and written language of instruction, even in Protestant northern Europe. Seneca's stoic tragedies, full of stirring rhetoric and striking *sententiae*, were a schoolmaster's dream (just as their violent plots and noble sentiments were surely a schoolboy's delight). At the Rotherham School near Sheffield, weekly lessons in Shakespeare's time consisted of two afternoons of Horace and two afternoons of Seneca's tragedies, which the students translated into English. There was no more engrossing way to perfect a student's Latin than by reading, memorizing, and reciting the plays of Seneca, Plautus, and Terence. Latin drama also served a ceremonial and financial function; schools presented plays as public entertainments for their patrons. Seneca was performed at the Inns of Court, Oxford, and Cambridge. The University of Salamanca had a statute mandating that a comedy by Plautus or Terence be presented on Corpus Christi. Jesuit schools organized performances to attract and recruit young intellectuals to their order.

In his native Spain, Seneca (and Cinthio's Senecan adaptations) became the classical models with which dramatists like Juan de la Cueva and Cristóbal de Virtués tried to discipline the vital but unruly popular theater. If the Iberian's example of intensifying drama through classical form and compression proved only intermittently influential, the stunning sensationalism of his plots made a lasting impression. His latter-day countrymen outdid him in devising spectacular revenges, horrifying ghosts, inspiring declamations, and lurid pageants of seduction, rape, incest, and murder. Miguel de Cervantes displayed more restraint in his classical tragedy, *El cerco de Numancia* (*The Siege of Numantia*, c. 1580), but he, too, used Seneca as a model.

Less rooted in the economics of popular theater than the Spanish stage, French drama quickly assimilated the formal principles of classical tragedy. The French knew some Greek tragedy from the Latin translations of Erasmus and others, but in France, too, Seneca remained the most accessible model. French theater observed the classical unities of time, place, and action as well as the restrictions against comedy and low diction longer than any other tradition. For better and worse, Seneca remained a model for French tragedy from early plays like La Péruse's *Médée* (1553), a direct adaptation of Seneca's *Medea*, to neoclassical masterpieces like Pierre Corneille's *Médée* (1635) and Jean Racine's *Andromaque* (1667) and *Phèdre* (1677). As George Saintsbury observed, Seneca's influence pervaded French tragic theater, "from Jodelle, through Garnier and Montchrestien and even Hardy, through Corneille and Racine and Voltaire, leaving his traces even on Victor Hugo."

The sheer volume of Renaissance translations, adaptations, and imitations attest to Seneca's preeminent popularity. He was the first classical poet to be translated *in toto* into English. The Jesuit Jasper Heywood, who called Seneca "the flowre of all writers," published his free adaptation of *Troas* in 1559, followed by increasingly more faithful versions of *Thyestes* (1560) and *Hercules Furens* (1561). Other eager Elizabethan translators soon followed. By 1581 Thomas Newton was able to collect Seneca's *Tenne Tragedies* in one volume. (At that time only one Greek tragedy was available in English, a 1566 version of Euripides' *Phoenissae* translated from an Italian Senecan adaptation and retitled *Jocasta;* it remained the only Greek translation until the next century.) Seneca's plays became the model for both the traditions of English tragedy—the courtly dramas of Samuel Daniel and Fulke Greville, sponsored by the learned Countess of Pembroke, and the popular theater of Thomas Kyd and Christopher Marlowe. *Gorboduc* (1562), the first blank verse tragedy, imitated Seneca, but it was Kyd's *The Spanish Tragedy* (c. 1585) that first made the Senecan conventions come alive in English.

It would be difficult to overstate the influence of Seneca on Elizabethan tragedy. English dramatists absorbed him from every side—directly from the Latin, from French and Italian adaptations, and from Newton's popular *Tenne Tragedies*. Thomas Nash, like most learned Elizabethans, deplored writers who could not read the Latin classics in the original and "feed on nought but the crummes that fal from the translators trencher," but in 1589 even he recognized the inspirational impact these translations had on his contemporaries: "Yet English *Seneca* read by candle light yeeldes manie good sentences. . . . and if you intreate him faire in a frostie morning, he will affoord you whole *Hamlets*, I should say handfulls of tragical speeches."

Seneca provided the formal pattern for Elizabethan tragedy. He gave Tudor playwrights the five-act structure to frame the dramatic action with a beginning, middle, and end (rather than the episodic form of most medieval drama). He introduced a cast of helpful secondary characters to keep the narrative moving: the messenger to report important (and usually violent) off-stage events, the female confidante to elicit private thoughts from the heroine, the loyal friend or servant to listen to and advise the hero, as well as a decidedly un-Athenian version of a chorus that moralizes on events but never participates in them. Seneca also introduced the catalyzing figure of the ghost who returns from death to provoke revenge. The classical stature of Seneca's tragedies also gave the Elizabethans permission to use violent and sensational plots featuring murder, suicide, adultery, incest, trickery, insanity, and vengeance. All of these attributes came together in the most influential Senecan contribution to English drama—the revenge tragedy. Modeled mostly on Seneca's *Thyestes*, these "tragedies of blood" combined violence, intrigue, and constant psychological tension. Is it any wonder they became the most popular genre of the Elizabethan stage? Senecan revenge tragedy gave shape not only to Kyd's crowd-pleasing *Spanish Tragedy* and Tourneur's adorably lurid *Revenger's Tragedy* but also to Shakespeare's innovative psychological drama, *Hamlet*.

Seneca's other contribution to English tragedy was magnificent language. He showed playwrights the lofty alternatives to the drab verse of earlier drama. In style as in subject matter, Seneca is the poet of extremes. His verse is never better than when at its most expansive or its most concise. His extended, emotional speeches, in which the language and the passions build to explosive levels, dazzled the word-drunk Elizabethans. If Seneca's dramatic orations, with their sonorous allusions, musical syntax, and dizzy rhetorical turns, encouraged hurricanes of theatrical bombast, they also demonstrated how mixing the techniques of poetry and oratory could create dramatic verse of powerful eloquence. To understand how Seneca's great speeches sound in Latin, an English-speaker need go no further than Elizabethans like Marlowe who patterned their dramatic verse after his high tragic style:

> If all the pens that ever poets held
> Had fed the feeling of their masters' thoughts,
> And every sweetness that inspired their hearts,
> Their minds, and muses on admired themes;
> If all the heavenly quintessence they still
> From their immortal flowers of poesy,
> Wherein, as in a mirror, we perceive
> The highest reaches of a human wit;
> If these had made one poem's period,
> And all combined in beauty's worthiness,
> Yet should there hover in their restless heads
> One thought, one grace, one wonder, at the least,
> Which into words no virtue can digest.

This passage from *Tamburlaine the Great* displays the lush, declamatory, hyperbolic language of Senecan drama. The characters in tragedy do not lead quotidian lives. They suffer the extremities of ambition, lust, horror, pain, and remorse, and they require speech capable of carrying their extraordinary burdens. The syntax is often overtly rhetorical, as when Marlowe piles one hypothetical phrase on another, and the phrasing is often pointed, as in the calculated and balanced alliterations in key lines, but the total effect is poetic.

Renaissance playwrights also learned from Seneca the theatrical impact of brevity. Ingenious one-liners are not a conspicuous feature of folk drama; striking aphorism is, however, the trademark of Seneca's theatrical language. Lapidary *sententiae* end major speeches, announce turning points in soliloquies, and add edge to important conversations. Seneca handled the traditional Greek technique of stichomythia (verse dialogue in which characters trade one-line repartees) with unsurpassed brilliance. Seneca has had many detractors, but no one has ever questioned his genius for aphorism.

It is no accident that the *sententia* is a characteristic Roman form. Latin is the ideal medium for epigram. It is an extremely economical language. Since Latin is an inflected language, in which the endings of words signal their grammatical functions, most prepositions and auxiliary verbs are unnecessary. It also lacks articles. Consequently, Latin can say something in about half the words English would require. Word order is also almost entirely flexible, so a poet can freely arrange the language to achieve the maximum musical and semantic effect. If poetry depends on language being used in the most concise, expressive, and memorable way, the advantages of *lingua Latina* are self-evident.

Seneca's fellow Iberian, Martial, became the greatest epigrammatic poet in European literature, but Seneca had little interest in the epigram as an independent literary form. In both his verse and his prose he used it as a means of punctuating and intensifying longer works. His prose is celebrated for its quotable maxims:

> There is no great genius without some touch of madness.

> It is not the man who has too little, but the man who craves more, that is poor.

> The best ideas are common property.

> What nature requires is obtainable, and within easy reach. It's for the superfluous we sweat.

His verse epigrams, however, show even greater compression. Seneca carefully matches his syntax to his meter, making the aphoristic sentence fit exactly into a single line of verse (a trick far less common in Latin poetry than an English-speaker would imagine). His pointed lines have the brevity, clarity, balance, and polish characteristic of the form.

*Curae leves locuuntur, ingentes stupent.*
[Light griefs speak easily, the great ones are struck dumb.]

*Prima quae vitam dedit hora, carpit.*
[The first hour that gave life also began to take it away.]

The difficulty in translating these *sententiae* is evident in the wordy, literal paraphrases. The Latin is so compact and evocative that to make them seem idiomatic in English, one usually adds words that are not in the Latin. To the Elizabethans this was an artistic challenge to pursue. Scholars like John Cunliffe and E. F. Watling have traced Senecan quotations through Elizabethan literature. One can follow a single Seneca *sententia* through half a dozen English poets. In the *Agamemnon* Seneca penned a resonant line about how one crime leads to another:

*Per scelera semper sceleribus tutum est iter.*
[The safe journey through crimes is always by more crimes.]

In 1566 John Studley translated this line as a slightly limp fourteener:

The safest path to mischiefe is by mischiefe open still.

For the next half-century Seneca's line echoed across the English stage:

The safest passage is from bad to worse.
(Thomas Hughes, *The Misfortunes of Arthur*)

Black deed only through black deed safely flies.
(John Marston, *The Malcontent*)

Things bad begun make strong themselves by ill.
(William Shakespeare, *Macbeth*)

Small mischiefs are by greater made secure.
(John Webster, *The White Devil*)

One deadly sin, then, help to cure another.
(John Massinger, *Duke of Milan*)

In his *Catiline*, however, Ben Jonson, the best Latinist of them all, admitted defeat and let his version run over the line break:

The ills that I have done cannot be safe
But by attempting greater.

It would be misleading, however, to suggest that it was merely
the form of Seneca's language that fascinated Renaissance writers. In
epigram more than in any other literary form, style and substance
are inseparable. The dark, worldly fatalism of Seneca, his admission
of the wildest passions, his heady mixture of intellect and emotion all
came over into modern European literature along with the poetic
language and dramatic forms that embodied them.

Seneca demonstrates a particular gift for creating epigrammatic
dialogue. His stichomythia usually interlocks each line with the next
by repeating key words or ideas, usually with an ironic twist. When
Lycus and Megara argue over Hercules' heroism in *Hercules Furens*, they spar verbally in antithetical epigrams. In his 1927 essay
"Seneca in Elizabethan Translation," which remains the most profound modern defense of the tragedian (as well as the last time a
major English-language writer discussed Seneca at any length), T. S.
Eliot half-heartedly praised Seneca's dialogue as "an effective stage
trick," but then he added thoughtfully, "it is something more; it is
the crossing of one rhythm pattern with another." Renaissance tragedians admired Seneca's technique. One hears it in Kyd, Marlowe,
Jonson, and Shakespeare. Here is an exchange from the greatest
English Senecan play, *Hamlet:*

HAMLET: Now, mother, what's the matter?

QUEEN: Hamlet, thou hast thy father much offended.

HAMLET: Mother, you have my father much offended.

QUEEN: Come, come, you answer with an idle tongue.

HAMLET: Go, go, you question with a wicked tongue.

The careful shaping and compression of speech into formal
patterns exercised immense influence on European dramatic poets.
In England, Seneca's expansive and epigrammatic style helped determine the development of blank verse. Eliot considered Seneca
crucial to the Elizabethan sense of dramatic poetry: "The art of
dramatic language, we must remember, is as near to oratory as to
ordinary speech or to other poetry. If the Elizabethans distorted and
travestied Seneca in some ways . . . they also learned from him the
essentials of declaimed verse."

Ironically, it was only in Italy, where the Senecan revival had begun, that no tragic theater emerged comparable to the traditions of England, France, and Spain. Today the influential Italian playwrights of the mid-sixteenth century, like Cinthio and Ludovico Dolce, survive mainly as figures of literary history. The failure of Renaissance Italy to develop a national theater has fascinated critics, and many complex theories have been offered in explanation. Surely near the heart of the problem, however, lurks Seneca.

Italian tragedy was the creation of self-conscious intellectuals cut off from a viable tradition of popular theater. They tried to recreate classical tragedy for a sophisticated audience of nobles, courtiers, and intelligentsia. Choosing Seneca as a model, however, they began to exploit the stylized and lyric elements of drama at the expense of its narrative and realistic features. From the beginning, Cinthio and Dolce incorporated *intermedi* (music, madrigals, and choruses) between the acts. Within fifty years Italian artists had developed the ritual and lyric potentials of the Senecan aesthetic to their logical end—opera. In 1597 the first opera, *Dafne*, was produced by three members of the Florentine *camerata*, a coterie of poets, musicians, aristocrats, and intellectuals. By 1607, when Claudio Monteverdi premiered his *Orfeo*, opera had found its first genius. His final work, *L'incoronazione di Poppea* (*The Coronation of Poppea*, 1642), became opera's first incontestable masterpiece. Not coincidentally it tells the same story as the pseudo-Senecan play, *Octavia*, and Seneca himself is one of the major characters. If opera eventually became Italy's true tragic theater, the new art form owed as much to Seneca as to its professed model, Greek tragedy. Indeed the dark masterpieces of Italian Romantic lyric tragedy by Donizetti, Bellini, and Verdi not only share a common dramatic aesthetic with Seneca; they also provide the best analogy for a modern audience as to how Roman tragedy achieves its emotional effects. Three centuries after Cinthio's death, his dream of recreating the grave majesty of Seneca's tragedies had become a reality—not in the theaters of Italy but in its opera houses.

## III

Lucius Annaeus Seneca was born in 4 B.C. in the southern Spanish city of Cordova, into a family of equestrian rank, immense wealth, and intellectual distinction. His father, Lucius Annaeus Seneca the Elder (often known as Seneca the Rhetorician, to distinguish him from his more famous son), was an influential author in his own right. He wrote a now-lost history of Rome, but his most celebrated works were two treatises on rhetoric, *Controversiae (Debates)* in ten books and *Suasoriae (Persuasive Arguments)* in two books, both of which survive in fragmentary form. It is hard for contemporary readers to understand the cultural importance of these books. Rhetoric was the basis of Roman education. Boys preparing for either public or intellectual life pursued a curriculum of rhetorical study, which included logic, moral philosophy, literature, memory training, oratory, and expository writing. A famous rhetorician like Seneca the Elder, therefore, commanded the sort of intellectual and social authority in Rome that today we might associate with a millionaire president of an Ivy League university who had also won the Nobel Prize in economics. Today Seneca the Elder's treatises survive mainly for their documentary value on Roman education, but for centuries they fascinated European writers, educators, and politicians. Montaigne cites them approvingly, and as late as the early seventeenth century, both Ben Jonson and Blaise Pascal could quote them with the expectation that their audiences would recognize the citation.

Each of Seneca the Elder's children was in some way remarkable. His oldest son, Annaeus Novatus, became proconsul of Achaia, the Roman governor of Southern Greece. A sensible but aloof man, he was careful to stay out of local religious squabbles. He appears under his adopted name, Junius Gallio, in the Acts of the Apostles (18:12–16) when Athenian Jews charged Saint Paul with blasphemy. Refusing to punish Paul unless the synagogue elders could demonstrate some crime beyond disagreeable opinions, Gallio watched indifferently as the Greek crowd suddenly beat up Paul's accusers. (How annoying it must have been to a worldly Roman to govern the argumentative zealots of these ardent Asiatic cults.) The youngest son, Annaeus Mela, concentrated his energy on increasing the considerable family fortune. He eventually became the agent who managed much of Nero's business. More important, Mela raised a son named Marcus Annaeus Lucanus, whom posterity remembers as Lucan, Rome's last great epic poet. His historical poem, *De Bello Civili* (*On the Civil War*), sometimes called *Pharsalia*, chronicled the war between Caesar and Pompey. Lucan's youthful fame made Nero, who fancied himself Rome's greatest poet, actor, musician, and charioteer, so wildly jealous that the emperor forbade him from reciting or publishing his poems. Our Latinless age no longer reads Lucan, but his former stature among European poets is demonstrated by Dante. In Canto IV of the *Inferno*, Virgil's ghost is met in Limbo by the shades of four great poets—Homer, Horace, Ovid, and Lucan—who, with Virgil ("*l'altissimo poeta*," the highest poet) constitute Dante's nominees for the greatest poets of antiquity. Seneca the Elder, Seneca the Younger, and Lucan represent an extraordinary constellation of talent. Has any other family produced three such distinguished writers in three successive generations? The achievement seems unique. There was little chance for a fourth generation. In A.D. 65 all three brothers and the twenty-six-year-old Lucan died by suicide in the aftermath of Piso's failed conspiracy against Nero's life.

The accomplishments of Seneca the Elder's middle son, Lucius Annaeus, however, take precedence in this distinguished clan. He became a major figure in drama, philosophy, and politics while amassing one of the greatest fortunes in the Roman world. As was the custom in his family, Seneca was brought to Rome as an infant. He studied Stoic and Pythagorean philosophy. Despite the slurs on his character by partisan contemporaries, Seneca appears to have had a sober, disciplined, and introspective character linked with a pragmatic and politic mind. Drawn to ideological purism, he had too much common sense and sociability to become an extremist. One incident from Seneca's youth illustrates the two sides of his character. Excited by Pythagoreanism, Seneca became a strict vegetarian. When the elder Seneca discovered his son's new enthusiasm, he warned him of the liabilities in public life of becoming known as an eccentric. His son accepted the advice.

Like many writers, Seneca was a sickly youth. At one point his health was so bad he considered suicide but held back out of consideration for his aged father. The young Seneca traveled for his health to Egypt, to visit his aunt, who was married to the prefect. When he returned to Rome, he worked with conspicuous success in several areas—politics, law, teaching, and literature. First he gained the junior senatorial office of *quaestor* (magistrate) and then became *tribunus plebis* (public advocate). These positions were the traditional starting points for an important political career. He grew famous for his persuasive addresses in the Senate and his sharp, memorable writing. The Greek historian Dio Cassius attests that Caligula envied Seneca's eloquence and planned to execute him, but his advisors assured the emperor that the philosopher would soon die of consumption. Learning of Caligula's designs, Seneca took the hint and retired from public life. (No one knows when Seneca wrote most of his plays and philosophical treatises, but one assumes that, like many out-of-power politicians, this active man did not waste his recurrent periods of enforced leisure.)

After the demented Caligula died at the hands of the Praetorian guard in A.D. 41, the moderate but erratic Claudius assumed the throne. By now the Republican institutions of pre-imperial Rome had been mostly corrupted or destroyed under the first four Caesars. Assassination, coerced suicide, and exile had decimated the patrician class. The integrity and authority of the Senate had eroded. Rome was the administrative and financial center for a vast empire of sixty million souls, where immense fortunes and sumptuous luxuries were available to those sufficiently clever, aggressive, or ruthless. In this venal and unstable environment, Seneca returned to public life.

Seneca's reentry into politics was short and disastrous. Within the year, he somehow became involved in the vicious power struggles of the Claudian house. Accused of adultery with a member of the royal family, he was exiled to mountainous and lawless Corsica (*Corsica terribilis*, he called it in a poem). During his hard, eight-year exile, Seneca lost both wife and son. He filled the years of grief and isolation, however, by writing some of his most influential philosophical works—two of his three surviving "consolations" (eloquent Stoic essays on death and bereavement) and probably *De Ira* (*On Anger*), a treatise on controlling the emotions.

Today few people read these erstwhile classics. They have little to offer the academic student of philosophy. Although early Stoics were rigidly systematic, Seneca is mostly unconcerned with philosophical systems. He belongs to that antiquated and discredited trade called moral philosophy. Undoubtedly, he studied the epistemology and cosmology of the Stoa, but he shows little interest in the ontology of knowledge. Closer to Montaigne and Marcus Aurelius than to Plato or Aristotle, Seneca the philosopher writes as a candid and reflective man obsessed with the question of how the average thinking person leads a good and happy life in the face of pain, uncertainty, and death. His vision of philosophy is relentlessly practical. For Seneca, philosophy meant trying to live correctly and honestly by means of reason. If Seneca hardly ranks as a major philosopher, he remains Stoicism's most eloquent apologist and perhaps Europe's first great essayist. Posterity prized his lucid, concise, and eminently quotable prose. In the Middle Ages whole anthologies were devoted to *sententiae* from Seneca's lapidary Latin. Elizabethan schoolboys memorized his maxims. A glovemaker's son from Stratford, for instance, remembered Seneca's pithy *"Tanta stultitia mortalium est"* and translated it quite literally as "what fools these mortals be."

In A.D. 48 Messalina, Claudius's wife, outraged Rome by bigamously marrying her lover. The uxorious Claudius could not bring himself to punish Messalina, but his advisors sent the Praetorian guard to kill her. Claudius heard the news at table and went on with his meal. The compliant emperor was soon pushed into an incestuous marriage with his niece, the crafty, iron-willed Agrippina. Foremost among the new empress's ambitions was that her son, Lucius Domitius Ahenobarbus, be designated heir to the throne. When Claudius finally adopted him in A.D. 50, the boy assumed the old Claudian family name by which he is remembered—Nero. Agrippina needed a capable mentor for her talented son. She also wanted to create public good will for the boy. She successfully maneuvered to recall the widely respected Seneca from Corsica to serve as twelve-year-old Nero's private tutor. She also secured him the position of *praetor* (one of the twelve high officials who administered public justice and managed the large government bureaus). Agrippina assumed that Seneca, no friend to Claudius, who had banished him, would prove a grateful ally.

Returning to Rome, Seneca found himself at the center of political power. For the next thirteen years he would be one of the most powerful men in the empire. Meanwhile Agrippina worked to place her son on the throne. In A.D. 54 Agrippina fed Claudius poisoned mushrooms. He did not die at once, so his wife administered a second dose, possibly, Suetonius reports, by means of an enema. Claudius's popular son, Britannicus, was kept in the palace to console the grieving widow while Nero was quickly spirited by the general Sextus Afranius Burrus to the camp of the Praetorian guards. When Burrus announced Claudius's death, the guards asked for Britannicus, but they knew their general wanted Nero. After Nero promised them generous gifts, the guards proclaimed him *imperator*. Shortly thereafter Britannicus died of poisoning (personally administered, Suetonius reports, by Nero).

Although the teenaged Nero was now emperor, an uneasy coalition of Seneca, Burrus, and Agrippina ruled Rome. Seneca became the *de facto* prime minister while Burrus handled military affairs, and Agrippina pursued her assorted intrigues. For the first five years this arrangement worked well. Seneca and Burrus kept Nero on a moderate course. Half a century later the emperor Trajan called this period the best governed in the history of imperial Rome. Seneca also became the first political speechwriter on record. He penned Nero's eloquent eulogy for Claudius. Old timers were shocked—the earlier Caesars had all been magnificent orators. The new emperor was different in other ways, too. He was an aesthete devoted, Tacitus reports not altogether approvingly, to sculpture, painting, poetry, singing, and riding. Seneca did his best to direct and amuse the temperamental young emperor. After Claudius was posthumously declared a god, Seneca wrote a ribald, cruel, and only intermittently funny satire, the *Apocolocyntosis* (the *Pumpkinification*), in which the bumbling Claudius arrives in heaven, seeking to become a god, only to be sent to Hades where, after much ungentle buffoonery, he ends up as a minor bureaucrat. (There may have been a later section, since lost, in which the emperor metamorphoses into a pumpkin— hence the title.) This grotesque burlesque has not added luster to Seneca's reputation.

As Nero grew older, he escaped Seneca's control. From the remarks of Tacitus, Suetonius, and Dio Cassius, we can intuit the many compromises Seneca accepted to maintain his slipping moral influence. Once again we see the conflict at the heart of Seneca's character. He was austere and noble minded; he was also cannily practical. He wrote Nero his great epistolary essays *De Vita Beata* (*On the Happy Life*), *De Clementia* (*On Clemency*), and *De Beneficiis* (*On Benefits*), classic statements of the Stoic world-view. But Seneca also provided Nero with less-attractive guidance. After Nero spectacularly bungled the murder of his mother (in a specially constructed boat that fell apart and sank when secret lead weights were dropped), he sent for Seneca and Burrus in the middle of the night for emergency advice. They were shocked but realistic enough to know that Nero was not going to be talked out of completing the murder. They held their noses and helped finish the job. Tacitus claims that Seneca even wrote Nero's self-serving letter to the Senate justifying the murder on the political grounds that Agrippina had tried to become co-ruler.

Caught in this murderous web of court intrigue, Seneca watched as Nero's reign degenerated into a bizarre spectacle of political violence, sexual excess, and artistic buffoonery. He and Burrus tried to curb each of Nero's new manias—from chariot racing to courtesans. Posterity has not judged Seneca's later years with Nero gently. He and Burrus did what was necessary to maintain their influence. The Roman mind was ruthlessly pragmatic. Even as he sank into moral compromise, Seneca probably saw himself effecting public good by keeping away the gang of pimps, charioteers, actors, gamblers, eunuchs, and dancers who served as Nero's other confidantes. Seneca's detractors rarely point out that his moral treatises are full of self-critical confessions that his own conduct falls short of his ideals. As Michael Grant observes, "struggling with ill-health and confronted by all the perils that contemporary court and society had to offer, he did at least always try to accept the least of possible evils."

Seneca eventually became too deeply involved in Nero's regime to escape the corruptions of power. If his enemy Suillius can be believed, Seneca's consolation came less from philosophy than from wealth; he reportedly appropriated the estates of people who died childless. There were also vague accusations of usury and extortion (directed mostly at his brother Mela). Tacitus implies, however, that the bulk of his wealth came as gifts from Nero. By whatever means, Seneca amassed a huge estate. His houses and gardens surpassed the emperor's. He owned the finest vineyards in Italy. When Burrus died (possibly by poison) in A.D. 62, Seneca tried to retire from politics. He offered Nero most of his property, but the emperor refused his resignation. Seneca nonetheless dismissed his retinue, renounced his extravagant public trappings, moved into the country, and avoided Rome.

With Burrus dead and Seneca departed from court, Nero had nothing to stop his plots and passions. He ordered assassinations on the slightest pretext and intrigued to marry his beautiful and vicious mistress, Poppaea. He divorced his conspicuously virtuous wife, Octavia (the daughter of Claudius), on the grounds of barrenness; later he had her executed on overtly false charges of adultery with a slave. (This incident provides the plot of the fascinating pseudo-Senecan play *Octavia*, the earliest surviving European play about current political events.) Nero was devoted to Poppaea, but one day, pregnant and ill, she complained when he came home late from the races. Losing his temper, he kicked her to death. Nero's love was no protection from Nero's anger.

Nero also loved Seneca. Having lost his natural father at three, the future emperor had a turbulent and insecure childhood dominated by Agrippina's obsessive affection (which, Tacitus believed, eventually became incestuous). Nero had no love for his stepfather, Claudius; but, just as his mother was settling into her loveless imperial alliance, Nero met Seneca. Tacitus claims that Nero was ten; Suetonius puts him at twelve. In either case the sensitive and unstable boy fell under the powerful influence of the nurturing older male who would guide him into adulthood. Seneca was brilliant, worldly, creative, and idealistic—a potent combination for an impressionable youth. Freud maintained that our superegos are formed mostly by our parents' moral values. Seneca, I suspect, became Nero's superego, his ethical conscience. Even as Nero sank into extravagant vice, he held on to Seneca as his closest counselor. Seneca represented parts of Nero's self-image that the emperor was loath to abandon entirely—at least outwardly. Nero's disreputable retinue hated the philosopher-poet. They filled the emperor's ears with rumors and accusations. But there is no persuasive evidence that the student turned decisively against his tutor, until the Pisonian conspiracy plunged Nero into a murderous fright. Only when Nero believed, perhaps wrongly, that the foster father on whom he had showered wealth and power had betrayed him did he turn murderous.

In A.D. 65 a group of politicians and military officers formed a plot to assassinate Nero. They secretly selected the handsome and affable patrician Gaius Calpurnius Piso as Nero's replacement. The morning of the assassination, however, a conspirator's servant informed Nero. As the size of the conspiracy became apparent, Nero panicked. Surrounding himself with guards and toadies, he embarked on a vast and bloody program of revenge. Lucan was almost certainly involved in the conspiracy. The poet whom Nero had silenced died defiantly in the grand style. Cutting his veins, he recited a stirring passage from the *Pharsalia* about a dying soldier. The entire Annaeus clan, however, was now doomed. (Also murdered in the aftermath was Petronius Arbiter, author of the first European novel, the *Satyricon*). Seneca's death, however, was the most famous consequence of Nero's campaign. Described at length by Tacitus in his *Annals*, Seneca's suicide became the Roman equivalent of Socrates' death in Athens.

Nero sent a colonel of the imperial bodyguards to Seneca's villa to accuse the philosopher of complicity in the conspiracy. Seneca sent back an aloof rebuttal. Nero then dispatched his troops to compel Seneca to suicide. He was not allowed to make a will. According to Tacitus, Seneca turned to his friends and said, "Being forbidden . . . to show gratitude for your services, I leave you my one remaining possession, and my best: the pattern of my life."

He ended saying loudly enough for Nero's troops to hear, "After murdering his mother and brother, it only remained for him to kill his teacher and tutor." Seneca cut his wrists, but his body was so lean from his austere life that he didn't bleed sufficiently. He then drank a cup of hemlock, but it did not act fast enough. He was placed in a warm bath and then taken into a steam bath where he suffocated. He was, according to his own instructions, cremated without ceremony.

Three years later, with Gaul and Spain in revolt, Galba's army marching on Rome, and the Senate voting on the emperor's execution, the terrified Nero fled to a house outside the capital. Lacking the courage to commit suicide, he asked his attendants to set him an example by killing themselves. When they refused, he begged his secretary to help him cut his own throat before troops arrived to arrest him. "How ugly and vulgar my life has become," he moaned. The last emperor of the Julian line bled to death on a squalid couch surrounded by disgusted servants. Hearing the news, Galba proclaimed himself emperor. As Seneca had observed, "however many people a tyrant slaughters, he cannot kill his successor."

IV

Seneca was the first great Latin writer to spend his adult life in a totalitarian state. He had no personal memories of the Republic. The "Golden Age" of Augustus had ended during his adolescence. His Rome was the autocracy of Tiberius, Caligula, Claudius, and Nero, where political power superseded law, morality, and tradition. Seneca's character was rooted in the austere, rural disciplines of the early Republic, but he lived mostly in a decadent, imperial capital. Beyond the familiar spectacles of gladiatorial butchery and official corruption, Seneca's Rome saw a race horse proclaimed consul, pimps serve as state counselors, and a mad emperor deify himself. Political succession consisted of assassination and military coup d'état. Public reformers who were not skilled opportunists were mostly killed or exiled. "If only the Roman people had a single neck," lamented Caligula. Roman artists and intellectuals still assiduously emulated the Greeks, but the capital's ruling class mostly behaved like army officers in a Latin American police state. This polluted milieu colored Seneca's artistic vision as decisively as Athenian democracy shaped Aeschylus's dramaturgy. If, as David Slavitt has suggested, Seneca's tragedies concern "the limits of the cruelty men and women can visit upon one another," his Rome gave an honest author few other topics.

Since the little attention Seneca receives today comes from classicists, he is habitually examined in relation to the Greeks. But these conventional comparisons obscure his true character, as indeed they distort the understanding of most Roman literature. It is more illuminating to compare Seneca to twentieth-century writers, not only to dramatists like Antonin Artaud, but to the poets of the modern totalitarian state, like Osip Mandelstam, Anna Akhmatova,

Marina Tsvetayeva, Gottfried Benn, and Miklos Radnoti. His artistic life had more in common with the careers of Mikhail Bulgakov or Dimitri Shostakovich than with those of Aeschylus or Sophocles. The central theme of Seneca's tragedies is how to endure a world in which there is no justice, no safety from tyrants, no guarantees—political or divine—of human dignity. These questions were not theoretical in Nero's Rome. Seneca's tragedies have frequently been censured for their obsession with terror and violence; yet any ten pages of Suetonius's *The Twelve Caesars* contain greater horrors than Seneca ever mounted on the stage. To criticize Seneca's tragedies for their violence is like dismissing Alexander Solzhenitsyn's *Cancer Ward* because it is gloomy.

Our knowledge of Roman tragedy is haphazard and incomplete. Seneca is the only tragedian whose work has survived except in fragments. A considerable amount of information, however, exists about pre-Senecan Latin tragedy, including at least a hundred play titles and many tempting fragments from highly regarded dramatists like Gnaeus Nevius, Quintus Ennius, Lucius Accius, and Marcus Pacuvius (whom Cicero, who died before Seneca's birth, considered Rome's foremost tragic poet). "Heard melodies are sweet," wrote Keats, dying in Rome, "but those unheard are sweeter." Studying Latin tragedy, one is always painfully conscious of how much has been lost, how little one knows for sure, how much else depends on speculation. Only two lines remain from Ovid's celebrated *Medea* and nothing at all from Julius Caesar's version of *Oedipus*. And yet we know the fact about Roman drama most relevant for studying Seneca: while Latin tragedy originally grew out of translation and imitation of the Greek repertory, it gradually developed its own style and character. By the time Seneca came to the theater, the Roman tragic tradition had already flourished for two and a half centuries—longer, that is, than the history of American literature. While Romans held the Greeks supreme in the genre (as Elizabethan poets later considered the Romans their superiors), they also boasted a huge dramatic literature full of acknowledged masterpieces. Seneca's relation to Greek drama is, therefore, more complex than his detractors usually allow. Four centuries of continuous dramatic activity stood between him and Euripides, including a rich and diverse theatrical tradition in Latin.

Aeschylus wrote more than ninety plays; Sophocles produced at least one hundred and ten. Only seven tragedies by each dramatist have survived. No one knows how many plays Seneca wrote, but posterity possesses ten tragedies linked to his name: *Hercules Furens* (*The Madness of Hercules*), *Troades* (*Trojan Women*), *Phoenissae* (*Phoenician Women*), *Medea*, *Phaedra* (also titled *Hippolytus*), *Oedipus*, *Agamemnon*, *Thyestes*, *Hercules Oetaeus* (*Hercules on Oeta*), and *Octavia*. Some of these plays present textual problems. The text of *Phoenissae* is incomplete, whereas the *Hercules Oetaeus*, the longest surviving classical tragedy, seems to have been greatly expanded by a later author. The compelling *Octavia*, the only extant *fabula praetexta* or Roman history play, was probably written by one of Seneca's followers, since the tragedian himself appears as a character. (Its unusual structure and dangerous political subject, however, may suggest that the tragedian wrote it for private performance.) If we place these three problem texts to one side, Seneca, like Aeschylus and Sophocles, survives with seven complete tragedies of undisputed authorship. This is not many plays from which to understand the entire tradition of Roman tragedy, but it does provide enough depth and diversity to judge the merits of an individual author.

## V

If Seneca's plays survived the sack of Rome, the burning of libraries, the leaky roofs of monasteries, the appetites of beetle larvae, and the slow erosions of rot and mildew, they have not had a conspicuously easier time among modern critics, who dismiss them both for too closely resembling Greek models and for too freely departing from them. As Frederick Ahl has observed, "no field of literary study rivals that of Latin poetry in so systematically belittling the quality of its works and authors." And no genre has suffered more consistent disparagement than Roman tragedy. The critical challenge in assessing Seneca is quite simple—to see his plays as works of art in their own right, and to understand how they fit into the tradition of European tragedy. To begin this task, however, one must be willing to see the changes he made in dramatic style and structure as conscious innovations, not as unintentional failings. For all his learned borrowing from Euripides, Aeschylus, and Sophocles, Seneca's aesthetic has little in common with Periclean tragedy. His dramaturgy marks not only a deliberate departure from the Greek tradition but a radical reconception of the genre from narrative to lyric terms.

From Aristotle to the Enlightenment influential theories of tragedy have emphasized the connection between the genre's emotional force and its characteristic narrative concentration and coherence. Sophocles was the first playwright to understand the power tragic theater gains by carefully arranging the story line. The tragic mode, he realized, unlike epic, comedy, or romance, cannot easily assimilate episodic material. Sophocles' innovation was not lost on Aristotle, who called plotting "the first principle . . . the soul of tragedy." Two and a half millennia before Edgar Allan Poe explained that the short story must integrate every element of the work to create a single pattern of effect, the Athenians had applied this aesthetic to tragedy. Italian Renaissance commentators, reading the *Poetics* through the lens of Seneca, mistakenly extrapolated Aristotle's practical observations on Sophoclean compression into a general theory of the dramatic unities of time, place, and action. Though it is now mandatory to mock the Italian aestheticians and their Enlightenment disciples, surely these cognoscenti understood something essential about the poetic integrity of tragic drama, even if they expressed it too schematically.

Classical tragedy achieves its harrowing impact through extreme compression and integration—of plotting, language, character, imagery, and ideas. The Greek tragedians carefully foreshadowed and foreshortened the central dramatic action to create a single narrative line that moves in measured steps to a fateful and usually dire conclusion while also ironically underpinning key events along the way. The Italians were correct in observing that such plotting works most naturally when a play unfolds in a single setting during a short period of time and focuses on the actions of a single character. In Sophocles' *Oedipus Rex*, for instance, Oedipus rarely leaves the stage except during the choral dances; even during his few exits the onstage action still focuses mostly on him. No one can dispute the dramatic effectiveness of the Sophoclean method. Playwrights from Euripides to Agatha Christie have employed it to create theatrical intensity and suspense. There is, however, no reason to believe that linear narrative is the only method suitable for tragedy.

Seneca's plots focus less narrowly on a single protagonist or the unfolding of a single narrative line. In *Hercules Furens*, for instance, the title character does not even appear until the third act, and no sooner does Hercules enter than he rushes away to his next battle. Euripides' *Herakles*, which served as Seneca's chief source, also delays the hero's entry until midway, but the radical difference between the Athenian and Senecan aesthetics becomes obvious when one studies what each dramatist does when Hercules is offstage. Euripides presents the plot of *Herakles* in straightforward, narrative terms. As the play opens, Amphitryon (Herakles' stepfather) and Megara (Herakles' wife) bemoan the hero's absence. While Herakles has gone into the underworld to complete his last labor, the capture of Cerberus, Lycus has usurped the throne of Thebes. He has also slaughtered all the royal family except Megara and her children. Impoverished and unprotected, Amphitryon and Megara wait for Lycus to kill them. Soon the tyrant, who believes Herakles will never return from Hades, arrives and orders their deaths. Herakles' family prepare for their execution by going into their house to dress the children in burial garments. When they return to face execution, they witness Herakles' arrival. After a long exchange with his family, the hero leads them to safety in their house. Ignorant of Herakles' return, Lycus returns with his henchmen to kill the family. He goes into the house, where Herakles kills him. The first half of the play is now complete. Herakles has rescued his family, but the audience understands the bitter irony of his deed. Soon the hero will go mad and kill his wife and children.

Compared to Euripides' linear exposition, the first three acts of Seneca's *Hercules Furens* initially seem diffuse and indirect. Most of the Euripidean story is present. Indeed, Seneca even added a striking plot twist—Lycus offers to spare Megara and her family if she will marry him to give legitimacy to his rule. But despite his reputation for peroration, Seneca has compressed the traditional plot into a fraction of Euripides' length. He handles the narrative scenes expertly, and his new material on Lycus and Megara is dramatically arresting. Seneca's provocative originality, however, comes from

what he adds. The first act of *Hercules Furens* is a single, extended
soliloquy by the goddess Juno. Her tense and angry scene, which
lasts 124 lines in the Latin, begins at a high emotional pitch and
modulates ever higher to an almost unbearable level of passion.
Standing beneath the night sky of Thebes, Juno starts by venting her
anger at her notoriously unfaithful husband (and brother), Jupiter:

> Call me sister of the thunder god.
> That is the only title I have left.
> Once I was wife and queen to Jupiter,
> But now, abandoned by his love and shamed
> By his perpetual adultery,
> I leave my palace to his mistresses.
> Why not choose earth when heaven is a whorehouse?

Seneca's characters usually view nature subjectively. They amplify
their emotions until their passions color the world around them.
While his Juno would never condescend to mere fairness, she has
good reason for finding the constellations infuriating; most of them
commemorate the deification of Jupiter's paramours and illegitimate
offspring.

> Even the Zodiac has now become
> A pantheon of prostitutes and bastards.
> Look at Callisto shining in the north,
> That glittering slut now guides the Argive fleet.
> Or see how Taurus rises in the south,
> Not only messenger of spring's warm nights
> But the gross trophy of Europa's rape!
> Or count the stormy Pleiades—those nymphs
> Who terrorize the waves, once warmed Jove's bed.
> Watch young Orion swaggering with his sword,
> A vulgar upstart challenging the gods,
> While gaudy Perseus flaunts his golden star.
> Gape at the constellations Jove awarded
> Castor and Pollux, his twin bastard sons.
> And now not only Bacchus and his mother
> Parade their ill-begotten rank in heaven,
> But my great husband, lord of lechery,
> Discarding his last shred of decency,
> Has crowned his drunken bastard's slut with stars!

Juno's tirade is quintessential Seneca, simultaneously learned, theatrical, and emotional. He piles one example of Jove's infidelity on another until Juno's language and emotions reach an exploding point. Senecan tragedy is not for those who delight in economy and understatement. The goddess soon moves on to the real object of her hatred, Hercules, whom she has tried to destroy since infancy. Now that he has completed his final labor by capturing Cerberus, she fears Jove will deify him. She recounts his exploits derisively and then rehearses all the possibilities for vengeance. Only one method, she realizes, can overcome the hero's unconquerable strength— madness. She then summons up the hellish furies who will carry out her plan:

> . . . There is
> A cavern buried deep in Tartarus
> Where guilty souls are tortured through eternity
> By unappeasable guardians of pain.
> I summon up those primal deities.
> Come to me, Discord, goddess of destruction.
> Bring up the secret horrors of the damned
> That even Hercules has never seen.
> Come to me goddesses of Violence
> And rash Impiety whose filthy hands
> Are stained with family blood. Come to me, Error.
> And come to me, you whom I most desire,
> Goddess of Madness, who turns men on themselves,
> You who will be the spur of my revenge.

Juno's speech must rank among drama's most extravagant and ardent expressions of female anger, a poetic equivalent of an operatic diva's grandest scene. It is a dazzling mix of poetry, rhetoric, and theater, written in Seneca's characteristically flamboyant and allusive style. But, once finished, Juno walks offstage never to reappear. A choral ode follows, and then Seneca uses the second act to present the traditional plot. Hercules arrives at the opening of the third act, dragging Cerberus in chains and accompanied by Theseus, whom he has freed from the underworld. Learning of Lycus's audacious crimes, Hercules immediately leaves to seek revenge. Theseus is now alone with Megara and Amphitryon, and Seneca adds another series of speeches unlike anything in Euripides.

Seneca devotes most of the third act of *Hercules Furens* to a sequence of poetic set pieces describing the underworld. Amphitryon is eager to know about the afterlife and his stepson's adventures in Hades. He asks Theseus a series of brief questions, to each of which Theseus replies at length. Theseus's speeches constitute a remarkable narrative poem (Seneca's dark and revisionary response to the *catabasis*, the descent into the underworld, in Virgil's *Aeneid*) that presents a horrifying vision of the afterlife:

> There are no grassy meadows bright with flowers,
> No fields of ripened corn swaying in the wind,
> No soft green vistas for the eye, or groves
> Where branches bend with slowly sweetening fruit,
> No breezes spiced with odors of the plum.
> But only wasteland everywhere, the fields
> Unwatered and untilled, the soil exhausted
> And nothing moving on the silent land.
> And this is how life ends—
> This barren place, this country of despair,
> Where no wind blows and darkness never lifts,
> With hopeless sorrow twisting every shadow.
> Dying is bitter, but eternity
> Confined in this black place is worse.

While Theseus's speeches tell of Hercules' exploits, they—like Juno's tirade—seem to exist independently as poems in their own right. Largely narrative in structure, they are primarily lyric in effect; they vividly convey the private anger, terror, and agony of their speakers. One finds similar episodes in all of the other plays: Creon's description of Tiresias's sacrifice in *Oedipus*, the messenger's account of Hippolytus's death in *Phaedra*, the ghost of Aggripina's soliloquy in *Octavia*, and, perhaps the most powerful, the messenger's chilling depiction of Atreus butchering his nephews in *Thyestes*. It is always dangerous to guess an author's intention, but one suspects that Seneca conceived of these speeches as daring *coups de théâtre*, show-stopping recitations that push the genre of tragic drama to the furthest limit of the form. The scenes contain some of Seneca's finest poetry; if they did not imaginatively overpower the audience, the dramatic fabric of the play would disintegrate. These moments must be magnificent, or they are nothing.

Surely a major reason for Seneca's current obscurity in this Latinless age has been the inadequacy of most translations in conveying the essentially poetic quality of his dramatic language.

Juno's tirade and Theseus's narration are so much longer, more ostentatious, and more elaborate than the play's narrative requires that the reader is left with only two possible explanations. First is the conventional view that the playwright is dramatically incompetent. (This is Muller's charge, that Seneca is "indifferent to form" and lacks "economy, purity, symmetry, appropriateness of any sort.") The second interpretation is that Seneca knows exactly what he is doing here (and in similar places throughout his other plays) but that his artistic aims differ radically from his Greek predecessors.

This observation leads to the central issue in assessing Seneca's tragedies: In what context shall they be judged? Works of art are always evaluated, explicitly or implicity, against a tradition. The concept of genre—be it revenge tragedy, bedroom farce, Hollywood western, or avant-garde theater piece—assumes a set of shared expectations between artist and audience concerning subject, form, and style. Tradition is necessarily a dynamic concept; only dead traditions do not change. Significant new works alter or enlarge their genres, just as mediocre or derivative works exhaust or debase a tradition. The death of verse tragedy came at the hands of a thousand uninspired neoclassical playwrights whose sober imitations slowly strangled the tradition. By the twentieth century only isolated acts of poetic genius, like García Lorca's *Blood Wedding*, could temporarily resurrect the genre; even brilliant attempts like Eliot's *The Family Reunion* or W. H. Auden and Christopher Isherwood's *The Ascent of F-6* only charmed the corpse halfway out of the grave.

Seneca's plays, however, do not fit comfortably into either the dominant ancient or the modern traditions of European tragedy. Classical scholars, who are trained to compare ancient texts with their sources and parallels, habitually evaluate Seneca retrospectively in relation to earlier Greek drama. This method implicitly overemphasizes the conservative elements in Seneca's dramas and ignores the revisionary nature of his aesthetic. As Moses Hadas observed, "if we choose to call Seneca's plays Greek tragedies, we must pronounce them debased." Judged by the Aristotelian aesthetic of tragedy as a public, narrative genre, Seneca's plays hardly make sense. His asymmetrical expositions, lyric digressions, subjective psychology, scene-stealing ancillary characters, and spectacular violence mock Athenian taste and decorum. Likewise Seneca's plays make little dramatic sense judged by the assumptions of realist drama, especially the works of Henrik Ibsen, who invented the most influential form of modern prose tragedy. Judged as realist drama, Seneca's plays appear bombastic, lurid, schematic, and dramatically inert. They rely too exclusively on the power of speech to portray human action, rather than presenting the action itself. Their characteristic eloquence often misses the elusive truths that slip between and behind words. His sensational plots explore emotional extremes at the expense of understanding the pathos of the ordinary. Seneca is no more satisfactory as Eugene O'Neill than as Euripides.

Neither aesthetic, however, seems intrinsically appropriate to the author of *Hercules Furens, Phaedra,* and *Thyestes.* Seneca's concept of tragedy is neither narrative nor sociological; it is lyric and poetic. If he is to be understood as a dramatist, he must be seen as an innovator, the creator of a new theatrical genre—lyric tragedy. While the new genre was historically rooted in the Athenian tradition, by selectively emphasizing and exploring certain features of the original form it developed into a distinctive type of tragic theater. Seneca's highly allusive style, which incorporates a myriad of elements large and small from earlier Greek and Roman writers, has blinded many critics to the sheer novelty of his artistic aims. In this sense Seneca resembled modernist poets like Pound, Eliot, Montale, Radnoti, and Mandelstam; he was meticulously attentive to the tradition he had transformed. Unless one recognizes the unconventional innovative nature of Seneca's lyric tragedies, their form will never make satisfactory sense.

Lyric poetry presents the sensibilities of a speaker at a particular moment, often in a specific place and time. It seeks to capture with compelling exactitude a single, intensely unified experience. The lyric mode is subjective, heightened, and emotional. Originally sung, lyric poetry still aspires to the conditions of music. One might characterize lyric tragedy, therefore, as a form of spoken drama that aspires to the conditions of opera. While it presents a story (because lyric tragedy no less than opera needs narrative structure to provide cohesion), the plot is primarily a means to the genre's real artistic end, the vivid depiction and amplification of its characters' subjective experience. The purpose of plotting, therefore, is not to create narrative suspense but to lead the spectator through a sequence of extended lyric moments that combine into a powerfully expressive total design.

Seneca builds his tragedies around a series of arresting, emotional, lyric moments—verbal arias, duets, and choruses—designed to move the audience to a heightened emotional state. If one reads Seneca looking primarily for the story, one will inevitably be disappointed. His tragedies are well-plotted, but Seneca rarely explores the expressive possibilities of narrative. His central artistic concern is to convey the most extreme states of human suffering. Eliot was correct, therefore, in asserting, in "Seneca in Elizabethan Translation," that " 'plot' in the sense in which we find plot in *The Spanish Tragedy* does not exist for Seneca." Slyly, Eliot went on to observe: "He took a story perfectly well known to everybody, and interested his auditors entirely by his embellishments of description and narrative and by smartness and pungency of dialogue; suspense and surprise attached solely to verbal effect."

One might push Eliot's insight even further to reach the essence of Senecan tragedy. Perhaps Seneca's particular genius lay in understanding that the only way he could charge the familiar tragic plots with their original cathartic intensity—especially to a Roman audience inured to violence and injustice, whether in the Coliseum or the imperial court—was by putting his auditors inside his character's sensibility. Seneca was not concerned with creating suspense or surprise; he wanted pity and terror. He willingly traded narrative complexity, symmetry, and momentum for the opportunity to achieve imaginative force and immediacy. Seneca has been rightly praised for the psychological complexity of his protagonists. His Hercules, Phaedra, Thyestes, Medea, and Oedipus are not flat stereotypes; their personalities contain the virtues, weaknesses, and contradictory impulses that Aristotle demanded for the complex character of the tragic protagonist. Seneca, however, puts this deep psychology to unusual ends; he is less interested in how his characters act in tragic circumstances than in how they feel. What inspires him both as a dramatist and a poet is imagining from the inside what it is like to experience unbearable levels of pain and passion.

The subjectivity of Senecan lyric tragedy leads to a structural idiosyncrasy in the plays. The most important connections between scenes are not always logical or narrative but imagistic and emotional. Lyric poetry often works most effectively by talking around a subject rather than addressing it directly. Seneca's originality as a dramatist was the incorporation of elaborately crafted scenes that are tangential to a play's plot but central to its subtext. Juno's dazzling soliloquy in *Hercules Furens* is largely superfluous to the narrative. Likewise Theseus's extensive descriptions of the underworld could have been compressed into a single speech. What Seneca accomplishes by expanding these episodes is to submerge his audience in the psychic environment of the play. Juno's uncontrollable rage sets the tense emotional tone of the story; her fear of Hercules ironically prefigures the terror others will feel during his murderous rampage. When she describes his vainglorious conquest of the underworld, her palpable horror suggests the terrible consequences of his profanation of death's mysteries. Theseus's own obsession with the darkness and emptiness of hell implies Hercules' unrecognized vulnerability to its destructive effects. No one can escape the primal forces he has unleashed by opening the gates of hell. Juno and Theseus's powerful set pieces saturate the audience with the images, ideas, and sensations needed to understand the play's horrifying climax. As Seneca demonstrates, there are other ways than narrative to foreshadow tragic events and establish dramatic irony.

One also sees the essentially lyric nature of Seneca's tragedy in his use of the chorus. Greek tragedy began as a series of choral songs and dances. Thespis reportedly created drama by introducing a single actor impersonating a mythic or legendary character who conversed with the chorus. Aeschylus, Sophocles, and Euripides added more actors and elaborated the narrative elements, but the role of the chorus remained primary to Greek tragedy. Even in Euripides, it remained on the stage during the entire drama and represented the public nature of the genre. Seneca has frequently been criticized for denying his chorus any meaningful role in the action. If Seneca's plays were fully staged—and there is much debate on the issue of how they were performed—then the chorus must have frequently disappeared into the wings. It rarely speaks except during the elaborate choral odes between each act. While

Seneca denies the chorus a dramatic role, he gives it a central function in the lyric structure of his plays. His long choral odes explore,
amplify, and supplement the mood of the plays. They frame the
dramatic scenes around them in poetic terms. These odes show
Seneca's largely unrecognized gift as a lyric poet. The final chorus
from *Oedipus,* to choose one example out of many, opens with rare
elegance and power:

> Fatis agimur; cedite fatis.
> non sollicitae possunt curae
> mutare rati stamina fusi.
> quidquid patimur mortale genus,
> quidquid facimus venit ex alto,
> servatque suae decreta colus
> Lachesis nulla revoluta manu.
> omnia secto tramite vadunt.
> primusque dies dedit extremum.

One need not know Latin to appreciate the overt musicality of
these lines. Sounds echo across and between lines. The language is
stately and epigrammatically exact (most lines have only four carefully chosen and arranged words). To catch the flavor of the passage a
Latinless reader might profit from looking at more than one translation. E. F. Watling conveys the majestic tone of the original, while
Rachel Hadas emulates its lapidary compression:

> Fate guides us; let Fate have her way.
> No anxious thought of ours can change
> The pattern of the web of destiny.
> All that we do, all that is done to us,
> Mortals on earth, comes from a power above.
> Lachesis measures out the portions
> Spun from her distaff, and no other hand
> Can turn the spindle back.
> All creatures move on their appointed paths;
> In their beginning is their end.
>                                    (Watling)

> By fate propelled, to fate we yield.
> No fussy gestures set us free.
> It is decreed, our human doom,

all from above. Lachesis' laws
(tightly she grasps them) point one way.
Through narrow channels our lives move:
our first day singles out our last.

(Hadas)

Seneca's transformation of the chorus into an entirely lyric and meditative device also highlights a fundamental difference between his conception of drama and the modern ideal. Despite his occasional employment of spectacle—Hercules' entry dragging Cerberus, Medea's exit in a chariot drawn by flying dragons, or Atreus uncovering a platter to reveal the heads of Thyestes' sons—the dramatic action in Seneca's plays is overwhelmingly located in the language. Just as the bel canto tragedies of Donizetti and Bellini assumed the human voice's ability to convey everything essential to the drama, lyric tragedy rests on the assumption that poetic speech can articulate everything necessary to create tragic theater. Needless to say, contemporary theater no longer assumes the clarifying power of speech—whether in poetry or prose—as the central dynamic of drama. If anything unites the divergent aesthetics of Samuel Beckett, Edward Albee, Joe Orton, David Mamet, Caryl Churchill, and Harold Pinter, it is a belief in the deceptions of speech and the expressive power of the inarticulate.

Can it be sheer coincidence, however, that it was those ages that understood and appreciated Seneca's aesthetic that produced the most enduring verse tragedies since the Greeks? When Seneca's reputation stood at its highest in England, France, Spain, and Italy, those traditions created the finest poetic drama in their histories. Can it also be mere chance that, as Seneca fell out of favor in Western Europe, poetic tragedy became a marginal theatrical genre? (Eastern Europe, never entirely part of Latin culture, followed a different course of development.) This is not the same as saying that Seneca's presence or absence had these effects on drama, only that a culture's ability to hear and understand how Seneca's plays worked reflected a broader faculty to marry poetry and serious drama. An unqualified conviction that tragedy requires the intensification of poetic speech is not only the tenet that separates Seneca from contemporary drama; it is also the belief that divides Marlowe, Shakespeare, and Racine from Büchner, Ibsen, and O'Neill.

Seneca's tragedies represent the ultimate development of poetic drama. While they outwardly fulfill the narrative requirements of theater, the effects they pursue are intrinsically poetic. Lyric tragedy balances on the border between what Aristotle called the "imitated human action" of drama and the purely verbal representation of poetry. If one pushed Seneca's aesthetic any farther, the dramatic structure would disintegrate; one would be left with a dramatic poetic sequence, like Tennyson's *Maud*, Hardy's *The Dynasts*, or Pound's *Homage to Sextus Propertius.*

Judged by their proper standards, the lyric tragedies of Seneca are considerable achievements. His much abused *Thyestes*, the most violent and gruesome play in the Western canon, is a dark and disturbing masterpiece. It was not only for its sensational plot that this play became one of the most influential tragedies ever written. Its feverish emotion and poetic energy make it an overwhelming experience to read. The sexually charged *Phaedra* and razor-edged *Medea*, which Eliot considered Seneca's best plays, are equally compelling. *Hercules Furens*, which Eliot raided for both "Marina" and *The Waste Land*, is Seneca's most innovative tragedy. Alternately violent, visionary, phantasmagoric, and poetic, it demonstrates the imaginative possibilities of lyric tragedy. (The often splendid *Hercules Oetaeus* is less successful in dramatic terms, but with its great length, large cast, and double chorus, it shows the Senecan lyric form pushing beyond the limits of theatrical tragedy. *Hercules Oetaeus* is an unacknowledged ancestor of both dramatic poems like Goethe's *Faust* and romantic grand operas like Berlioz's Virgilian *Les Troyens*.) Seneca's *Oedipus* will always suffer in comparison to Sophocles' masterpiece, but read on its own terms, it is a potent poetic drama and may illustrate most vividly the existential bleakness of Seneca's vision.

In Sophocles' *Oedipus the King*, the final scenes lay the groundwork for a new social order. Although Oedipus's individual suffering remains primary, it is depicted in a civic context. Creon is already implicitly in charge. As he leads the blinded Oedipus away, the promise of health and prosperity returns to Thebes. In Seneca's *Oedipus*, however, the dramatic focus remains mercilessly on the suffering king; he has no comforters. In Sophocles, Oedipus blinds himself out of shame; he cannot bear to see his children or face his father in the underworld. Seneca's Oedipus puts out his eyes because death would be too easy; he wants to protract his agony and make his suffering commensurate with his sins. When Seneca's Oedipus staggers out of Thebes, alone and unconsoled, he may grimly take his curse with him, but the author offers no hint that his suffering will redeem the city.

Seneca's tragic vision admits no escape from evil, no defense against the mindless brutality of fate. The gods may witness human suffering, but they will do nothing to prevent or ameliorate it. There is no welcome *deus ex machina*. When divinities intervene, they come like raging Juno in *Hercules Furens* or avenging Venus and Neptune in *Phaedra*. The supernatural world is represented by vindictive spirits and hellish demigods, as in the opening of *Thyestes*, where a demonic Fury drives the ghost of Tantalus out of Hell to provoke his grandson Atreus to unspeakable revenge. The eternal realm is less likely to endow the mortal world with grace than to pollute it with madness and evil. Hercules may have escaped physically from the underworld in *Hercules Furens*, but its forbidden knowledge has infected his spirit in ways he will not understand until too late. The end of *Thyestes* may be the bleakest conclusion in all tragedy. Atreus has killed and dismembered his nephews and tricked his brother Thyestes into publicly eating his own children at a banquet. Evil is joyfully triumphant. The innocent have been unspeakably destroyed. The hero has no shred of dignity left, only shame, horror, and defeat. And yet Seneca has kept the reader fixed and fascinated during the terrifying spectacle. He has managed the difficult but essential feat of tragic theater—to lure the audience to the edge of an abyss to watch a fellow human's sudden fall to destruction, to make them feel the injustice and agony of the doomed without ever wanting to turn away.

## VI

A genius for tragic drama is the rarest literary talent. In the history of European theater from the beginning of Athenian drama in 535 B.C. (when Peisistratus established the first public competition in tragedy) until the advent of Realism, only a few writers have managed to create enduring bodies of work in the genre. After naming the supreme masters of tragedy—Aeschylus, Sophocles, Euripides, Shakespeare, Corneille, and Racine—whom else can we list without sensing a significant falling off in ambition, intensity, or quality? Goethe's *Faust* may be a masterpiece, but it is no tragedy, and his other plays lack the dark intensity that characterizes the tragic mode. The once influential tragedies of Alfieri, Voltaire, Hugo, and Grillparzer now seem like elegant but dusty museum pieces. The best plays of Marlowe, Ford, and Webster remain vivid but also remind one of how uneven the rest of their work is. There are individual tragedies that stand on the higher levels of the genre— Schiller's *Maria Stuart*, Büchner's *Woyzeck*, Marlowe's *Edward II*, Pushkin's *Boris Godunov*, Musset's *Lorenzaccio*, and Milton's *Samson Agonistes*—but their authors (with the possible exception of Schiller) did not create total dramatic *oeuvres* equal to these isolated masterpieces. Perhaps a few tragedians, like Büchner and Marlowe, possessed a commensurate, native genius for the form but had no time to develop. Sophocles lived to be ninety and wrote until the end; Büchner died of typhus at twenty-three, and Marlowe was killed in a tavern brawl at twenty-nine (an age at which Shakespeare was still a journeyman dramatist). Had they lived, they might have immensely enriched the canon of tragedy, but such is the difficulty of the genre that even their truncated careers stand out.

The tradition of tragedy is a jagged, discontinuous line. The gaps and failures represent its problematic character more truthfully than its rare and often isolated triumphs. An extraordinary number of Europe's greatest writers struggled unsuccessfully with the form. In nineteenth-century England alone, Byron, Wordsworth, Coleridge, Keats, Shelley, Landor, Hunt, Browning, Arnold, Tennyson, and Swinburne attempted to revive tragic theater. But the genre not only requires a double genius in poetry and theater; it also demands a fierce dialectical imagination that can face the unjust and irrational mockery of fate without flinching. If few authors possess the mandatory gifts, fewer ages permit the necessary vision.

It is against this small and fitful tradition that Seneca's work must be judged. He does not stand with the handful of tragedy's supreme masters. He lacks the genius for dramatic narrative of Shakespeare and Sophocles. He rarely achieves the perfect imaginative balance and compression of Racine. He lacks the innate theatricality of Euripides. And yet, once his plays are understood on their own terms, his dark, lyric tragedies can hold their own against the rest of the tradition. Seneca's plays display poetic integrity, psychological depth, linguistic force, and unsurpassed emotional intensity. The sheer originality of Seneca's concept of tragedy and the frenetic energy of his dramatic execution give his plays extraordinary impact. No dramatist has ever portrayed a darker vision of human existence. No tragedians except Shakespeare and Sophocles exerted a stronger influence on posterity. Seneca's plays were the matrix from which the Renaissance gave birth to modern tragedy. If his reputation has long been in decline, it is time to ask how much of that falling off reflected not only a general disparagement of all Latin literature but also a distrust of poetry itself as a dramatic medium. Readers willing to approach Seneca without preconceptions will find a profound and original tragic poet. "Time discovers truth," he once wrote. Perhaps our time will rediscover him.

Dana Gioia

# OEDIPUS

Translated by Rachel Hadas

# INTRODUCTION

I translated Seneca's *Oedipus* without first reading the play through. My expectations were vague—clotted rhetoric, exaggerated ghastliness, echoes of Sophocles' more celebrated work of the same name—and I vaguely hoped some of them would be disappointed. I wanted, if possible, to be surprised.

I wasn't surprised, and I was. The note of despair, for example, was struck as hard as I had expected, but sooner and more frequently: not only does Seneca's chorus detail the ravages of the plague, but so too, immediately and repeatedly, does Oedipus himself. The feeling this play gives us, that we are supping full of horrors, owes something to the sparse yet packed quality of Seneca's Latin, where every word tells, and more, no doubt, to the celebrated grimness of the Senecan imagination. More specifically, this Oedipus is burdened from the outset with such a sense of doom that Sophocles' hero looks positively jaunty by comparison. Oedipus's opening soliloquy in this play combines flashback and lamentation, description and foreboding. The speaker is vulnerable, fearful, so close at all times to awareness of his own guilt that the suspenseful pacing with which Sophocles endowed his version of the tale invariably suffers.

Not that Seneca's handling of plot is inept. We have many taut and telling exchanges between Oedipus and Jocasta or Creon or the elderly shepherd; this Oedipus has the familiar characteristics of anger, haste, and courage. But because the darkness of both past and present is such a threatening reality in the Senecan play, atmosphere constantly looms larger than story. It is entirely characteristic of Seneca's vision and technique that the two most distinctive innovations in his *Oedipus* are Tiresias's daughter, Manto, who (ostensibly for the benefit of her blind father but of course also for us) gives

3

an enthrallingly gruesome account of an inauspicious sacrifice, and Creon's lengthy account of his journey to the underworld to consult the ghost of Laius. (If, by the way, some of Seneca's descriptions of the anarchy caused by the plague recall Lucretius on a similar subject, the pathetic picture of souls flocking through the nether world is reminiscent of Virgil.)

Neither of these elaborate accounts advances the plot very far. Are they then mere bravura pieces, providing the listeners with the expected thrills of horror? Partly, no doubt. But they also open the world of the play to the dimension of the unearthly, the ghostly, which infuses *Oedipus* more with the mood of *Hamlet* or *Macbeth* than with the rational temper which, as Bernard Knox has pointed out, is a recurrent theme in Sophocles' tragedy of Oedipus.

If ghosts throng the underworld and omens shadow the sunlight, this comes as no great surprise. But the increasing psychological inevitability and pathos that mark the latter part of this play took me aback; I stepped up the pace of my translating, in time with the quicker rhythms of the action. I had not expected these lofty, doom-laden figures to be changing before my eyes, yet this is what I found. The changes are, to be sure, not in their final deeds, but in the degree of freedom with which these deeds are pondered and decided upon. Thus we see through the messenger's eyes Oedipus in the process of changing his mind: committing suicide isn't the right course of action, blinding himself is. In an abbreviated version of this same desperate introspection, this final grasping at choice in a world that permits so little freedom, Jocasta too changes her mind: first she asks Oedipus to kill her, then, in a few lines, debates where the proper place is for her to stab herself and promptly does the deed.

As the tragedy ends, Oedipus, in Dana Gioia's words, "staggers out of Thebes, alone and unconsoled." The only ray of hope is that since he "grimly take[s] his curse with him" (Gioia), the city may be cleansed by his departure. But what we witness is Oedipus's invitation: "wasting, black plague, dementia, come here, / be my companions!" rather than any reestablishment of order and health at Thebes; the close of the play is stark indeed.

In translating this play, I soon found that rhymed couplets (the rhyme is approximate at times, but the metrical framework stays firm) provided the energy of pace, the dignity of diction, and the occasional aphoristic prickle needed both for extended speeches and for stichomythia. For the choruses, a very different texture was needed, and I settled on a vaguely accentual (three-beat) alliterative line rather in the mode of Auden's *Age of Anxiety*.

Indeed, anxiety pervades the world of the play, as it did New York City in the fall of 1991, when I was working on my translation. Entering and reentering the merciless terrain of *Oedipus*, writing with one hand and eating hot Chinese soup with the other or getting ten lines done in the Hungarian Pastry Shop, provided the pleasures not only of problem solving but—amidst the fears and miasmas of our time—of truth telling.

I should add, finally, that the English versions that guided me as I worked were two: Frank Justus Miller's (Loeb, 1917), fairly clear but impossibly stilted, and the clearer and more concise but only slightly less archaizing prose version by my father, Moses Hadas (Library of Liberal Arts, 1965). I deliberately avoided reading other poetic renderings; I wanted to find my own, and no one else's, way of letting Seneca speak out, with all his eloquence and grimness, his horror and his glory.

Rachel Hadas

# OEDIPUS

## CHARACTERS

OEDIPUS, king of Thebes
JOCASTA, queen of Thebes
CREON, brother of Jocasta
TIRESIAS, a blind prophet
MANTO, daughter of Tiresias
OLD MAN, messenger from Corinth
PHORBAS, former shepherd of King Laius
MESSENGER
CHORUS of Theban Elders

OEDIPUS: Rising resignedly through smears of grey,
the sun slinks back to drive the dark away.
To houses stricken with this ravenous plague
it brings a lurid light:
each dawn uncovers wreckage from last night.
Who would want to be a king, I ask—
horrors heaped behind a grinning mask!
Rocks that jut out into the open sea
are drubbed by breakers on the quietest day,
vulnerable and naked as a king                    10
daily exposed to every passing thing.
I shunned the scepter that my sire would leave me.
Exiled and bold, without a care to grieve me,
I wandered; and—I swear it by the sky!—
blindly stumbled into royalty.
Oh God, unspeakable the things I fear—

7

by my own hand somehow to kill my sire,
or so the Delphic oracle gives out.
And something even worse is hinted at
than murdering my father—some vile curse                    20
too foul to speak of. Phoebus in my eyes
flashes the bed where my own father lies!
This threatening image made me leave the place.
My life at home was innocent, I say;
my effort was forever to obey
the laws of Nature. But when what you fear
is so enormous, though it may appear
impossible, you shudder all the time:
*Can I, could I commit this dreadful crime?*
Yes, Fate's concocting something just for me,                    30
now, now this instant!
                              How can this not be,
when right and left my kinsmen are mown down?
Some special hell's reserved for me alone.
The city crumbles—fodder fresh at hand
for Death's forever hungry maw. I stand
safe and sound as far as I can see,
but still a doomed man, still Apollo's prey,
marked by the aura of foreboding fate:
the very life I've lived pollutes the state.                    40
We burn with fever, but no breezes cool
our faces, and the August sun adds fuel
to feed the summer's flames. The streams dry up
and the thin grass grows colorless with drought.
Dirce's depleted, Ismenus so low
that through its sluggish waters bare banks show.
Down a dark sky the sun's pale sister slinks;
daylight dwindles to a feeble wink.
Even on clear nights, no stars appear;
a black miasma shrouds the atmosphere.                    50
Heaven's happy houses, palaces of gods,
look dim, diminished. Grain within the pod
nods its golden top, then dries and dies.

No group's immune from such calamities:
all ages and both sexes are cut down.
The dreadful plague joins babies and old men,
parents and children. A shared funeral pyre
is common: for each family, one fire.
Few are the survivors left to mourn;
most of them are ash within the urn.                              60
All funeral rites now are abbreviated.
Who's left to weep? The city's decimated.
The monstrousness of what's befallen us
keeps us from weeping. Tears are little use
when a bewildered father lifts his son
onto the pyre. The mother, crazed, brings one,
then scurries back again to fetch another
for the same flames that just consumed his brother.
Lamentations may be at their height;
they're interrupted as fresh griefs break out.                    70
Pyres people have reserved for their own use
are loaded with another family's corpse.
Fire is precious now, so people steal it.
Shame? In our wretchedness we do not feel it.
We lack the graves to cover up the bones.
Fire is sufficient—yet it hardly burns
more than a fraction truly through and through.
Earth is lacking, timber's lacking too
for mounds and pyres. And no prayer or skill
can help the sick; the healers too fall ill.                      80
I kneel in supplication. Let me die
before this town collapses utterly!
Let me not be the last to linger on,
let not the final funeral be mine!
Oh savage gods, oh Fate on your black throne,
does death say no to me and me alone,
that death so greedy for my countrymen?
Oh, leave this place polluted by your past!
Death is your legacy, a single vast
infection stretching up into the sky!                             90

Oh sinister sojourner! Who but I
visited you upon this wretched town?
Years ago I should have left for home.

JOCASTA: Oedipus, why lament so wretchedly?
It would be kinglier, if you ask me,
to stand firm, look your problems in the eye.
As the state of things gets slippery,
all the more firm should your comportment be.
It's hardly brave to turn your back on fate.

OEDIPUS: The charge of cowardice is far-fetched, remote;          100
our royal nature knows no pangs or qualms.
Should bristling Mars be facing me in arms,
I'd be audacious, I would fight back
even at giants leading the attack.
The Sphinx, that riddling monster, I defied,
who wove the web where many others died.
I faced that prophet with her bloody gums
and stood my ground—ground that was white with bones!
When from the cliff's edge she loomed over me,
already slavering for her future prey,                           110
her wings were poised for flight, her tensile tail
a waiting whiplash. Fearful, all in all!
And yet I posed my riddle. Next, a shriek—
and her impatient claws ripped at the rock
and not my entrails. But that tangled mess,
her dark enigma, I solved nonetheless
(*Aside*) [*Some editors give the following brief speech to Jocasta.*]
What foolishness, the death you now implore!
It would have been appropriate before.
You killed the Sphinx, this scepter is your meed.
But still she fights against me! Even dead,                      120
she drags the city down with her to hell.
One way remains; Phoebus alone can tell.

CHORUS: People are dying all over the city.
Empty fields. Where are the farmers?

This is how it used to be:
Theban armies galloping East
to pitch their tents in the land of dawn
saw the Arabs rich with spices,
Parthians who shot behind their backs;
got as far as the Red Sea                               130
where hot sun burns the natives brown.
Our forebears were unconquered people;
we are dying. Savage doom
grinds us down. Every hour
a fresh procession moves along,
slowly shuffling toward Death.
Mournful parade, marking time:
seven gates gaping are too narrow
for travelers flocking toward the tomb.
For the sad survivors, gridlock!                        140
Funeral blocks funeral.
First to fall sick were sleepy sheep:
poisonous pasturage they cropped.
Hand held high for the fatal blow
stands the priest; the gold-horned bull
slowly sinks. The neck-gash gapes
under the massive ax's blow;
but not by blood the steel is stained.
Black pus oozes from the wound.
The horse collapses on the track;                       150
off his side the rider tumbles.
Abandoned cattle lie down to die.
Herds are shrinking, bulls are sick,
shepherds fail their feeble flocks,
dying leave livestock doomed to die.
No longer do wolves frighten deer;
lions' roars dwindle into whimpers.
Stored-up viper venom dries,
clots, so serpents choke and strangle.
Boughs of trees no longer pour                          160
shadows onto bluish hills;
arable land turns hard and dry;

grapevines no longer droop with fruit.
All's plague-stricken, all's plague-sickened:
the plague lays waste to everything.
A mob of Furies, torches smoking,
has smashed the gates of the world below.
Hell's hot river, flowing fire,
changes course and waters us.
Dank Death opens wide his jaws,                170
spreads his wings. The ferryman
poles his boat on the murky stream—
tough old man, but his arms are weary,
so many victims to row over.
They say the mastiff Cerberus
has broken loose and haunts the living.
Earth herself's been heard to howl;
hypertrophied phantoms stalk
our woodlands, where the trembling trees
shake down snow from their branches.            180
The river Dirce's gummed with blood;
hounds are heard to bay by moonlight.
Worse than death, new forms of dying!
Heavy languor weighs the limbs,
faces flush, a rash breaks out,
heads are scorched by burning fever,
cheeks swell with a flux of blood,
ears are ringing, blackish bile
drains through nostrils, ruptures veins.
Guts are wrung by a rattling retch.             190
They hug cold stones against their chests.
A gleam of freedom for the sick
when the nurse feetfirst is carted out:
they rush to fountains, scarf down water.
Over the altars sufferers sprawl
to pray for death—the kindest gods
may grant so much. Shrines are piled high
with offerings not to please the gods
but to allay their endless hunger.

OEDIPUS: Who is that approaching hastily?                    200
    The noble Creon, so it seems to me,
    or my sick spirit spins some fantasy.

CHORUS: Creon! The answer to the city's prayer.

OEDIPUS: I shudder, wondering which way Fate will steer.
    My shaky mood could waver either way.
    When joys and griefs so close together lie,
    the mind is doubtful. How much should one see?
    How much is best to know? I'm dubious.
    Brother-in-law, do you bring help to us?
    Let me hear it now, if there's good news!            210

CREON: The answer's tangled and ambiguous.

OEDIPUS: Half-hearted help in time of suffering
    is no help.

CREON:       But god's words are riddling.

OEDIPUS: Speak! I can deal with ambiguity.
    Solving riddles is my specialty.

CREON: Laius's murder—such is god's command—
    must be avenged by exile from our land;
    only then can skies turned clear once more
    give us our fill of unpolluted air.                    220

OEDIPUS: Who was our great king's killer? Answer me!
    Whom Phoebus named—he pays the penalty.

CREON: May I make bold to speak of things so vile
    to sight and hearing that my guts congeal,
    my limbs go numb?
                All reverence, I trod
    into the holy precinct of the god
    and raised my pious hands in ritual prayer.

Parnassus' peaks responded with a roar!
Apollo's laurel shook as in a gale,                                230
and the Castalian springs stood stony-still.
The wild-haired priestess, in the grip of god,
shrieked out supernaturally loud:
   Kind stars will shine on Thebes once more;
   First show this regicide the door!
   King-killer, your identity
   Apollo knows, and perfectly.
   Short-lived will all your triumph be
   And war will be your legacy
   To the same city whence you came,                      240
   And to the sons you leave behind,
   Mother-lover, doomed and blind.

OEDIPUS: What heaven now is urging me to do
   was owed to Laius' ashes long ago,
   to shield his scepter from all insolence.
   Kings must look out for kings—it's common sense
   to fear the living and ignore the dead.

CREON: But greater fears thrust piety aside.

OEDIPUS: What fear absolved you from such pious debts?

CREON: It was the baleful Sphinx and all her threats.            250

OEDIPUS: Let that old crime be expiated now!
   Whatever god is good to us below—
   Jupiter, who celestial laws ordains;
   Phoebus Apollo, whose bright beauty shines,
   who rules by revolution twelve great signs;
   night-wandering Phoebe, sun's fair sister moon;
   and in his roving chariot Neptune;
   and you, Lord Pluto, guardian of night,
   whose dwelling places only lack for light,
   listen! May he who cut King Laius down                  260
   no shelter find in countryside or town.

Disgraced by incest and its tainted brood,
may he trudge an exile's weary road,
may he slay his own father! That's my curse,
the very fate I've fled. What could be worse?
By both my kingdoms—present, past—I swear
he will find no forgiveness anywhere!
By my childhood faith I swear it too;
and, father Neptune, let me mention you,
who wash my Corinth with your double tide.                    270
Apollo, witness all that I've just said.
So may my father end his days in peace,
and Merope know only his embrace.
Nothing can free the culprit from my grip!
But where did the appalling crime take place?
He fell—in battle? Or into a trap?

CREON: He was en route to the Castalian wood.
Overgrown and dark with leaves, the road
divides into three branches on the plain.
One leads to Phocis, town the god of wine                     280
favors. Twin-peaked Parnassus from that place
gently rises into heaven's space;
next toward the Isthmus and its double sea
the second goes; and then, meanderingly,
the third through fields and valleys takes its course
and finally arrives at Elis' source,
a chilly stream. Here, unsuspecting, he
was set upon by robbers suddenly.
They were armed, and no one saw the crime.
Aha! Tiresias, in the nick of time!                           290
Trembling and slow, yet summoned here by god,
by his daughter Manto he is led.

OEDIPUS: Please, confidant of gods, Apollo's friend:
name the victim whom the gods demand!

TIRESIAS: Sire, if I crave delays, if my tongue's slow,
let not this come as a surprise to you.

Much truth lies hidden from a sightless man.
But since both god and country spur me on,
I follow. Let us pick the Fates apart!
If warm blood only flowed into my heart,                          300
then from my breast Apollo could have spoken.
Well then! Drive to the altar an unbroken
heifer, and a bull of gleaming white.
My daughter, who supplies your father's sight,
describe each step of the prophetic rite.

MANTO: A perfect victim waits for sacrifice.

TIRESIAS: Then call upon the gods with reverent voice
and sprinkle incense on the altars now.
Heap it high!

MANTO:                        What you command, I do.          310

TIRESIAS: And are there flames now to devour their prey?

MANTO: A light flashed suddenly, then died away.

TIRESIAS: But did the flame seem steadfast, bright, and clear?
Did it point straight upward in the air
unfolding its high crest, or did it falter,
so murky smoke wound all about the altar?

MANTO: As Iris makes her many colors one,
yet separate, when she brings in the rain,
curving her bow across a thunderhead,
so you would hesitate to name this shade.                         320
The flame was many-faced and mutable:
deep blue with orange patches for a while,
then red as blood, then blackness. Finally
it snuffed out to invisibility.
But now the angry flame is splitting—see!—
the sparks of sacred fire shun one another.
Father, as I stare at it, I shudder!

OEDIPUS

The wine's poured out and turns at once to blood;
thick smoke enwraps the king's head like a shroud
and, denser by the minute, blocks his sight                          330
as a dark cloud effaces wan daylight.
Father, what does this mean?

TIRESIAS:                                        I stand amazed.
Confusion tugs my reeling mind both ways.
What shall I say? The signs are bad, not good,
but too obscure to be well understood.
The gods—who like to make their anger clear—
are undecided now, it would appear;
their wish is both to threaten and conceal.
Shame for some unknown cause is what they feel.                      340
Drive bullocks to the altar speedily!
Do they allow rough handling placidly?

MANTO: Head held high, the bull was facing East,
then shrank in terror from the sun's bright face.

TIRESIAS: How many blows are needed for the kill?

MANTO: The heifer shoved herself against the steel
and thus with but a single blow she fell.
The bull, though twice struck, wanders here and there,
bleeding his listless soul into thin air.

TIRESIAS: Does the blood spurt from just one narrow cut             350
or from a larger wound ooze slowly out?

MANTO: From the wide chasm of its cloven breast,
a rapid flood of gore streams from one beast.
The other's wound, though deep, is nearly dry;
the blood runs backward, spilling out through eye
and mouth.

TIRESIAS:                                Ill-omened sacrifice of dread!
Describe the entrails now to me instead.

MANTO: Father! The entrails are not gently shaking,
　　but with a violence that sets me quaking,                    360
　　splashed with fresh blood. The heart lies deep within;
　　rot and infection run through every vein.
　　The one-lobed liver oozes with black bile,
　　and—for a single ruler this bodes ill—
　　identically bulging twin heads grow,
　　on both of them transparent membranes through
　　which things best hidden are allowed to show.
　　Sturdy and thick, the side that means bad luck
　　has seven veins. A ridge that runs, oblique,
　　behind these, blocks them. Everything is wrong!              370
　　The organs lie where none of them belong.
　　On the right-hand side a lung lies bleeding,
　　unable to expand enough for breathing;
　　on the left side no heart, a gaping hole,
　　no soft-stretched membrane covering it all.
　　Anarchic creature, lawless in the womb!
　　And where does this protuberance come from?
　　Oh, monstrous! In this virgin animal
　　a fetus grows—deformed, unnatural,
　　ectopic pregnancy! With a bawling moan                        380
　　it tries to urge its twitching limbs along.
　　All the entrails are stained with lurid gore.
　　Carcasses heave, straining to rise once more;
　　a disemboweled bullock tries to wound
　　the priest! I let the guts fall to the ground.
　　This growl you hear, now rising to a roar:
　　fire, altar, hearth are giving voice to fear!

OEDIPUS: Tell me the worst. I am prepared to hear
　　instructions from portents truly dire.
　　Somehow disasters often calm one's thought.                  390

TIRESIAS: You'll wish woes back whose remedies you sought!

OEDIPUS: Tell me—the gods want me to know it too—
　　someone is stained with regicide, but who?

TIRESIAS: Nor birds that slice the sky in airy flight
   nor sacrificial guts can drag to light
   the buried name. We'll find some other way:
   from gloomy shores unvisited by day
   summon the king, who, freed for this from hell,
   his murderer's identity will tell.
   We'll unseal Hades, and the shades we'll ask           400
   to rise from death and help.
                            Whose is this task?
   Not yours; for royalty it is profane
   to glimpse that kingdom where the dead souls reign.

OEDIPUS: Creon, successor to my kingdom, who
   is better suited to this task than you?

TIRESIAS: Then let the people roar their Bacchic hymn
   while we approach Death's kingdom dark and dim.

CHORUS: Tie back your flowing hair with ivy bands
   and grasp the thyrsus in your soft white hands.         410

   Here, come here, heavenly brightness.
   Bacchus, come! Thebes implores you.
   Toward us turn your fresh face,
   radiant beauty! Conquer clouds,
   hungry Fate, threats of doom.
   Wreathe your head with spring flowers,
   Eastern veils, ivy berries;
   toss your hair, then twist it back.
   For fear of furious Juno once
   long ago you changed your shape,               420
   dressed as a girl with golden hair,
   a sash around your saffron gown,
   and ever since you've sighed for softness,
   long loose robes flowing down.
   Easterners who drink the Ganges,
   Northerners who break the ice
   of Araxes saw you seated,

long-robed lions close beside you,
in your chariot of gold.
Disreputable old Silenus                                           430
trails behind you on a donkey;
ivy frames his flabby face.
His followers begin to dance!
Wild feet stamping to the beat,
Bassarids prance along behind you,
mountaintop to mountaintop,
till the women of this town
suddenly behold a Maenad,
holy fawnskin wrapped around her,
brandishing the Bacchic wand.                                      440
Frenzied women tear their hair;
then Pentheus is ripped apart,
the spell is broken. Did this happen?
Glossy Bacchus' foster mother,
Ino, wreathed with rings of sea nymphs,
lives in caves beneath the ocean;
a brand-new boy-child rules the waves,
divine Palaemon, Bacchus' cousin.
Tyrrhenian troops kidnapped you,
but Nereus soothed the swelling seas,                              450
turned blue depths to verdant meadows.
Plane trees put out bright green foliage,
Apollo's laurel flourishes,
loud birds chatter in the branches.
Around the oars ivy clings;
around the mast grapevines twine.
At the prow a lion roars;
at the stern a tiger crouches.
Into the sea the pirates dive.
Once in the water, transformation!                                 460
Their arms drop off; chests and bellies
meet in the middle, merge to one;
from their flanks wee hands dangle;
curved backs slide into the water;
tails like crescents slice the sea.

A school of dolphins swims after the fleet.
In Lydia the Pactolus
river's rich waves carry you
past burning banks in a float of gold.
Massagetes who drink milk and blood                    470
unstring their bows, lay down their arrows.
Lands of Lycurgus who wields the ax
have also known the power of Bacchus.
The Zalaces know when he passes
as do tribes of wind-blown nomads
washed in the waters of cold Maeotis
and those beneath Arcadian stars.
Scattered Gelonians he has tamed;
he has disarmed the Amazons!
Their faces fell; they bit the dust,                   480
laid down their arrows on the ground,
and metamorphosed into Maenads.
Then Pentheus was torn asunder;
holy Cithaeron ran with blood;
into the woods the women fled.
And in his stepmother's despite,
Argos also worships Bacchus.
Naxos, jewel of the Aegean,
bestowed a virgin bride on him,
a better husband than her first,                       490
that cruel deserter Theseus.
From the rocks wine spouted forth;
rivulets crisscrossed the meadows;
earth drank deep of sweetest liquors.
Snowy milk gushed in radiant streams
and old wine steeped in Lesbian thyme.
To highest heaven they lead the bride.
Long-haired Apollo chants the hymn;
twin Cupids twirl the wedding torches;
his fiery weapons Jupiter                               500
lays down, abjures the thunderbolt
at Bacchus's epiphany.
While the bright stars run in their courses,

while river Ocean rings the globe,
while the full moon collects her fires,
while the Morning Star predicts each dawn,
while the Great Bear hangs over the sea,
we shall worship, worship Bacchus
of the clear and shining face!

OEDIPUS: You're horrified—I see it in your eyes.                510
   Still, tell us whom god says to sacrifice.

CREON: What you command fear bids me to withhold.

OEDIPUS: Even if our town's disaster leaves you cold,
   think of the fortunes of those kin to you!

CREON: Avid your hunger for such knowledge *now*,
   but you will come to rue the things you know.

OEDIPUS: So ignorance of all catastrophe
   and ostrich tactics are a remedy?

CREON: With such a bitter pill, who'd want a cure?

OEDIPUS: Say what you know! Or else you can be sure,             520
   taught by tortures: kings' wrath reaches far.

CREON: Kings come to hate words they themselves have bidden.

OEDIPUS: Unless your words uncover what is hidden,
   the underworld will soon receive your ghost!

CREON: Is staying silent too much to request?

OEDIPUS: Too much free speech spells danger for a king,
   yet silence is still deadlier a thing.

CREON: Silence being criminal, what can a man do?

OEDIPUS: The man who will not speak subverts the law.

CREON: Well, let me speak. The words are wrung from me;      530
   I beg that you will hear them patiently.

OEDIPUS: Who's forced to speak should pay no penalty.

CREON: A somber grove of trees stands far from town
   near Dirce's valley; rivulets run down.
   One cypress, loftiest in all that place,
   clasps the whole forest in its green embrace;
   like open arms an ancient oak holds out
   its great curved branches, riddled now with rot.
   Great chunks of one long years have nibbled at;
   another's crooked, split clear to the root.                     540
   In this place bitter-berried laurels grow,
   and slender linden trees, and myrtle too;
   alders whose timber sails the seven seas
   and knotty pine exposed to every breeze.
   Amidst all these trees, an enormous one
   shades the smaller saplings from the sun.
   Its giant branches, spreading far and wide,
   furnish a kind of fort for all the wood.
   Beneath this tree, untouched by light of day,
   an icy river wends its sluggish way.                             550
   Spongy swamps are everywhere about.
   When the old priest approached this gloomy spot
   forever veiled in its peculiar night,
   a ditch was swiftly dug, and glowing coals
   flung into it (snatched first from funerals).
   The priest, now garbed in a funereal gown,
   takes a branch and waves it up and down.
   Cloaked in deep mourning, the old man moves on;
   his inky robes are trailing on the ground,
   his white hair tied with sprigs of deadly yew.                   560
   Black-fleeced sheep and oxen of dark hue
   are dragged away. The fed flames leap and thrive

as in their ghastly fire the victims writhe.
Dead spirits and their king the priest invokes
first; then the keeper of Lake Lethe's lock;
chants magic spells; and, foaming at the mouth,
repeats a charm that has the power to soothe
or to compel the shades that flit about.
Next upon the altar he pours out
blood; burns whole victims; fills the trench with gore.          570
Then a stream of snowy milk he pours
and, with his left hand, wine; and calls again
upon the spirits in a wilder tone.
Hecate's hounds were howling, and the sound
three times made the whole valley floor resound.
"They hear me!" cries the priest. "What I have said
has burst blind Chaos and released the dead."
The whole wood cringed; its leaves stood up like hair.
Stout oaks split open, forests quaked with fear,
the earth shrank back and gave a dreadful groan.                 580
Indignant at this breach of Acheron,
or else travailing to give passage to
the dead, she shrieked, all barriers burst through!
Or triple Cerberus it might have been,
angrily worrying his massive chain.
Then earth yawned. An enormous gulf spread wide.
And I beheld the shadowy pools inside,
and pallid gods of quintessential night.
My thick blood clotted in my veins with fright
as troops of savage creatures leaped out, stood                  590
in arms before me—that whole snaky brood
of brothers sprung once from the dragon's teeth.
Then grim Erinys and blind Fury shrieked,
and Horror, and whatever teeming forms
in such eternal darkness breed by swarms—
hair-tearing Grief, and Sickness, her poor head
scarcely upright; Old Age, and looming Dread;
and hungry Plague, who gobbles nations up.
At such a spectacle our spirits stop.
Even the girl, who from her father knew                          600

such necromancy, was astonished too.
But her undaunted sire Tiresias
summoned the bloodless throng of ghosts to us.
Like clouds they float, and the fresh air drink in.
More than the leaves of autumn whirling down,
more than spring flowers massed in fullest bloom
among which a great globe of bees appears,
more than the waves that wash Ionian shores,
more than the birds that, fleeing winter chills,
crisscross the skies, exchanging snow for Nile's          610
warm waters—far more numerous than all
these were the ghosts responsive to his call.
Trembling, they flock where shade is to be found.
Zethus first emerges from the ground,
clutching a fierce bull by the horns. And then,
a lyre in his left hand, comes Amphion,
the sweetness of whose melodies split stone.
Then Niobe, safe now among her sons,
with haughty gaze re-counts her ghostly brood;
then Agave, a far worse mother, mad                       620
and raving still. Along with her she brings
the Maenad troops who tore apart the king.
And mutilated Pentheus follows them,
still furiously angry, threatening doom.
Repeatedly called forth, a certain shade
far from the others lifts his guilty head
and tries to hide. The priest renews his pleas
and finally we glimpse the hidden face—
Laius! I shudder at the very sound.
The sight was fearful: blood was all around,              630
his filthy hair was matted in a mass.
He raged at us:
                    "Oh Cadmus' horrid house,
ever rejoicing to shed kindred blood,
brandish your thyrsus, savage your own brood
sooner than commit what is the true
desire of every man in Thebes to do—
sleep with his mother! Not heavenly wrath, my town,

no, nothing but your own crimes drags you down!
You suffer—not from stormwinds from the south,                    640
nor from earth parched by a destructive drought,
but from your king, who bought his reign with blood
and occupies the bed his father should—
appalling offspring of the monstrous womb
that bore him first, then swelled again by him.
Returning to the source from which he'd come,
he did a deed that even wild beasts shun,
himself begetting brothers of his own—
a knottier tangle than the Sphinx by far!
You wield that blood-stained scepter; I, your sire,             650
still unavenged, will haunt you everywhere.
Fury as bridesmaid keeps me company—
her hissing whiplash cracks resoundingly.
Your whole incestuous household I'll lay low,
plotting violence for its overthrow.
So take your king and fling him far from here,
an exile, to whatever land can bear
his poisoned presence. Once he leaves this place,
it will recapture springtime's verdant grace,
life-giving air we'll once again breathe deep                  660
as in the forests beauty wakes from sleep.
Plague, death, destruction, labor, waste, and pain,
exiled with him, will never come again.
And even as he hastens to find ways
of quick escaping, I'll concoct delays.
With nothing but a staff to guide each step,
a wavering path of blackness he shall grope.
You Theban elders, exile is for you
to force on him; I'll darken his sky too."

OEDIPUS: My arms and legs, my bones begin to freeze—           670
I've done the dreaded deed. Or so he says;
yet Merope, still Polybus's spouse,
rinses the stain of incest from my house,
and Polybus is living! So you see
the crime of murder can't be laid on me.

From either charge each parent clears my name,
from murder, incest—no room's left for crime.
All Thebans mourned their good king Laius' loss
long before I set foot in this place.
A god is angry, or the old priest lies—                              680
no, you're conspiring right under my nose.
The prophet blames the gods for my disgrace
and meanwhile plots for you to take my place.

CREON: And see my sister driven from the throne?
  If kinship's sacred bonds were, on their own,
  not strong enough to hold me safely here,
  then fortune's pinnacle of sheer desire
  would scare me off. But you must prudently
  lay down this burden, let yourself go free.
  Retire from kingship, and be more secure                           690
  henceforth living in a humbler sphere.

OEDIPUS: Resign the kingship—that's what you advise?

CREON: Advice is for those who still have a choice.
  For you no way is open but your fate.

OEDIPUS: It never fails! Those hungry to be great
  praise leisure and repose and moderation
  as if these never masked a man's ambition.

CREON: So all my years of loyalty to you
  prove nothing?

OEDIPUS:                                Loyalty helps traitors too!   700

CREON: I'm free of royal burdens, yet to me
  things royalty delights in wend their way.
  Crowds of people mill about my gate,
  and not a single day succeeds to night
  that lacks in a munificent selection
  of tokens of your powerful affection.

Rich food and clothing, every kind of aid—
with such fine fortune, what else could I need?

OEDIPUS: The thing you lack. There are no bounds for greed.

CREON: Condemned, defenseless, then, am I to fall?                    710

OEDIPUS: But did you show regard for me at all,
    you and Tiresias listen to my side?
    I'm guilty—no! I follow where you lead.

CREON: And if I'm innocent?

OEDIPUS:                                    You might as well
    learn now—kings fear whatever's possible
    as well as what is certain.

CREON:                                    Any king
    frightened by phantoms merits the real thing.

OEDIPUS: But once he is set free, the guilty man              720
    responds with hatred. Kill him if you can.

CREON: And so breed hatred.

OEDIPUS:                                    Who's afraid of hate
    fails to see fear guards the royal gate.

CREON: Harsh rulers with fierce scepters in their hand
    fear those they terrorize; don't understand
    the way fears haunt us, always coming back.

OEDIPUS: Shut up the miscreant in a hollow rock!
    And guard him there with vigilance, while I
    go to the palace, seat of royalty.                              730

CHORUS: Oedipus, you are not to blame,
    but ancient grudges of the gods

against the house of Labdacus.
Castalia's grove was kind to Cadmus,
Dirce's stream cooled colonists
out of the East, when Agenor's son,
tired of tracking Jupiter's
thieveries throughout the world,
rested, trembling, beneath our trees,
kowtowing to the kidnapper.                                         740
Apollo's advice to him: Forever
follow the path of a straying heifer
never broken to yoke or plough.
But giving up the chase, he named
our race for that unlucky creature.
From that time on our land has teemed
with monsters. In valleys vipers rise
higher than oaks and pine trees, hissing,
dark blue heads above the treetops,
bodies stretched along the ground.                                 750
Or boiling with its bloody breed,
Earth spills over with men in arms.
Horns and trumpets bray for battle,
new lips and tongues are put to use
first to utter a battle cry.
The fields are full of kindred folk.
Worthy of the seed they spring from,
their lives last a single day:
after the morning star they rise,
before the evening star they fall.                                 760
Mother Earth shuddered at such creation,
feared her bellicose new brood
until the generation gave
away, and Earth saw her offspring—
bodies now—back in her bosom.
May the civil strife be done with!
May Thebes know no other battles!
And Actaeon, Cadmus' grandson—
his own forehead sprouted horns,
as pursued by his own hounds                                       770

headlong over woods and mountains
fled Actaeon, swiftly, swiftly,
crashing through groves, over boulders,
trembling at fluttering feather lures,
escaping snares he'd set himself.
In a peaceful mountain pool
finally he saw himself—
saw the antlers, saw the face
of an animal, in that same
tranquil pool where the goddess                          780
savage in her chastity
had bathed her gleaming arms and legs.

OEDIPUS: Worries and fears are spinning in my head.
    Through no one's deed but mine is Laius dead,
    or so the gods of heaven and hell proclaim.
    And yet my mind feels guiltless all the same.
    Better than the gods know me, I know
    myself. Yet memory yields up this dim clue:
    a man my staff has struck . . . and down he goes,
    given over to the gods below,                        790
    but not before he shoulders me aside
    (he older and I younger): "Off the road!"
    All this was not nearby but far away,
    near Phocis, where the road divides in three.
    (*Enter* JOCASTA; OEDIPUS *addresses her*)
    Wife and companion, answer this for me.
    When Laius died, how old a man was he?
    Bowed down by years of age, or in his prime?

JOCASTA: Between the two, yet near the older time.

OEDIPUS: And did great throngs cling closely to his side?

JOCASTA: Many of them mistook the path and strayed;      800
    a faithful few contrived to keep close by.

OEDIPUS: Of those good friends, did no one die but he?

JOCASTA: One gave his life through faith and loyalty.

OEDIPUS: (*Aside*) Now I have him! Number, place agree—
but tell me when.

JOCASTA:                          Ten harvests have gone by.

(*Enter* OLD MAN)

OLD MAN: Sire, Corinth's people call upon you now
to rule them. Death has laid your father low.

OEDIPUS: Fortune's attacking me from every side!
Tell me exactly how Polybus died.                         810

OLD MAN: His aged spirit drifted off in dreams.

OEDIPUS: My father was not murdered then, it seems.
Clean hands I now raise heavenward, and swear
they're free at last of any libelous smear.
Yet of my fears the greater part remain.

OLD MAN: Such cares will vanish once you're on the throne.

OEDIPUS: My father's kingdom willingly I take;
the image of my mother makes me quake.

OLD MAN: You fear the mother who so anxiously
awaits your coming?                                       820

OEDIPUS:                   Out of piety.

OLD MAN: And leave her widowed and abandoned?

OEDIPUS:                  There
you touch upon the very thing I fear.

OLD MAN: This buried fear that tortures you must be
  spoken! No secret will leak out through me.

OEDIPUS: Warned by the Delphic Oracle, I dread
  to pollute my mother's marriage bed.

OLD MAN: Reject such fears—they never can come true.
  Merope did not give birth to you.                              830

OEDIPUS: I was adopted? What good could this do?

OLD MAN: The sons of kings keep watch on loyalty.

OEDIPUS: How did you learn my secret history?

OLD MAN: These very hands passed you, an infant, on
  to her who gave you birth.

OEDIPUS:                                    My mother's son
  you handed to her? Who gave me to you?

OLD MAN: A shepherd in high Mount Cithaeron's snow.

OEDIPUS: That wild place? What brought you there that day?

OLD MAN: A herdsman follows livestock as they stray.        840

OEDIPUS: Now name whatever marks you know I bear.

OLD MAN: Your feet were pierced with iron. From that scar
  and the resulting swelling, you are lame;
  the wound that makes you limp gave you your name.

OEDIPUS: And who was he—for I still want to know—
  who gave my person as a gift to you?

OLD MAN: The royal herdsman, under whom a whole
  flock of minor shepherds served as well.

OEDIPUS: His name?

OLD MAN:                    An old man's early memory grows    850
  faint and flabby, fading with disuse.

OEDIPUS: But could you recognize the fellow's face?

OLD MAN: Perhaps I might. What's buried in the space
  of bygone years some little mark can show.

OEDIPUS: Then towards the altars all our herds must go
  together with their shepherds—quickly, too.
  The leaders of each flock—slaves, call them out!

OLD MAN: Whether the cause is chance or foresight, let
  those things stay hidden which have seen no light
  for many years! We seek to lay truth bare,                860
  but often what we find is sheer despair.

OEDIPUS: What evil worse than this is there to fear?

OLD MAN: Terrible woe, of that you can be sure.
  The people's welfare and the king's meet here
  in equal balance. Don't touch either one;
  leave fate unchallenged to unfold alone.

OEDIPUS: I'd never meddle when the state's serene;
  if anarchy's at hand, I intervene.

OLD MAN: What more than royal blood can tempt you so?
  Beware; the parentage you learn, you'll rue.               870

OEDIPUS: Whoever I may be, I need to know!
  Here comes old Phorbas, weighted down with years:
  King Laius' flocks were all once in his care.
  (*To* OLD MAN)
  Are they familiar, this man's face or name?

OLD MAN: I think I recognize him. All the same,
   his face is strange—and yet not quite unknown.
   (*To* PHORBAS)
   Was it you who during Laius' reign
   drove his rich herds along Cithaeron's plain?

PHORBAS: Cithaeron's pastureland was always prime.
   I'd feed my flocks there in the summertime.                    880

OLD MAN: Do you know me?

PHORBAS:                          My memory isn't clear.

OEDIPUS: Did you once give a boy to this man here?
   Speak up! You're blushing, fumbling for ways
   to shape your words, but truth hates such delays.

PHORBAS: You stir up waters that for years have lain
   stagnant.

OEDIPUS:        Must torture force you to speak plain?

PHORBAS: I did give him the child. No gift—a blight
   that never could have lived to see the light.                  890

OLD MAN: Ill-omened words! He lives—and will, I pray,
   live on.

OEDIPUS:        Why should he perish, as you say?

PHORBAS: An iron rod pierced both his feet, and bound
   his legs together; the resulting wound
   foully festered. He was at death's door.

OEDIPUS: (*Aside*)
   Fate's close at hand. Why question any more?
   (*To* PHORBAS)
   Who was that baby? Tell me.

PHORBAS:                  Loyalty
   forbids an answer.                                      900

OEDIPUS:             Bring fire, somebody!
   Flames will drive such fidelity away.

PHORBAS: Must truth be sought by such a cruel path?
   Pardon, I beg.

OEDIPUS:           I may seem full of wrath,
   but vengeance lies right within your reach.
   Whose was that boy? I want a truthful speech.
   What woman's child?

PHORBAS:          Your own wife gave him birth.

OEDIPUS: Ah, open up and swallow me, oh earth!       910
   Father of shadows, blast with blackest curses
   that man who roles of son and sire reverses.
   Stones at my head, you citizens, let fly;
   take arms against me. Father, son will vie
   to injure me. Husbands and brothers—let
   them arm themselves against me! Let the poor
   sick populace snatch brands from every pyre
   to hurl at me. For my whole generation
   I'm a miasma, harm for civilization.
   Hated by the gods from that vile day                920
   I first drew breath and feebly tried to cry,
   what else am I now fit for but to die?
   (Aside)
   But summon up your spirits now. It's time
   to dare atrocities that match your crime.
   Back to the palace! Let Jocasta preen;
   her dynasty's enriched by many a son.

CHORUS: If I could fashion my own fate,
   I'd glide along caressing winds.
   No violent gales would capsize me.

Let gentle breezes push my boat                              930
while cautiously I steer my life
along the path of moderation.
Young Icarus feared the king of Crete,
yet boldly reached out for the stars;
he tried to order his false wings
to vie with skimming birds in flight.
Now deep waters bear his name;
nothing else is left of him.
Daedalus, the old survivor,
halted halfway up the sky                                    940
waiting for his winged son
(as a bird flees from the hawk
to gather up her fear-flung brood)
till, damned by his attempt to soar,
his hands entangled in false wings,
the boy splashed down into the sea.
All that exceeds the norm is left
hanging on the edge of doom.
What is this noise outside the door?
A stricken servant of the king                               950
hammers a fist against his head.
What news?

MESSENGER: Once Oedipus perceived the whole foul dread
    that was his birthright, onto his own head
    he showered curses, and with hurrying feet
    sped to the palace, mulling on his fate.
    A savage lion on the Libyan plain
    rages and roars and tosses its gold mane;
    so, wild of eye, distorted by his passion,
    he groaned—no, howled. An icy perspiration            960
    covered his body, as a foaming tide
    of long quiescent sorrows overflowed.
    Some appalling stroke is in his mind
    to match his fate—and bring it to an end.
    "Why am I waiting? Why delay?" he moans.
    "Stab me, someone! Shatter me with stones,

or let a fire consume my sins to ash!
Tigers and vultures, batten on my flesh!
Accursed Cithaeron, lair of nothing good,
send out wild beasts against me from your wood,                 970
set a pack of slavering hounds on me
or the ferocious queen, mad Agave!
My soul, death's nothing fearful, no offense;
death preserves the good man's innocence."
These were his words. He drew his sword, and then:
"Is this the way? Such dreadful crimes with one
blow to be dissolved, the penalty
forever paid? Yes, for your father die—
punishment enough for that. But not
for her who bore you, on whom you begot                          980
an evil breed of offspring—not for her!
If you're the sinner, she's the sufferer,
utterly ruined. And your country bleeds!
Suicide can't atone for these misdeeds.
No, let that nature who in fashioning me
forsook her laws and standards utterly
transform herself once more on my behalf
to punish me with freakish shapes of wrath.
Let me live a brand new life, then die,
only to be reborn to misery,                                     990
a never-ending cycle. This takes thought:
some unique form of punishment stretched out,
some death continual, lingering; some way
where, shunned by live and dead alike, I'll stray
toward slow extinction, not a sudden end.
How can you shrink from such a sentence, friend?"
Sobs like a sudden rainstorm wet his face.
"Weeping is useless, tears a mere disgrace.
Ah, but if my eyes themselves I scrape
out of their sockets, then—like tears in shape—                 1000
they can rain down. Gods of connubial night,
let this be your sacrifice: my sight!"
These were his words. Cheeks blazing fiery red,
delirious, eyes starting from his head,

of desperation's violent power full,
he groaned. His fingers clawed into his skull.
His eyes wait, avid, ready for his hands,
and rush to meet them, eager for the wound.
His nails rake out all lingering shreds of light,
ripping loose the very roots of sight.                              1010
All blind and empty! Still, his hand's employed
scraping the hollow, picking at the void.
His maddened ravings too go on and on,
but somehow their immediacy is gone.
Now that he is finally free of sight,
he lifts his head to catch a glimpse of night.
Scanning the heavens with his empty eyes,
he rips away a lingering ribbon, cries
to all the gods triumphantly: "I pray
you, spare Thebes now! I've paid the penalty;              1020
I've found a sure way to make old wrongs right.
My dark past matches this unending night."
Now from his mangled face a shower of gore
bursts out afresh, blood spraying everywhere.

CHORUS: By fate propelled, to fate we yield.
    No fussy gestures set us free.
    It is decreed, our human doom,
    all from above. Lachesis' laws
    (tightly she grasps them) point one way.
    Through narrow channels our lives move:                 1030
    our first day singles out our last.
    No god can cause events to swerve
    which, meshed in motives, roll along;
    each life proceeds untouched by prayer.
    To some men, fear's the greatest bane:
    afraid of what is fated, blind,
    they blunder right into their fate.
    Listen, the door! The king himself—
    eyeless, unguided—gropes this way.

OEDIPUS: All is well, the deed is done at last.                                  1040
    I've paid the penalty for my murderous past.
    How sweet the shadows are! Some grateful god
    has poured a cloud of blackness on my head,
    pardoned my crimes. The sun's unwinking lid
    I have escaped. It's not, you parricide,
    to any exercise of your own might
    that you owe this deliverance. Rather, light
    shuns you.
              I finally have a truthful face.

CHORUS: Here comes Jocasta at a frantic pace,                                     1050
    beside herself, delirious, like the queen
    who, frenzied, tore the head from her own son
    and understood too late what she had done.
    She hesitates to speak to him. In her,
    desire and pity alternate with fear.
    Though such calamities must banish shame,
    her voice still falters as she speaks to him.

JOCASTA: What shall I call you? Son? You are, I know,
    a son who will not speak to me, or show
    his empty features.                                                          1060

OEDIPUS:               Leave me, let me be!
    What enemy would restore my sight to me?
    My mother's voice—I recognize the tone—
    means that all my efforts are in vain.
    For us to meet again is blasphemy.
    Our crimes should be divided by some sea
    as vast as our own sins; some country far
    from here should shelter us, strange as a star.
    Only a planet alien to this place
    (if there is any) could be home to us.                                        1070

JOCASTA: You are not guilty! Fate's to blame, not you!

OEDIPUS: Oh mother, spare your breath, and my ears too—
　　by my mutilated face I plead
　　and by the hideous mingling of our blood
　　and by our double kinship, fair and foul.

JOCASTA: What are you waiting for, oh coward soul?
　　You were his crime's companion, yet he
　　alone now faces punishment. Why not me?
　　Incestuous creature, through whose dreadful deed
　　every human decency lies dead,                                    1080
　　end it! Free your ill spirit with a blade!
　　Not even if god were thundering at my head
　　with all his glittering bolts aimed straight at me
　　could I ever pay the penalty,
　　hellish mother that I am. I see
　　no way but death—and death will find a way.
　　(*to* OEDIPUS)
　　Come, parricide; your mother needs a stroke
　　to kill her too. Come and complete your work!
　　(*She grabs his sword*)
　　Better to seize the sword that struck him down,
　　my husband—no, my husband was his son!—                 1090
　　the sword I'll plunge into my breast or neck.
　　Come on, sword, quickly! Choose a place to strike.
　　I know the place: I'll pierce that fruitful womb
　　that brought to birth a husband and a son.

　　(*Stabs herself*)

CHORUS: Her cold hand heavy on the wound,
　　she lies. Blood forces out the sword.

OEDIPUS: Oh god in charge of truth, what have you done?
　　Another death? My father was the one
　　I owed to fate, but—doubly guilty now—
　　I've killed my father and my mother too.                          1100
　　She never would have perished but for me.
　　Lying Apollo, in my cruelty

I surpass my own vile destiny!
With trembling fingers, wandering through the gloom
with hands outstretched and groping, you must roam—
and quickly, too—one foot before the other—
but careful lest you stumble on your mother!
All you with bodies burdened by disease
and fighting for your lives, I leave this place.
Look up! For even as I move away,                    1110
a gentler spirit animates the sky.
Whoever at death's door somehow lives on,
let him now gulp great draughts of oxygen.
Go offer hope to those resigned to die;
the pestilence leaves Thebes along with me.
Destructive Fates and sickness' trembling fear,
wasting, black plague, dementia—come here,
be my companions! All to me are dear.
(*Exit*)

# THE MADNESS
# OF HERCULES

*(HERCULES FURENS)*

Translated by Dana Gioia

# INTRODUCTION

Almost everyone agrees with the principle that a translation should be faithful, but the practical question is always, to what? Abstract principles are useful to a translator only insofar as they lead to specific solutions. The serious translator must inevitably decide which particular features of the original he or she wants to re-create in the new language. The question is particularly problematic in the case of that difficult, doomed, and necessary undertaking—translating poetry. While translation is undoubtedly a creative act, it is also unavoidably an interpretive one. The translator must identify, though not necessarily disclose, what he or she considers the artistic essence of the original. I raise these issues because my translation of *Hercules Furens* assumes the essentially poetic character of Seneca's tragedy. I have tried to be as faithful as possible to the literal sense of the Latin without sacrificing the poetry.

The power of Seneca's plays resides preeminently in their language, and no play displays this characteristic more conspicuously than *Hercules Furens*. The drama moves forward by pushing language to its extremes of intensity and expression. The cathartic effect of the tragedy depends on Seneca's bold projection of the tormented inner lives of his characters, who suffer from the gnawing cancers of horror, fear, hatred, remorse, and grief. To communicate the piercing immediacy of these emotions, Seneca exploits the varied resources of literary speech—poetry, oratory, narrative, dialogue, and aphorism. Although his language can be complex, learned, and allusive, it is always carefully shaped for dramatic effect. A translator must never forget that Seneca's lines were meant to be performed aloud. If the excitement of performance (the sense of the speaker pushing his or her ability to the limit) is lost, *Hercules Furens* loses its narrative drive and dramatic tension. If the sonorous physicality of the language is lost, the play loses its unifying energy. Without the dazzle of its poetry, *Hercules Furens* disappears.

The power of a classic resonates as much in its strangeness as in its familiarity. One essential quality of *Hercules Furens* that I wanted to re-create was its profound foreignness to our contemporary assumptions of drama. Although not part of a public ritual like the tragedies of Aeschylus, Seneca's play nonetheless unfolds according to a prescribed ceremonial protocol. *Hercules Furens* exalts in its own fixed forms and conventions, an attitude utterly at odds with modern notions of high art. The temptation for a translator is to make the play more like a contemporary drama, but it is always a mistake to "improve" an original—to adapt it, that is, to the exigencies of current taste—unless one plans to create a new work of art that can stand independent of the original. A translator should not try to remove the strangeness from an original but to convey it effectively. I have made no cuts or significant alterations. But, while taking every word into account, I have resolutely avoided translating the text word by word or even phrase by phrase. I have, instead, tried to bring it across turn by imaginative turn. Reflecting the intricate shifts and shapes of the original seemed essential in capturing its quirky brilliance.

There is no way of doing a poetic translation that will please everyone. The more remote and difficult the text—the more, that is, the original requires imaginative transposition—the greater the room for dissatisfaction. Faced with the impossibility of satisfying others, I decided to please myself, by translating the play as I saw it produced in the theater of my imagination. *Hercules Furens* is Seneca's *Inferno*, a vision of hell without the consolations of Christian redemption. The tragedy's world-view is so dark that only the emotional energy and formal magnificence of the language make its existential bleakness bearable. To translate the play persuasively required finding poetic equivalents in English capable of sustaining its almost intolerable levels of tension and horror while also admitting interludes of philosophical reflection. I hope my formal solutions do not displease the shade of Seneca. This translation of *Hercules Furens* was not written to be read silently on the page but to be spoken and heard. It is consciously intended as a performing version. To a director wishing to mount the play I offer the following suggestions:

1.  Acting style: Seneca's tragedy has almost nothing in common with contemporary realistic drama. Its energy depends on its poetry being brought to life by the human voice the way a prima donna seduces an opera house into submission or an old chanteuse brings a cabaret audience to tears. Nothing less than shameless self-confidence will suffice. Directors should revel in Seneca's artifice and view all notions of verisimilitude with suspicion. As in Nō drama, the splendor of the play for a Western audience resides at least partially in its foreignness. The performance may even require some form of overt stylization to distance the audience so that the dramatic action will seem to unfold in a mythic world purer than our own.

2.  The chorus: English-language theater has no tradition of choral recitation. I have translated the choral odes as Seneca wrote them, as continuous lyric poems. It would, however, be self-defeating to chant the odes in traditional choral style, since their poetry might well become lost in their performance. Although they could be recited by a single actor, the choruses would best be performed by two or three voices speaking alternately alone and in unison. The director should use his or her own discretion in dividing the lines among voices consistently with the theatrical vision of the production.

3.  Performing version: The translation re-creates the full text as it survives. A text of a play, however, is not theater. No one knows how the play was performed in Rome, but throughout the recorded history of drama, theatrical companies have edited and adapted their materials for performance. Shakespeare's company almost certainly cut and tailored his plays in production. Ibsen and O'Neill allowed cuts. Donizetti, Verdi, and even Wagner authorized streamlining of their tragic operas. A theatrical piece must work on stage. A director may want to cut the text of *Hercules Furens* slightly for performance. But a good director always cuts reluctantly and understands that every line removed must somehow be reflected in what remains.

Few classical texts have so thin a tradition in English translation as Seneca's *Hercules Furens*. I found only two previous verse translations—Jasper Heywood's 1561 version in bumptious fourteener couplets and Frank Justus Miller's 1907 rendition in blank verse. Heywood was the first English translator of Seneca. By the liberal standards of Tudor translation, he stayed close to Seneca's original in this play (unlike in his earlier *Troas*, to which he added a new character and inserted a chorus of his own invention). While Heywood's version has considerable historical interest, his unfortunate meter and haphazard versification make most of the play tough going. Only in the choruses, where he abandons fourteeners, do we occasionally hear a genuine poet.

Miller's translation, which is more widely known, as part of George E. Duckworth's *The Complete Roman Drama* (Random House, 1942), has the considerable virtue of fidelity. He brings Seneca's knotty Latin across line by line. Miller also provided the more or less literal prose translations for the 1917 Loeb Classical Library volumes. This seventy-five-year-old volume, which appears to be the most recent version of the play, proved invaluable to me, and I offer Professor Miller's shade my gratitude. Having studied Miller's Loeb version so carefully, however, I cannot resist nominating it as the most regularly iambic prose translation in the language. Hardly a sentence doesn't scan.

Invaluable to an amateur classicist like myself was John G. Fitch's exemplary critical Latin text and commentary, *Seneca's Hercules Furens* (Cornell University Press, 1987). Professor Fitch provides nearly five hundred pages of line-by-line commentary on the language, sources, allusions, and parallels of the Latin. If I sometimes departed from his readings, I always did so reluctantly. I also consulted Hugh MacMaster Kingery's 1908 edition, *Three Tragedies of Seneca*, which offered nothing quite so complete as Fitch's commentary but nonetheless helped me unravel some difficult passages.

Those books helped me with the Latin. I was fortunate in having a number of poets read portions of the English. I want to thank R. S. Gwynn, Paul Lake, Elizabeth Macklin, Charles Martin, David Mason, Robert McDowell, and David Slavitt for reading and commenting on sections of the play as it grew slowly act by act toward completion. I should also like to thank Anthony Lombardy, who read an early draft of my introduction.

Dana Gioia

# THE MADNESS OF HERCULES

## CHARACTERS

JUNO, queen of the gods, both sister and wife of Jupiter

AMPHITRYON, husband of Alcmena and stepfather to Hercules

MEGARA, wife of Hercules and daughter of King Creon

LYCUS, usurping king of Thebes who, before the play opens, has killed King Creon and his sons in battle

HERCULES, bastard son of Jupiter with Alcmena, but reputedly the son of Amphitryon

THESEUS, king of Athens, whom Hercules has just freed from the underworld

THREE CHILDREN, sons of Hercules and Megara (mute parts)

CHORUS of Thebans

BACKGROUND: Hercules is the illegitimate son of Jupiter and the mortal woman Alcmena. His nominal father is Amphitryon, Alcmena's husband, who loves Hercules as if he were his own child.

For several years Hercules has been exiled from his homeland, Thebes, and compelled by the gods to serve King Eurystheus. For his master, the hero has performed twelve dangerous and superhuman labors, each of which the king and his patroness, the goddess Juno, had hoped would destroy him.

As the play opens, Hercules has completed his final and most perilous labor, descending into the underworld to capture the three-headed dog, Cerberus. He is now free to return to his family in Thebes. His exploits have also brought him universal fame and demonstrated his worthiness to be deified by Jupiter. His lifelong ene-

49

my, Juno, is outraged at the possibility that Hercules will become
a god.

   The news of Hercules' safe return from the underworld has not
yet reached Thebes, where his family is in danger from Lycus, a
foreigner who has usurped the crown. Without Hercules, they have
no defender.

SCENE: *A public square of Thebes, in front of the palace of Hercules
and a temple dedicated to Jupiter and Ceres, beginning on the day of
Hercules' return to Thebes from the underworld.*


# ACT I


(*Enter* JUNO *alone. Late at night.*)

JUNO: Call me sister of the thunder god.
   That is the only title I have left.
   Once I was wife and queen to Jupiter,
   But now, abandoned by his love and shamed
   By his perpetual adultery,
   I leave my palace to his mistresses.
   Why not choose earth when heaven is a whorehouse?

   Even the Zodiac has now become
   A pantheon of prostitutes and bastards.
   Look at Callisto shining in the north,                    10
   That glittering slut now guides the Argive fleet.
   Or see how Taurus rises in the south,
   Not only messenger of spring's warm nights
   But the gross trophy of Europa's rape!
   Or count the stormy Pleiades—those nymphs
   Who terrorize the waves, once warmed Jove's bed.
   Watch young Orion swaggering with his sword,
   A vulgar upstart challenging the gods,
   While gaudy Perseus flaunts his golden star.

Gape at the constellations Jove awarded                        20
Castor and Pollux, his twin bastard sons.
And now not only Bacchus and his mother
Parade their ill-begotten rank in heaven,
But my great husband, lord of lechery,
Discarding his last shred of decency,
Has crowned his drunken bastard's slut with stars!

But why rehearse long-standing grievances?
Tonight I have to face new aggravation—
From Thebes! This crude, depressing, backward land,
Less a nation than a vast bordello,                            30
Full of ripe country girls eager to make me
Stepmother to my husband's indiscretions.
And now Alcmena will be deified
To occupy my place among the gods.
And Hercules, her son by Jupiter,
Is ready to assume his promised star.

I hate this Hercules. Even his begetting
Covered me with universal shame.
When Jupiter first coupled with Alcmena,
He cost the world a day, ordering Phoebus                      40
To hold the rising chariots of the sun
Beneath the eastern waves—because one night
Was not enough to satisfy his lust.
I will not cool my anger in the waves,
But fuel it like a blacksmith's raging furnace
To forge a blade of merciless revenge.
My only peace will be eternal war.

But with what weapons? Every savage beast
Spawned by the blighted earth, every foul monster
Born by the angry sea or storm-tossed air—                    50
Each filthy, vicious, pestilential fiend
Hercules has destroyed or overcome.
He leaves each battle freshened and renewed.
He revels in my cruelest challenges.

He takes the deadly labors I impose
And turns them to his credit. Pointlessly
My hate has made a hero out of him.
My anger proved the mother of his glory.
His reputation stretches with the sun
From where bright Phoebus rises in the east          60
To where it darkens Ethiopia's tribes.
Across the world he's worshiped like a god.

There are no monsters left—and, if there were,
Why bother sending him to conquer them?
I fretted more in setting his twelve labors
Than that young braggart did in their completion.
Each time I sent him to his death, he smiled,
Always returning smugly with his trophies—
The lion's skin stretched out across his shield,
His arrowheads dipped in the hydra's poison.          70

And now his conquests reach beyond the earth.
He batters down the gates of hell itself
And brings back spoils from the defeated depths.
I watched him come before the throne of Jove.
Yes, watched in horror, as he shamelessly
Displayed the sacred beast which he had seized
From Jove's own brother, having brushed aside
The guardians of hell as casually
As hands might wave aside a smudge of smoke.
What next? Why not bring Pluto bound in chains,          80
Enslave a deity equal to Jove
And occupy his throne to rule the dead?
Was it not blasphemous enough for Hercules
To trespass Hades, roving like a bandit,
Then break death's law returning to the light?
The door stands open to the afterlife,
The crowded shadows whisper of escape,
The solemn mysteries of death revealed.

But Hercules is proud of breaking laws.
He takes a boy's delight in boasting how 90
He meets my every challenge. He insults me,
Parading throughout Greece triumphantly,
Leading the sacred Cerberus to show
The terrifying mysteries of the grave
To every craning shopkeeper and schoolboy.
I watched the daylight shrink in fear. I saw
The blazing noon turn gray as the foul, black,
Three-headed beast was circled by the crowd.
I watched the holy guardian of death,
Loaded with chains, gaped at like a sideshow, 100
And I was sick with shame that I, the queen
Of all the gods, had given the command.

But these are minor matters now—compared
With what I fear. Why wouldn't Hercules,
Who has subdued both earth and underworld,
Not try to conquer heaven next and seize
His father's office? Bacchus peacefully
Claimed his immortal place among the stars,
But Hercules knows nothing but brute force.
He will use violence to make his claim. 110
It will not bother such a man to rule
A decimated and demolished kingdom.

Now each new triumph multiplies his pride,
And he has learned by shouldering the sky
That he is strong enough to conquer heaven.
He freed encumbered Atlas from the weight
Of holding up the star-filled firmament,
But that immeasurable mass did not
Bend Hercules. Though I had hoped to crush him,
Unwavering he carried it erect 120
And proved his strength was greater than the gods'.

The time has come to turn my anger loose,
To set it like a pack of starving wolves

Howling after this ambitious brute—
To corner him, to rip him flesh from bone!
I will not delegate my huge revenge,
Nor will I use more monsters as my proxy.
He easily destroyed the ten great beasts
King Eurystheus found. That method failed.
No, even if the Titans were unchained,                           130
Who challenged Jove, or if the burning caves
Of Aetna were unbarred to free the buried
Giant whose slightest movements shake the earth,
Or the cold moon poured down its cruelest fiends,
I would not pit them all against this man.
But there is one sure way to conquer him.
I will make Hercules destroy himself.

Let my voice shake the deepest pit of hell
And wake the Furies, daughters of the Night.
Come to me, sisters, with your hair alive                        140
In leaping flame, your dripping claws clamped tight
Around your scourges made of thrashing snakes.

And as for Hercules, let him proceed,
The arrogant fool, seeking his divinity,
So confident he is superior
To other men. Let him assume he's left
The underworld and all its ghosts behind.

For I will show him hell on earth! There is
A cavern buried deep in Tartarus
Where guilty souls are tortured through eternity                 150
By unappeasable guardians of pain.
I summon up those primal deities.
Come to me, Discord, goddess of Destruction.
Bring up the secret horrors of the damned
That even Hercules has never seen.
Come to me goddesses of Violence
And rash Impiety whose filthy hands
Are stained with family blood. Come to me, Error.

And come to me, you whom I most desire,
Goddess of Madness who turns men on themselves,          160
You who will be the spur of my revenge.

Now servants of the underworld, begin!
The fires of vengeance rage. Alecto, lead
The hissing Furies out of hell, and let
Each loathsome goddess snatch a burning brand
From the infernal pyre. Now to our work!
Revenge the desecration of the Styx.
Shatter his sanity. Make his soul burn
More furiously than Aetna's deadly furnace.
And make me mad as well, blinded by hate,                170
Senseless with anger, famished for his blood,
If it takes madness to conceive a plan
To break his mind and compel Hercules
To turn his strength to self-destructive fury.

The first act of my madness is a prayer—
For Hercules—"May he return home safe,
His strength intact, and find his little sons
Happy and healthy." Why resent his vigor?
I want him strong today. I want the same
Great force that conquered me to be his conqueror.      180
I crave occasion to applaud this hero,
Who triumphed over death's dominion,
As he begs for death and grovels for oblivion,
And, if I haven't always been a good
Stepmother to my husband's gifted son,
Today I'll make amends. I'll stand beside him
When frenzy blurs his sight, and help him send
Each arrow to its unsuspected mark.
I'll be his staunchest ally in the fight.
And when he finishes his giddy slaughter,               190
I'll have him raise his dripping hands to Jove
And ask for his admission into heaven!

I see the first bright tracings of the dawn.
The plan is set, and now I must be gone.

(*Enter a* CHORUS *of Theban elders*)

CHORUS: Now the stars begin to fade
    Like an army put to flight,
    Burying their scattered campfires,
    Routed by the morning's light.

    Fading in the northern sky,
    Soon the Great Bear will be gone.                    200
    One by one its seven stars
    Disappear into the dawn.

    Blazing from the mountaintop,
    Phoebus rises on his steeds.
    In the vineyards of the Bacchae
    Sunlight down the hillside bleeds.

    Phoebe, goddess of the Moon,
    Flees the sun's advancing beams.
    Hunger, Worry, aching Labor
    Shake the peasant from his dreams.                   210

    Shepherds leading out their flocks
    Find the meadows frosted white.
    Bullocks gambol in the pasture.
    Lambs are frisking in delight.

    Hidden in the highest treetops,
    Mournful nightingales have sung
    Philomela's ancient sorrows,
    Comforting their starving young.

    Now the other birds awaken,
    Loud with music of their kind.                       220

Sailors setting forth to danger
See their canvas swell with wind.

On the harbor rocks, a fisher
Baits his hook of keen design,
While another smiles to feel
The struggling prey caught on his line.

Such is the lot of common people.
Who praise each day for its rewards,
Grateful for peace, they envy no one
But prize the small joys life affords.                    230

Let ambition rule the City
Where truth and virtue are sold short,
Where suitors sleep in rich men's doorways,
And poets lisp their lies in Court.

Let the miser count his riches
Always aching to have more.
Each new coin adds to his nightmare
Of his death unloved and poor.

Noble politicians preach
Virtue to the shifting mob,                               240
Defenders of a commonwealth
No one else but they can rob.

The happy few who live in peace
Realize it may not last.
The slightest change of fortune may
Leave joy and comfort in the past.

While fate permits, enjoy this life.
Death stalks us all with steady pace.
The wheel of Time turns just one way.
The steps we take we can't retrace.                       250

The Fates themselves who measure life
Cannot lengthen what they've spun.
Why tempt death by seeking glory?
Why hurry to oblivion?

Only Hercules descended
Into death before his hour,
Then escaped the grieving kingdom,
Unrestrained by Pluto's power.

But on the preappointed day,
Implacable, the Fates return.                          260
Heroes thought invincible
Fall to ashes for the urn.

Let others seek far-reaching glory,
Salute the crowd from triumph's car,
Gain immortality in story,
Be deified in shining star.

But grant me just one quiet acre,
A humble cottage far from trouble,
To live out my alloted span,
Though great cities fall to rubble.                    270

CHORUS LEADER: But, look, Megara's coming. How sad she
     seems.
   Her hair's in disarray, and her three children
   Clutch at her skirt while old Amphitryon,
   Hercules' stepfather, hobbles after her.

## ACT II

(*Enter* MEGARA, *her* THREE CHILDREN, *and* AMPHITRYON. *Being
mortal, they do not know that* HERCULES *has safely left the underworld. They approach the altars of Jupiter and Demeter.*)

AMPHITRYON: O Jupiter, great ruler of Olympus,
   Chief judge of all the world, have mercy on us!
   Please set some limit to our suffering.
   I've never woken to a painless dawn.
   My son gains nothing from his awful toil.
   Each evil challenge that he overcomes        280
   Is just a step to one more dangerous.
   There's always some new foe awaiting him.
   Before he can return to us at home
   He must pursue some perilous new goal.
   He has no rest except the instant spent
   Hearing Eurystheus's next command.

   Juno has persecuted him since birth.
   Even his cradle was not free from danger.
   He had to fight off monsters before he knew
   What monsters were. Once Juno sent two huge        290
   Serpents to kill him. But, as their crested heads
   Rose to attack, the infant crept toward them,
   His wide eyes meeting their ferocious gaze.
   He calmly seized a serpent in each hand
   And pulled their thrashing bodies from the floor.
   His tiny fingers slowly crushed their throats.
   Such was his early practice for the Hydra.

   You know the hardships brought by his twelve labors—
   Of how he struggled for a year to track
   The swift, gold-antlered stag of Maenalus;        300
   And how he found the fierce Nemean lion

Then crushed the roaring monster in his arms.
Need I recall how, seizing Diomedes,
He fed the king to his man-eating steeds?
Or how he killed the Eurymanthian boar
Who terrorized the forests of Arcadia,
And caught the Cretan bull that had destroyed
A hundred towns? Or how in distant Spain
He slaughtered the three-headed Geryon
And took the giant's oxen as his booty?                               310
That herd now grazes on our own Mount Cithaeron.
When ordered to explore the tropic deserts
Of Northern Africa where the fierce noon
Scorches the sand, he stood between two mountains
And pushing them apart, made a wide path
For the cool ocean waters to pour in.
He found the grove of the Hesperides
And stole its golden apples from the dragon.
And did he not at last destroy by fire
The fierce, nine-headed Hydra of the swamp?                           320
He shot down all the bronze Stymphalian birds
Whose swarming wings could block the noonday sun.
He seized the armored belt of Queen Hippolyta,
The virgin monarch of the Amazons.
He even put his noble hands to work
And cleaned the filthy stables of Augeas.

What good did all this do him? Hercules
Is banished from the world that he defended.
The earth has lost the man who gave it peace.
Now crime not only prospers but assumes                               330
The public guise of virtue. Good men obey
The wicked. Might makes right. And fear is law.
With my own eyes I saw King Creon's sons
Cut down by Lycus's usurping hand,
As they attempted to defend their father.
Then Lycus murdered the old king himself.
I watched in horror as he seized the crown
By cutting off the royal corpse's head.

There are not tears enough to mourn for Thebes—
Country of gods that now fears its own master,                     340
Proud land whose fertile meadows once produced
A squad of soldiers sprung from dragon's teeth,
City whose walls were built by Jove's own son,
Amphion who could move great blocks of stone
By playing on his magic lyre, great kingdom
Which more than once the Father of the Gods
Left heaven's height to visit in full state,
Fair city which has welcomed gods and made gods
And, dare I say, will soon produce more gods,
How shamefully you are enslaved! How low                          350
The royal race of Cadmus now has fallen.
We now obey a low-born foreigner,
Who exiled from his homeland, tramples ours.

But Hercules, who could avenge these crimes,
A man who has already ousted tyrants,
Is far away. The gods make him obey
A king he would not countenance at home.
Now Lycus rules the Thebes of Hercules.

But not for long. My son will soon return
To punish these transgressions. He will find                      360
Some way to come back from the underworld
And see the stars again. And if he can't
Find an escape from hell, then he will make one.
I pray that he will come back safely and soon,
Return a victor to his vanquished land.

MEGARA: Come back to me, dear husband. Fight your way
    Up through the darkness. If there is no path
    For your escape, then rip the earth apart
    To make one, even if it means that all
    The secret spawn of hell stream after you.                    370
    Remember how you once pushed hills apart
    To make a new course for the river Peneus.
    You tore the sides off mountains, as you scooped

A sheltered valley for the rushing water
Leaping through the huge cleft your arms created.

Now for your parents, children, homeland, wife
Carve such a passage. If death weighs you down,
Bear its dark burden. Carry back with you
All the lost things that greedy time has hoarded.
Drive the forgetful, frightened dead before you            380
Trembling into the light. Make them your cattle.
It would be unworthy of you to return
Without some spoils beyond what was commanded.

But I've been speaking thoughtlessly—ignoring
The dangers we now face. O Hercules,
Will I never again hold you in my arms
Or tell you how the years apart have hurt me?
How often I imagine chiding you,
Half teasing, half in tears. Have you forgotten me?

To you, great Jupiter, king of the gods,                   390
I promise sacrifice—one hundred bulls,
Of finest breed, unbroken by the yoke.
To you, kind Ceres, goddess of the crop,
I vow that I'll perform your secret rites,
Go silent to your temple in Eleusis
And light the torches sacred to your name.
Then will my husband lead my brothers back
Out of the underworld and will restore
My murdered father to his stolen throne.

But if some power holds you in its thrall,                 400
Then we must follow you to Acheron.
So come at once, my love, to rescue us.
Or drag us down. We have no hope but you.
No other god will mend our shattered fortunes.

AMPHITRYON: Dear daughter-in-law, you must have some faith.
You are a loyal wife. You've shown such care

In raising our brave Hercules' sons.
Summon some courage yourself. He'll come back.
He always does, the greater for his labor.

MEGARA: The things unhappy people want too much                    410
    They start believing in.

AMPHITRYON:                 I disagree.
    The danger is that those who fear too much
    Believe their problems are unsolvable.
    Fear makes the world seem darker than it is.

MEGARA: Submerged in darkness, buried in the earth,
    Crushed beneath the weight of all the world,
    What chance has he to reach the sunlit air?

AMPHITRYON: The same he had when crossing the scorched
      desert.
    He made his way through shifting hills of sand
    That crashed and crested like a storm-swept sea.            420
    Or when his bark was shipwrecked by the tides
    On Syrtes' lethal shoal, he picked his path
    Safely across the pounding surf to shore.

MEGARA: Malicious fortune seldom spares a man
    Because he is courageous. No one courts
    Danger so often with impunity.
    Follow death long enough, and you will find it.

    But here comes Lycus now—scowling and angry,
    As ugly on the surface as inside.
    Look how he swaggers with his stolen scepter.                430

(LYCUS *enters. He sees* MEGARA *and* AMPHITRYON *praying on the
other side of the stage but does not at first approach them.*)

LYCUS: (*In soliloquy*) Now I am sovereign over all Thebes,
    Its wealthy towns, its sloping countryside,

All the lush valley of the swift Ismenus,
Even the isthmus stretching to the south.
Stand on the summit of Mount Cithaeron
And everything you see in all directions
Is mine.

        But no one ever gave it to me.
I am no heir. I have no noble name
Or great estate of ancient lineage,
No lofty family tree or courtly title.                                    440
All I was given was ferocious courage.
Nobles who brag about their ancestors
Extol the virtues that belong to others.
But when you seize a dynasty, you hold it
Nervously in your hands. Only sheer force
Can keep it yours. Everything you possess
Against the people's will comes by the sword.
No kingdom built on foreign soil is safe.

But there exists one person who can help
Secure my throne—the king's surviving daughter.                          450
If I could take Megara as my bride,
Her ancient blood would give my new regime
Legitimacy in the public eye.
I hardly think she will refuse my suit.
Sharing my bed will let her share my throne.
But if she stubbornly declines my offer,
I have no choice but to annihilate
Both her and all the house of Hercules.
Popular opinion will surge against me,
But if there is one thing that monarchs know,                            460
It's how to bear the public's hatred calmly.

Now is my chance. Fortune rewards audacity.
There is Megara, praying at the altar,
Still wearing the black veil of a mourning widow.
And next to her is old Amphitryon,
The one who really fathered Hercules.

(MEGARA *rises from prayer and turns to observe* LYCUS)

MEGARA: (*To herself*) What does this pestilence who killed my
    kinsmen
    Now want from me? What scheme has he in mind?

LYCUS: (*Addressing* MEGARA)
    Dear Princess of the royal house of Thebes,
    I need a moment with you to discuss               470
    Matters of great importance to us both.
    We must be open minded. Life is so short.
    There is no good in nourishing resentment
    Or letting anger fester in the heart.
    Conflict will never end if both the victor
    And vanquished are unwilling to disarm.
    A lengthy civil war can have no winners.
    Picture a kingdom with its farms in ruins,
    The fields unplowed, the villages burned down,
    The commonwealth a heap of bones and ashes.     480
    A prudent victor wants the peace restored.
    The conquered know it is their only hope.
    So won't you join me in rebuilding Thebes?
    Come, share my throne. I offer you this pledge
    Of my good faith. Give me your hand in peace.
    Why stand so silently? Why be so scornful?

MEGARA: How can I touch a hand still smeared with blood
    From slaughtering my father and my brothers?
    You'll sooner find a sunset in the East
    Or snowflake's glitter in a roaring fire.         490
    Why not ask Sicily to uproot itself
    And join its rocky coast to Italy?
    Why not stand on Euboe's storm-swept shore
    And tell the crashing, white-capped waves to stop?

    You took my father from me and my kingdom,
    My brothers and my home—what else is left?
    And yet I still have something dearer to me

Than father, brother, kingdom, or estate—
My hatred of you! How much I detest
Having to share it with the common crowd.                    500
How minuscule my loathing is to theirs.
Go on and rule—bloated with arrogance,
Puffed up with self-importance. But remember.
The gods avenge such pride.

                        Look at our past—
How tragedy pursues the House of Thebes.
You know our queens not only suffered evil
But have inflicted it. And Oedipus
Whose murder and incest pollute the name
Of father, husband, child. Think how his sons
Killed one another squabbling for the crown,                    510
Or how Niobe saw her children slaughtered
And turned into a stone dripping with tears.
Even great Cadmus, founder of our city,
Was cursed and changed into a crested serpent
To crawl across the wastelands of Illyria.
These are the precedents of your regime.
Do what you will as tyrant but remember
One day the doom of Thebes will fall on you.

LYCUS: Calm down, my dear. Enough of this mad talk.
Even your headstrong husband, Hercules,                    520
Knew kings must be obeyed. I've conquered Thebes.
My power is absolute. I don't explain;
I give commands. But since it's you I talk to,
I'll say a few words on my own behalf.

Yes, your old father died in a cruel battle
Along with your two brothers. I'm afraid
Weapons of war observe no decencies.
Once swords are drawn, they are not easily
Held back or put away. Wars feed on blood.
You feel your father died defending his realm                    530
While I was motivated by ambition.

Perhaps that's true, but once a war is over
Most people don't care much about the cause.
The only thing that matters is the outcome.
So let's forget about the awful past—
It can't be changed. For when the victor wants
To lay his weapons down, it's not unreasonable
To hope the vanquished put away their hate.
I don't ask you to grovel on your knees
And swear allegiance to my sovereignty.                       540
I like the way you stand up for your rights.
High spirits are attractive in a woman.
You deserve to be my queen. Come marry me.

MEGARA: A chill of horror makes my body tremble.
I can't believe your shameful proposition.
When war erupted, I wasn't afraid.
I faced each terror calmly—even when
The fighting echoed round the city walls.
But when you mention marriage, then I shudder.
For the first time I truly realize                             550
I'm just another slave captured in war.
Load me with chains or make me suffer death
By slow starvation. No torture you devise
Will break my loyalty to Hercules.
If I must die, I swear I will die his.

LYCUS: Why waste your love on someone trapped in hell?

MEGARA: He challenged hell to earn a place in heaven.

LYCUS: But now the earth has crushed him with its weight.

MEGARA: No weight can crush a man who held up heaven.

LYCUS: What if I force you?

MEGARA:                        Force can only work          560
On someone who is still afraid of death.

LYCUS: I can be generous. What wedding gift
　　Shall I present my bride?

MEGARA:                            Your death or mine.

LYCUS: Have you gone crazy? Do you want to die?

MEGARA: In death at least I can rejoin my husband.

LYCUS: Why choose that slave when you can have a king?

MEGARA: That slave sent many vicious kings to death.

LYCUS: Why does he serve a king and do hard labor?

MEGARA: A hero earns his fame through valiant labor.

LYCUS: What valor comes from fighting animals?                570

MEGARA: Valor consists of conquering what men fear.

LYCUS: Why argue? Hercules is dead in hell.

MEGARA: One must risk death to merit immortality.

LYCUS: Who fathered him that he seeks immortality?

AMPHITRYON: My poor Megara, rest awhile, dear daughter.
　　Let me respond to these crude accusations.
　　It's hard to fathom how there can be doubt
　　Of Hercules' divine paternity.
　　After all his superhuman deeds,
　　After the peace he settled on the world              580
　　Through his exploits, after the many monsters
　　That he destroyed, and, most clearly of all,
　　After the perilous assault at Phlegra
　　Where fighting at Jove's side he helped defeat
　　The gruesome army of rebellious giants,

What need is there to prove his parentage?
His father is great Jupiter. To doubt that
Is to believe the hateful lies of Juno.

LYCUS: You blasphemous old fool, stop spouting nonsense!
The gods don't mate with ordinary people.                    590

AMPHITRYON: But many gods were born from such a union.

LYCUS: But were they slaves before they became gods?

AMPHITRYON: Apollo served as shepherd for Admetus.

LYCUS: But did he wander through the world, an exile?

AMPHITRYON: Apollo's mother was condemned to exile
And bore him on the wandering isle of Delos.

LYCUS: But did Apollo stoop to combat monsters?

AMPHITRYON: The young Apollo killed the dragon Python.

LYCUS: If Hercules is really half divine,
Why did the gods try killing him at birth?                   600

AMPHITRYON: Bacchus was born when thunderbolts ripped open
His mother's womb, and yet he later stood
Beside his father, Jove, the god of Thunder.
And Jupiter himself, who rules the stars
And shakes the heavens, spent his infancy
Hiding in a deep cave beneath Mount Ida.
The price of greatness is tremendous danger,
And suffering is the birthright of a god.

LYCUS: I would not call a wretched man divine.

AMPHITRYON: I would not dare to call a brave man
wretched.                                                    610

LYCUS: Brave wouldn't be the term I'd use describing
  A man who not so long ago gave both
  His club and lion skin to some young sweetheart,
  So he could dress up like a dancing girl.
  How brave to wear a flimsy Turkish gown
  And drench your curly hair with sweet perfume.
  How brave to waste your strength on spinning wool
  While swaying to a barbarous tambourine,
  Crowning your manly brow with a girl's turban.

AMPHITRYON: But Bacchus did not hesitate to wear          620
  His hair in ringlets sprinkled with perfume
  Or take his slender fennel staff in hand
  When he would prance about in flowing robes
  Blazoned with hems of oriental gold.
  After great deeds a hero must relax.

LYCUS: Was one great deed when he destroyed Oechalia
  And sacked the noble House of Eurytus—
  Raping the daughters, driving them to death?
  Neither Eurystheus nor Juno ordered
  That carnage. It was Hercules alone.                    630

AMPHITRYON: But Hercules has mainly done good deeds.
  He killed King Eryx in his own cruel game.
  And then destroyed Antaeus who had built
  An altar from his victims' bloody skulls.
  He slew Busiris who had sacrificed
  Innocent travelers in his savage rites.
  Cycnus who was invulnerable to swords,
  He strangled with his hands, and he alone
  Exterminated triple-bodied Geryon.
  You will be next. And, Lycus, please remember           640
  That even those dead tyrants never tried
  To trespass Hercules' marriage bed.

LYCUS: What Jove enjoys is lawful for a king.
  You gave your wife to Jove, and now your son

Will give me his. Megara learns from you
The ancient lesson that Jove taught your spouse—
All wives are free to take a better man.
But should she still refuse to marry me,
I will use force to sire an heir from her.

MEGARA: Ghost of King Creon! Dark family gods          650
Who haunt the House of Thebes. Relight the torches
That cursed the marriage of incestuous Oedipus
And bring this union your accustomed doom.
Come here, blood-thirsty daughters of Aegyptus,
Come, show me how you spent your bridal nights
By slaughtering your husbands in their beds.
You let one groom escape, now let me gladly
Complete your mission on my wedding night.

LYCUS: Since you not only still refuse my suit
But threaten violence against your king,                660
Then you must learn what royal power means.
Cling to your altar. No god can save you now—
Not even if the earth were split apart
And Hercules returned victorious.
(*Calling his attendants*)
Come, bring some wood. We'll make a bonfire here
And burn the temple up around these traitors.
We'll answer their vain prayers with death by fire.
Bring out the torches. Let one immense pyre
Exterminate this wife and all her brood.

AMPHITRYON: As father of Lord Hercules, I ask           670
One favor—let me be the first to die.

LYCUS: A king must learn to be a connoisseur
Of suffering. The cruelest punishment
Gives the condemned the opposite of what
They most desire. Let the miserable live
And send the happy ones to death by torture.
And so, old man, you'll burn along with them.

Now while my servants build the deadly pyre,
I'll go make sacrifice in Neptune's temple.
(*He exits*)

CHORUS:
Fortune envies the bold                                        680
And begrudges the righteous their share
Of life's rewards. O why
Should King Eurystheus
Enjoy such untroubled ease
While long-suffering Hercules
Whose shoulders once balanced the sky
Must invade each monster's lair,
Must kill the Hydra, and seize
From the watchful dragon's care
The fruit of the Hesperides?                                   690

He conquered the Scythian clans
Who wander the Asian plain.
He crossed the frozen sea
On its silent wastes of ice
To a harbor of motionless ships
Fixed on a frigid pier,
Where no waves broke on the shore,
And teams of long-haired men
Made paths through pathless snow—
A sea that changed with the year                              700
Where both ships and sledges go.

There the Queen of Amazons
Stripped off the golden belt
That shielded her snow-white breast,
Held out the glorious prize,
And offering it, she knelt
Looking up at her victor's eyes.

What reckless ambition forces
Hercules to plunder hell,

Down the trail that none retraces? 710
No winds will ever swell
The still waters of that stream.
No auspicious stars will guide
Lost sailors through its gloom.
The Styx is a motionless flood,
And ravenous Death drives down
The countless ranks who swarm
To the ferry we all must ride.

If only he could destroy
The savage laws of hell 720
And unravel the Fates' tight thread.
Once in Pylos he fought
The king of the numberless dead.
Though armed with his three-forked spear,
Pluto was wounded and fled,
For death was afraid to die.
Overturn the Kingdom of Fear!
Banish the darkness with light!
Make a pathway up to the sky!

Once Orpheus subdued with song 730
The desolate lords of the dead
And won his wife's release.
His art could charm the trees,
Make rocks weep, birds throng,
Stop a river in its bed.

The soundless vault of hell
Had never heard a song
Of such sad melody.
It echoed in every ear,
And even Eurydice cried 740
At her own destiny.
The solemn lords of the dead,
Who had relinquished tears,
And the judges who oversee

The punishment of the damned
All wept for Eurydice.

Then Pluto approved his petition.
"We are defeated," he said.
"You may lead her back to life,
But I put down one condition.                                   750
You must walk ahead of your wife
And not turn back your eyes
Till you leave the land of the dead
And reach the open skies."
But love could bear no delay.
Orpheus turned to his prize,
And Eurydice melted away.

The underworld was once subdued by song,
But now the darkness battles with the strong.


ACT III


(HERCULES *enters, accompanied by* THESEUS. *They have just returned from Hades and bring the sacred monster Cerberus as their
captive.*)

HERCULES: Lord of beloved light, glory of heaven,              760
    Driver of the noon's flaming chariot,
    Radiant face that warms the morning fields,
    Phoebus, forgive me if I make you witness
    This sacrilege. I have been forced to bring
    The darkest secrets of the dead to light.
    I ask you, Jupiter, the judge and king
    Of all divinities, conceal your face
    Behind your thunder clouds. And you, lord Neptune,
    Second in power, monarch of the sea,
    Dive deep beneath the waves. Let all the gods               770

Watching over the earth, avert their eyes,
So this enormity will not pollute them.

The earth's four distant corners did not hold
Dangers or punishment lethal enough
To placate Juno's famine for revenge.
I have seen places unapproached by man,
Darkness untouched by day. I have explored
The world of shadow and unending night
Where dismal Pluto reigns. And had it pleased me,
I could have crowned myself the king of hell.                    780
I conquered all the shapeless lands of darkness—
Blacker than night—subdued its joyless deities,
And routed death itself. Now I return.
What challenge worthy of my strength remains?
Command me, Juno. You have let me rest
Too long already. Tell me my next triumph!

But why are soldiers standing by the temple,
Guarding the doorway with their weapons drawn?

AMPHITRYON: Does hope deceive me? Is it really you,
Returning from the silent realm of death?                        790
Oh, my son, my arms and legs are trembling.
You've come at last to save our troubled city.
But do I really see you in the flesh
Or are you a ghost who comes to mock my sorrow?

(*He touches* HERCULES)

Oh, it is you! I know these steely arms,
These great broad shoulders, and this mighty club.

HERCULES: Why do you wear these filthy clothes, father?
And why is my Megara dressed in mourning?
My sons all look like beggars! What calamity
Has overwhelmed the House of Hercules?                           800

AMPHITRYON: King Creon has been murdered. Lycus has seized
   The throne of Thebes. And now he has condemned
   Your father, wife, and children to be killed.

HERCULES: Ungrateful country! Did no one try to help
   The House of Hercules? Of all the people
   I have protected, did not even one
   Come forward to protest these gross atrocities?
   But why waste time complaining about cowards?
   It is my honor Lycus has besmirched,
   And I myself will settle the account.                          810
   I'll gut him like a sacrificial beast
   And drink his filthy blood.

                              But, Theseus,
   You must stay here and guard my family.
   Some unexpected danger may appear.
   I must kill Lycus now. I have no time,
   Father, for your embraces. Nor, wife, for yours.
   Reunions have to wait. I must send Lycus
   Speeding to hell with news of my return.

(*He leaves, dragging Cerberus with him*)

THESEUS: Please wipe those tears away, dear queen. And, you,
   Stop crying, grandfather! Your son is safe.                    820
   If I know Hercules, Lycus will pay
   The penalty he owes the House of Creon.
   No, *will pay* is too slowly said—he *pays*.
   No, even that's too slow for Hercules—
   He *has already paid* the penalty.

AMPHITRYON: May some merciful god hear our prayers
   And rescue us from danger! Theseus,
   Courageous friend of my courageous son,
   Please tell us the whole story of his quest.
   Describe the journey to the underworld—                        830

How long was it? How hard? And tell us how
He bound the dog of Tartarus in chains?

THESEUS: You ask me to remember things so terrible
That even now it's frightening to think back.
I was a prisoner in the land of death so long
I still can't take the air I breathe for granted.
It seems too fresh and pure. See how I squint?
My eyes can hardly bear the light of day.

AMPHITRYON: You must control your fear, King Theseus,
Why deny yourself the best reward                               840
That comes from hardship? Terrors that we suffer
Often become quite sweet in the retelling.
Give us the truth, however terrible.

THESEUS: I ask permission then from all the gods,
Especially from Pluto, whose vast realm
Encompasses all creatures that are mortal,
And Proserpine, his captive queen. Allow me
To tell the secrets buried in the earth—
And to describe the sufferings of the dead.

There is a famous cliff on Sparta's coast,                      850
A headland covered by a thick-grown wood,
Where Cape Taenarus juts into the sea.
It's here the mouth of Hades opens up.
The high cliffs split apart, and a huge cave,
A gaping chasm, stretches its vast jaws
And makes an entrance wide enough
For all mankind.

                    At first the way is not
Entirely dark. Some daylight filters down
And gives the cave that same bleak iridescence
The sun shows in eclipse. But gradually                         860
The path descends into unending twilight.

Your vision blurs, and only feeble streaks
Of red and violet shimmer in the dark
Like the last fading embers of a sunset.

But then the pathway opens to a vast
And empty place, a hazy nothingness
That all the human race must come to fill.
The journey now seems easy. The path itself
Begins to draw you down. Like waves that sweep
Whole fleets of ships unwillingly off course,                    870
Wind pushes at your back. The dark turns ravenous,
And shadows stretch out from the walls to clutch—
They let no one return.

                              Now at the bottom
The river Lethe runs as boundary,
Quiet and smooth, curving across the plain.
One drink will wash away the memory
Of all life's sorrow. To prevent the souls
From turning back to find the world of light,
The peaceful river twists and twists again
Just as the slow Maeander River does                             880
In Phrygia, which bends back on itself
So many times that travelers scarcely know
Whether it seeks the seacoast or its source.

Beyond the Lethe, lies the foul Cocytus,
River of Tears, motionless as a swamp,
Where starving vultures and the mournful owl
Shriek overhead their prophecies of pain.
Here in the branches of a black-leafed yew
Sits drowsy Sleep, while desperate Famine lies
Writhing on the ground, stretching her wasted jaws.             890
Here futile Shame averts his burning face,
Always too late, and thin Anxiety
Stalks nervously, pursued by dark-eyed Fear.
Here is gnashing Pain and black-robed Sorrow,
Trembling Disease and iron-vested War,

And, last of all, Old Age, his staff in hand,
Tottering forward step by painful step.

AMPHITRYON: What grows there? Are there fields of grain or
    vineyards?

THESEUS: There are no grassy meadows bright with flowers,
    No fields of ripened corn swaying in the wind,                    900
    No soft green vistas for the eye, or groves
    Where branches bend with slowly sweetening fruit,
    No breezes spiced with odors of the plum.
    But only wasteland everywhere, the fields
    Unwatered and untilled, the soil exhausted
    And nothing moving on the silent land.
    And this is how life ends—
    This barren place, this country of despair,
    Where no wind blows and darkness never lifts
    With hopeless sorrow twisting every shadow.                       910
    Dying is bitter, but eternity
    Confined in this black place is worse.

AMPHITRYON: Tell us about the ruler of the land.
    Where does he govern his tribes of flitting shadows?

THESEUS: In Tartarus, the darkest part of hell,
    There is a place enshrouded in thick mist.
    Here from a single spring two rivers flow.
    The first is calm, the sacred river Styx,
    By which the gods must swear their binding oaths.
    The other is a swift and raging torrent,                          920
    The Acheron, whose leaping rapids make it
    Impossible to cross. Between the rivers
    Stands the palace of the underworld,
    Encircled by a double moat. The hall
    Is huge but hidden by dark groves of pine.
    The entrance has been carved from living rock,
    Out of a great cave. Here leads the path of souls.
    Here is the doorway to the underworld.

Beyond the gate, a field spreads out where Pluto,
Proud and forbidding, sits to judge the fate                    930
Of new arriving souls. His face is cruel,
And yet you see a strong resemblance there
To Jupiter and Neptune, his two brothers.
But if he looks like Jove, it is the Jove
Of blinding thunder. If hell is full of terror,
It is because all hell holds him in dread.

AMPHITRYON: Is it true that in the afterlife
Justice prevails at last, and guilty souls
Who have made no atonement for their crimes
Must pay the penalties long overdue?                            940

THESEUS: There are three judges for the dead, who sit
To pass belated sentence on the damned.
The first is Minos, once the king of Crete,
Next Rhadamanthus, last is Aeacus.
Each soul must suffer for its sins on earth.
The evils men inflict they now must suffer,
And torture takes the form of their own crimes.
I saw repressive tyrants chained in cells
And watched plebeians lash bloodthirsty kings.
But those who govern with compassion, those            950
Who have the power to hurt but have refrained,
Who rule their subjects without violence,
And master their own anger, these wise men
Not only will enjoy long, happy lives
But at life's end, they may be deified
Or else will reach the bright Elysian fields,
A paradise that they will help to govern.
Remember, kings, that shedding blood is evil.
The penalties you give return tenfold
When you face judgment in the afterlife.                        960

AMPHITRYON: But are the damned imprisoned in one place?
And are the legends true that say the guilty
Must suffer cruel eternal punishment?

THESEUS: Ixion turns forever on his wheel.
Sisyphus strains his neck against the stone.
Tantalus dips his blistered mouth to drink,
And the old man feels the cool stream touch his lips.
For once the water stays. He laps it greedily.
It splashes on his tongue—so cool and sweet—
And then it pulls away. He sits up weeping          970
And sees high hanging fruit that mocks his hunger.
But vultures glut on screaming Tityus.
The daughters of Danaus vainly bring
Their heavy water jars to fill the sieve.
The Cadmeids rage forever in their madness.
The drooling harpies snatch blind Phineus' meal.

AMPHITRYON: Tell me the story of my son's adventure.
Did Pluto willingly give up his beast?
Or did my son wage war to gain the prize?

THESEUS: A high, black cliff looms over that still shore,          980
And no waves break across the stagnant shallows,
Where ancient Charon tends his river ford.
His face is terrible, his clothes are rags.
He crowds the trembling phantoms to the raft
And ferries them across. His beard is grizzled,
His filthy cloak hangs from a shoulder knot,
His cheeks are sunken like a corpse, but he
Swings the huge pole to push the heavy craft.
Then emptying his raft across the river,
He brings the empty vessel back to load          990
The teeming shadows waiting on the shore.

When Hercules demanded to be ferried,
The frightened ghosts drew back. Charon cried sharply:
"What is your hurry, man? Why push so boldly?
Wait, as the others do!"

But Hercules
Refused to be delayed. Seizing Charon's pole,
He forced his way aboard. The massive raft,
Ample enough for countless shadows, groaned
Beneath his weight, and, as he rode across,
The overloaded boat rocked side to side,                          1000
Letting the swampy Lethe flood its bows.

The spirits of the monsters he had killed
Grew panicked at his sight. The warlike Centaurs
And Lapithae broke off their drunken battle.
The Hydra sank its heads into the swamp
And swam away to find a hiding place.

Soon Pluto's palace rose up into view
Where the ferocious dog of Hades stood
Guarding the kingdom. Tossing its three heads,
It cowed the shadows with its piercing barks.                     1010
Around each snarling head, its tangled mane
Bristled with vipers, and its thrashing tail
Ended in a hissing dragon's head—
Its shape was the embodiment of anger.

It heard the steps approaching and looked up,
Its neck alive with snakes, its ears erect
And keen enough to hear a shadow's footfall.
But when the son of Jupiter appeared
And stepped into the cave, the dog crouched snarling.
And the two foes each felt the thrill of danger.                  1020
Then suddenly the quiet cavern shook
With terrifying howls. The serpents thrashed
And hissed along its back. So deafening was
The savage barking from its triple throat
Even the blessed spirits froze with terror.

Then Hercules took off his lion skin,
Wrapped it around his left arm as a shield,

And thrust its head and jaws at Cerberus.
Defended by the bulky hide, he raised
His other arm and swung his massive club.                    1030
First left, then right, he beat the savage dog
From side to side in an incessant volley.
At last the dog gave up, spent from the combat.
Bruised and defeated, it lowered its three heads,
Surrendering the entrance. On their thrones
The king and queen of hell sat terrified.
Not only did they let him take the dog;
When Hercules demanded my release,
They gave me to him as a royal tribute.

Then stroking the repulsive monster's necks,               1040
He collared them with chains of adamant.
The sleepless guardian of hell forgot
Its famed ferocity. It drooped its ears,
Trembling and willing to be led away.
With muzzles down, it followed its new master,
The snake-tipped tail whiplashing side to side.

But when it neared the opening of the cave,
The unfamiliar gleam of sunlight hit
The beast's nocturnal eyes. The monster panicked.
Regaining courage, shaking the thick chains,               1050
It nearly dragged its conqueror back to hell.
Despite his efforts, Hercules lost ground.
He even asked for me to help him pull
The raging, frightened beast up to the surface.

When Cerberus first glimpsed the light of day
And saw the free expanse of open sky,
The beast collapsed. Clenching its eyes shut
To block the burning light, it cringed and shuddered.
Grinding its faces in the dust, it groaned
And crawled to hide in Hercules' shadow.                    1060

By then a cheering crowd began to gather.
They put on laurel wreaths and started singing,
Praising the exploits of great Hercules.

CHORUS LEADER: Eurystheus, Mycenae's first-born,
    Who won his crown by being drawn
    Untimely from his mother's womb,
    Sent you to conquer Acheron.

CHORUS: Only one labor was left to complete,
    To conquer the king of the third estate.
    Only one entrance led to the dark,                            1070
    The depths from which no mortal comes back.
    You made your way through fearful woods
    Surrounded by crowds of trembling shades—
    Great as the mobs that push through the streets
    To the Coliseum's pageants and fights,
    Great as the crowd in Elis that swarms
    To witness the sacred Olympian games,
    Great as the ranks on autumn nights
    Who celebrate Ceres' secret rites
    When initiates of Attic mysteries                             1080
    Walk in procession through sleepless cities—
    So large are the multitudes pressing down
    Toward Acheron's black and soundless plain.

    Some move slowly, hardly grieving,
    The years have dulled their taste for living.
    But others run, untouched by age,
    Maidens too young to have known marriage,
    Slender schoolboys with hair unshorn,
    And infants still lisping their mother's name.
    To ease the weeping children's fright                         1090
    They alone are given torches to light
    Their downward path, but the others must grope
    Through terrible blindness, step by step.

Spirits of the dead, what did you feel
When light dimmed, and each sad soul
First sensed earth's irresistible force
Pressing down on your helpless face?
The dense disorder of dark without shape,
The sickening cast of night, the deep                        1100
Stillness of a world without sound
And empty clouds in a windless land.

Let old age delay in bringing us there.
None come too late, and from that dim shore
None may return. Why should men
Hasten to find their oblivion?
The countless multitudes covering earth
Must come at last to the shadow of death
And sail on Cocytus' motionless tide.
For you, O Death, all things have been made.
Spare us today, who tomorrow are lost,                       1110
For you will surely command us at last.
Though you are patient, we hurry ourselves.
The hour of birth has cost us our lives.

To Thebes has come the joyful day.
On each high altar we will slay
Our choicest sacrificial beast.
Now to prepare the lavish feast.
Summon the workers from the field
To taste the fruits their labors yield.
Put down your plows and all join hands,                      1120
And dance to merry-making bands.
For Hercules returns to bring
Peace after all our suffering.
Peace stretches east where dawns must rise
And west where sunsets paint the skies
And reaches southward till it's passed
Where tropic suns no shadows cast.
To every shore the oceans border
Hercules has brought new order.

He crossed the rivers of the dead                          1130
And took the crown from Pluto's head.
Now he returns, and all is well.
Hail to the man who conquered hell!
The victor comes. Now let him wear
The wreath of poplar in his hair.


ACT IV


(HERCULES *enters. His hands and forearms are covered with blood.*)

HERCULES: I am avenged. With my own hands I've crushed
     The bloodied face of Lycus in the dust.
     Then I destroyed his henchmen. Those who shared
     The tyrant's power have shared his punishment.

     I must make offerings now to Jupiter                  1140
     And to the other gods who helped my victory.
     I'll heap the altars high with sacrifice
     And slaughter victims worthy of the deed.

     I'll honor Pallas, the ally of my struggles.
     Fierce mistress of the gorgon-headed shield.
     Attend me, Bacchus, slayer of Lycurgus—
     Your vine-wreathed staff conceals a deadly spear.
     You understand the pleasures of revenge!
     Hear me, twin gods, Apollo and Diana,
     Brave sister even quicker with your bow                1150
     Than your bold brother, master of the lyre.
     And I'll make sacrifice to any brother
     That I might have in heaven—unless, of course,
     He is the son of Juno!

                    Servants! Slaves!
     Drive in the cattle fattened for the kill.

Open the jars of precious Indian spice
And pour the aromatic Arab oils
Into the altar fire to make the smoke
Rise rich and savory up to the gods.
Weave me a wreath of poplar for a crown,                1160
And one of olive leaves for Theseus,
According to the custom of his city.

I lift my hands in prayer to Jupiter,
The Thunder God. May he protect our city,
The caves of Zethus, Dirce's famous stream,
The household gods of Cadmus, our first king.
Now heap the incense on the altar fire!

AMPHITRYON: But, son, you must first purify your hands!
They're splattered with the blood of those you killed.

HERCULES: I wish that I had brought the blood of Lycus       1170
To pour as my libation to the gods.
What finer wine could stain the altar stones?
No greater victim can be sacrificed
To Jupiter than a pernicious king.

AMPHITRYON: Pray to your father that your trials are finished.
Ask Jove that rest be granted to the weary.

HERCULES: Let me compose the prayer. It must be one
Worthy of both the Thunder God and me.

Let earth and sea and heaven hold their place.
Let timeless stars pursue their course unhindered,          1180
And universal peace descend on all
The nations. May untroubled countries use
Hard iron only to forge tools of trade.
May swords be buried. May even the sea
Lie blue and calm, unroiled by raging storms.
Let no more fires streak down from angry Jove.
And no more rivers flood with melting snow

The fresh-plowed fields. Let poisons disappear,
And no more deadly plants spring from the earth.
Let cruel and impious tyrants abdicate.                           1190
And if the earth must foster any evil,
Then let her bring these monsters forth today
I will destroy them all.

                        But what is this?
The noonday darkens. Shadows block the sun.
But why? There are no clouds. What makes the noon
Suddenly falter backward into dawn?
Why does the night return—black and untimely?
See how the stars fill up the daytime sky.
There is the Lion, burning in the South.
My earliest labor was to conquer him                             1200
Now he has broken from the Zodiac
And rages hot and famished for new prey.
He will consume the stars. Hear how he roars
Stretching his jaws, breathing deadly fire.
He shakes his head and flames leap from his mane.
Whatever stars the fruitful autumn brings,
Or cooling winter leads back to our view,
He'll overtake, and with one savage leap
Will crush the neck of Taurus, the sign of spring.

AMPHITRYON: What sudden sickness overcomes you, son?        1210
    Your glance darts back and forth across the skies.
    What grim hallucinations fill your eyes?

HERCULES: I have subdued the earth and pacified
    The swelling seas. Even the underworld
    Has felt my force. Now only heaven stands
    As the last labor worthy of my aim.
    The highest reaches of the universe,
    Heaven itself, must be my destiny.

    My father promised stars, but what if he
    Reneges his vow? The earth's immense expanse                1220

Is still not room enough for Hercules.
I claim my rightful place among divinities.
The company of gods all welcome me.
They open heaven's gate—all except Juno.
Will you unbar the sky and take me in?
Or must I batter down your stubborn gate?

If you delay too long, I will unchain
My grandfather, grim Saturn, from his cave
To oust my father's unpaternal reign.
I'll arm the Titans. I'll lead them in battle.                    1230
I'll rip up rocks, and with one hand I'll fling
The jagged peaks that centaurs climb as missiles.
I'll stack the highest mountains on each other
And build a pathway to the distant sky.
Chiron will look down from his star and gape
At Ossa and Olympus piled on Pelion,
His native mountains rising to the heavens.

AMPHITRYON: Stop this unspeakable, blasphemous raving!
Stop your proud heart from sinking into madness.

HERCULES: Look, the rebellious giants take up arms.               1240
Fierce Tityus has broken out of hell,
His chest torn open by the ravenous vulture.
See how he climbs to heaven for revenge.
Cithaeron shakes and great Mount Pellene totters.
The wooden peaks of Tempe are destroyed.
One fiend rips loose the pinnacle of Pindus.
Another seizes Oete as his weapon.
The Titan Mimas screams for blood . . .

                                    And now
The Furies crack their scourges, coming closer,
Closer, closer still. They scorch my face                         1250
With torches lit from dead men's burning bodies.
Tisiphone, the torturer of hell,
Her hair a hissing nest of oily snakes,

Stands in the portal of the underworld
Waving her torch. Bereft of Cerberus,
She cannot guard the gates of hell alone.

And look! Here are the children of the king,
My enemy, the filthy spawn of Lycus.
I'll kick them in the grave beside their father.
See how I send my arrows after them.                           1260
There is no better target for my bow.

AMPHITRYON: What blindness makes such violence possible?
Bending his massive bow, he draws his aim.
The arrow flies so forcefully it shrieks
Descending on its mark, a young boy's throat.
It hits the child and slices through his neck.

HERCULES: I'll kill the rest of them. I'll hunt them down
And drag them screaming from their hiding places.
Then I'll begin a war against Mycenae
To kill Eurystheus. I'll batter down
The high stone walls the Cyclops built his city.            1270

(*He starts to force open the doors of the temple in which his
two remaining sons have hidden.*)

I'll rip these doors apart and pull them off
Their splintered frames. Hear how the roofbeams crack.
Look how the light pours in the broken walls.
There is another of the dead king's brood
Trying to hide from me.

(HERCULES *seizes the child and drags him into the back of the
ruined temple, away from audience's view.*)

AMPHITRYON: (*Standing where he can see what is happening
inside the temple*)
                          Look how the boy
Trembles and tries to hug his father's knee.

His little voice breaks, begging. How can I
Witness this horror, this obscenity?
He grabs the pleading child and raises him                1280
High in the air. Then spinning him around,
He flings the body down with all his might.
Oh, hear the head smash open on the stones!
His splattered brains drip from the blood-soaked walls.

Now poor Megara holds her last small son.
Like hunted creatures driven from their lair,
Insane with fear, they try to find escape.

HERCULES: (*Unseen, addressing* MEGARA, *also in the temple*)
    Even if you hide with Jove himself,
    I'll find you, and I'll carry you away.

AMPHITRYON: (*Calling to* MEGARA)
    Where you are running to, child? What hiding place      1290
    Can you escape to? There is no citadel,
    No fortress strong enough to keep out Hercules.
    Don't run. Embrace him. Try to soothe his anger.

MEGARA: Husband, I beg you spare us from your rage.
    Do you not recognize your wife, Megara?
    Look at your son. He has your face and bearing.
    Look how the poor child reaches for his father.

HERCULES: At last I've cornered my stepmother, Juno.
    Now she will pay her debts to me in blood.
    I'll free my father from her shameful yoke.               1300
    But first I'll slaughter her repulsive child.

MEGARA: What are you doing? Killing flesh and blood!

AMPHITRYON: (*Watching what is happening in the temple*)
    Shaking with terror, recoiling from the furious
    Fire of his father's eyes, the smallest son,
    A child who's still too young for speech, collapsed

Before he felt the blow. He died of fear.
And now he turns his club against his wife.
Cracking her neck and spine, beating her head—
Blow after blow—until there's nothing left,
Nothing except her mutilated torso.                                    1310

I am too old to bear this agony.
But if my life now aches beyond endurance,
At least my death draws near. Aim your arrows at me!
Or raise the club you've splattered with the blood
Of all our family. Come kill the man
Who once was flattered to be called your father,
But who can never speak your praise again.

CHORUS: What is the use of seeking death, old man?
    Why whimper for oblivion? Run and hide.
    Let Hercules leave one crime uncommitted.                          1320

(HERCULES *re-enters from the temple*)

HERCULES: I've done it well. I have exterminated
    The dynasty of that obscene dictator.
    I've made the lofty sacrifice I promised.
    Juno, queen of gods, I've slaughtered all
    The bleating flock of your devoted worshipers
    And gladly drenched your altars with their blood.
    I'll go to Argos now and find more victims.

AMPHITRYON: You have not yet made full atonement, son.
    Complete your sacrifice. One victim more
    Still stands beside the altar, his neck bent,                      1330
    Waiting for the blow. I am that man.
    I give myself to death. I grovel for it.
    Now kill me!

(*He stands waiting, then speaks*)

What's wrong? Your face is blank,
Your eyes unfocused, and your hands are trembling.
Look, how his eyelids droop, his head sinks down.
He has collapsed! His knees have given way.
His body crashes like a great ash tree
Shaking the woods, or like the massive boulders
Men push into the sea to build a breakwater.
Are you alive? Or has this frenzy killed you,                1340
As it has killed your helpless family?

He is asleep. His chest heaves with each breath.
Give him some time for rest. The heavy sleep
May break his madness and purge his heart of evil.

But, servants, come and take away his weapons.
He may still be deranged when he awakes.

CHORUS: Let the deep sky and its creator mourn
With all the fruitful earth and wandering waves
That search the restless ocean. Mourn, bright sun,
Whose warm face blesses every land and sea               1350
Dispelling darkness; Hercules alone
Has journeyed equally
And seen your dwellings in both dusk and dawn.

Release his spirit from this monstrous curse.
Release him, gods, restore his darkened mind.
O Sleep, become his nurse,
Conquistador of pain, balm of mankind,
Life's gentler portion, Astrae's swift-winged son,
Indolent brother of rapacious death,
Who mixes truth and falsehood in a breath                1360
And grants us foretaste of oblivion,
Rest after journeys, harbor of our life,
Comrade at night and respite of the noon,
Blessing on both the peasant and the king,
Teacher correcting our instinctive fright,
Gently preparing us for endless night.

Sweetly and softly soothe his weary soul.
Bind him with torpor. Quietly control
His thrashing limbs. Reside in his wild breast
Until his reason is redeemed by rest.                                    1370

See how he suffers, writhing on the ground,
Twisted by nightmares. Still he has not found
The strength to overcome insanity.
Look how he tries to rest his clouded head
On his great club. He reaches desperately
To grasp the vanished staff with his blind hand.
And just as waves incited by the wind
In swelling whitecaps rise
Long after the high breeze that bore them dies,
He cannot shake the frenzy from his mind.                                1380

Subdue the tempest raging in his soul.
Restore his manly strength, and let him find
New sense of purpose. Or let him remain
Ruled by his passions, hopelessly insane.
Let his blurred reason stray beyond control.
Madness alone can hide this evil stain.
Because his guilt admits no innocence,
Only oblivion offers him defense.

Now let him beat his breast and strike the arms
That once held up the skies.                                             1390
Let heaven shake with his unhappy cries,
And let his wild screams reach the queen of hell.
To penetrate her kingdom's darkest cave
Where howling Cerberus chafes against his chain.
Let Chaos echo his outpouring pain,
And oceans tremble with each far-flung wave.
Let the sky weep that felt his arrows fly
To better use. No blows can be too strong
For such a heart afflicted by such wrong.
Let one lament three kingdoms unify.                                     1400

Now weep with him, you weapons who adorned
His neck as ornaments. Let his great quiver
Beat his broad back. Let his thick club of oak
Now brutally deliver
Wounds to his flesh. Such sorrows must be mourned,
And it is time his faithful weapons spoke.

Farewell, poor children, kindred in your doom,
Walk the dark path that won your father fame,
Which you will never share. You will not earn
Honor from punishing unrighteous kings,                       1410
Nor will you learn
To harden your smooth limbs in Grecian game,
Nor test your boyish strength in boxing rings.
You were too young to track the savage lion
And wound him with one well-shot javelin.
You could just aim the slender Scythian bow
To hunt small deer that always run in fright.
Now you must go into the Stygian night.

Go, spotless souls, whom evil has undone,
You who had barely crossed life's gleaming door—             1420
Before your father's madness struck you down.
Go serve the angry kings for evermore.


## ACT V


HERCULES: (*Waking with his sanity restored*)
    What place is this, what land, what corner of the world?
    Where am I? Do I stand beneath the rising sun?
    Or where the Great Bear spins above the frozen north?
    Or have I awoken in that farthest, western land
    Beyond the stormy gates of the Hesperides?
    What air is this I breathe? What soil now lies beneath
    My weary legs? Surely I have returned from hell.

Why do I see bodies, drenched in blood,                                1430
Lying beside my house? Are all my senses
Still clouded by the underworld's illusions?
Have grisly phantoms followed me from hell?
I shamefully confess I am afraid.
I don't know why, but all my being aches
With dark foreboding.

                Father, where are you?
Where is my wife, proud mother with her flock
Of children at her side? My shoulder's bare.
Where is the lion skin I always wear—
My shield in battle, and my bed at night?                              1440
Where is my bow? My arrows? Who would dare
Steal weapons from me while I still draw breath?
Where is a man so brave he does not fear
Even the sight of Hercules asleep?
I'd like to see the man who took such spoils.
I'd like to meet this hero. Show yourself.
What new son has my father sired now?
Did his begetting make the heavens wait
Still longer than the night stood still at mine?

What horror do I see? These are my sons,                               1450
Brutally murdered, lying in their blood.
And next to them my wife. Has some new Lycus
Seized power here? Who would dare risk such outrage
Now that I have returned? I ask the help
Of everyone—from the Ismenian valley
To the wide Attic plains, and every tribe
That lives between the twin Dardanian seas.
Come tell me who committed this grim carnage,
Or I will turn my anger loose on you.
Point out my enemy or be my enemy.                                     1460

Why do you hide, if you have conquered me?
Whether you seek revenge for my defeat
Of Diomedes and his murderous steeds,

For Geryon's flock, or for the Libyan lords
I once destroyed, I'm ready now to fight.
I stand here waiting—unarmored and unarmed—
Though you attack me, flaunting my own weapons.

Why does my father look away? And Theseus?
Don't hide your faces. Now is no time for tears.
I must find out who killed my family.                    1470
Tell me, father. Why won't you answer me?
Speak to me, Theseus, my trusted friend.

Both of them turn away—silent and ashamed.
Trying to hide the tears that stain their cheeks.
What good is shame in dealing with these horrors?
Was this the work of King Eurystheus,
Tyrant of Argos? Did some desperate band
Of dying Lycus's supporters come
To wreak such irretrievable disaster?
Father, by merit of my famous deeds,                     1480
And by your name which I have held above
All sacred names but one, I pray you tell me—
Who has destroyed our house? Who hunts me down?

AMPHITRYON: Let these evils pass you by in silence.

HERCULES: And let myself be unavenged?

AMPHITRYON:                            Revenge
    Will often bring more pain.

HERCULES:                      Has anyone
    Ever borne evil such as this, unmoved?

AMPHITRYON: Those who fear worse evils.

HERCULES:                              Worse than these, father?
    After today what sorrow can I fear?

AMPHITRYON: How small a part of your full pain you know.    1490

HERCULES: Pity me, father. I reach out to you.
　Why do you cringe?

　　　　　　　　　　He will not touch my hands.
　What guilt do they reveal? They're smeared with blood.
　And look—the arrows stained with my son's gore
　Are those I dipped in Hydra venom. I see—
　Those were my weapons. And I need not ask
　What hand has used them. What other man could bend
　The bow that even I can scarcely draw?

　I turn to you again. Father, tell me.
　Am I the guilty one? He is still silent.                        1500
　The guilt is mine.

AMPHITRYON:                            The pain is yours. The guilt
　Your stepmother's. Misfortune is no sin.

HERCULES: From every corner of the sky, rain down
　Your fiery thunderbolts. Father, if you've
　Forgotten me, at least avenge your slaughtered
　Grandchildren. Let the star-filled sky resound
　As deadly lightning cracks from pole to pole.

　Chain me to the jagged mountaintop
　That served as prison to Prometheus.
　Why keep that barren crag unoccupied?                          1510
　Confine me there in stony Caucasus
　To be devoured by savage birds of prey.

　Or lock my arms to the Symplegades,
　The clashing rocks that guard the Scythian sea,
　And let them torturously stretch my limbs
　Each time they pull apart, and when the cliffs
　Rush through the broiling sea to come together,

Then use my lacerated flesh to brake
Their grinding crash.

Or shall I build a pyre
Of massive height to burn away this flesh                1520
Abominably stained with family blood?
Yes, yes, it must be done.
And Hercules must go again to hell.

AMPHITRYON: His mind has not recovered from its frenzy,
But now his anger changes its direction,
Turning its fury on himself—a sign,
Surely, of madness.

HERCULES:                Home of the dark Furies,
Prison of the dead, country of the damned,
If you contain some place of banishment,
Hidden beneath the blackest pit of hell,                1530
Unseen by Cerberus, unknown to me,
Earth, hide me there, and I will seek it out
In the remotest end of Tartarus.

How savage is my heart. Oh, who can weep
Enough for you, my children, who now lie
Scattered before the house. Hardened by woe,
My eyes do not remember how to weep.
Give me my bow. Bring me back my arrows.

(*Addressing the bodies of each of his sons in turn*)

For you I'll break the arrows. And for you,
My son, I'll break the bow. To your poor ghost          1540
I'll burn my heavy club. And on your pyres
I'll toss the quiver and its poisoned shafts.
And then my arms will pay the penalty.
I'll burn them with their weapons, and these hands
That were the hands of my stepmother's hatred.

AMPHITRYON: Who would dare call insanity a crime?

HERCULES: Insanity can often lead to crime.

AMPHITRYON: But now your task is to be Hercules
And bear the heavy burden of disaster.

HERCULES: Insanity did not extinguish shame.                1550
I cannot bear to see the people flee
My unclean presence. Weapons, Theseus,
Give me my weapons. Return what you have stolen.
If I am sane, then trust me with my arms.
If I'm still mad, then run for safety, father.
And as for dying, I shall find a way.

AMPHITRYON: Whether you call me father or stepfather,
The sacred ties of family make us one.
By the gray hair that faithful sons respect,
I beg you spare your life. I'm an old man,                  1560
Lonely and weak, and you are the last pillar
Of our fallen house, the only light
Left shining in this black and evil hour.
I've never had a moment to enjoy you.
What fruit of all your labors fell to me?
I've only tasted fear—of stormy seas,
Of monstrous beasts, of every ruthless king
Who violates his people or the gods.
Always afraid for you, and always yearning,
A father aching for the sight and touch                     1570
Of his long-absent son.

HERCULES:                     Why should I keep
My soul imprisoned in this hateful light?
I see no reason. Everything I love
I've lost—my mind, my arms, my reputation,
My wife and children, and my strength. Now even
My fury vanishes. There is no power

That can redeem a spirit so polluted.
The only remedy for sin is death.

AMPHITRYON: You'll kill your father, too.

HERCULES:                           I will prevent that
By killing myself.

AMPHITRYON:          Before your father's eyes?                1580

HERCULES: I've taught him how to watch the unendurable.

AMPHITRYON: Remember all the glorious deeds you've done
And find the strength to pardon this one crime.

HERCULES: Should Hercules grant pardon to himself
Who never granted it to other men?
My glory came from labors others asked,
But this one was my doing. Father, help me.
Let loyalty move you, or horror at my fate,
Or pity for the downfall of my strength.
Return my weaponry. Let my right hand                        1590
Gain victory over fate.

THESEUS:                     Your father's prayers
Should be enough, but let me add my tears
To move you. Rise up! Show your fabled strength
And face adversity. Where is the courage
That never proved unequal to a fight?
Now demonstrate the greatness of your manhood
By holding back the wrath of Hercules.

HERCULES: If I live on, then I commit a sin,
But if I die, then I have suffered for it.
I ache to cleanse the world. I cannot bear                   1600
Viewing my monstrous being any longer—
Unholy, savage, driven, and untamed.

My hands must try a greater labor now
Than their last task. Why do they hesitate?
Are they courageous only in killing boys
And trembling mothers?

                                        Give me back my weapons,
Or I will strip the Thracian forests bare,
The groves of Bacchus, and of sacred Cithaeron,
To build a pyre to immolate myself.
Yes, I will pull down every house in Thebes                    1610
On its inhabitants, killing your nobles,
Collapsing every temple on its gods,
To crush myself beneath the city's rubble.

And if the weight of all the city walls
Does not cave in my shoulders, and the mass
Of Thebes' great seven gates can't bury me,
Then I will overturn the vault of heaven,
Which separates the world of gods from men,
And bring it crashing down upon my head.

AMPHITRYON: I give you back your arms.

HERCULES:                            Your words are worthy    1620
Of Hercules' father. Do you see
This arrow. It's the one that killed my son.

AMPHITRYON: But Juno shot that arrow from your hand.

HERCULES: But I will feel it now.

AMPHITRYON:                      Oh, my old heart,
Racing with fear, is pounding in my chest.

HERCULES: The arrow's in the notch.

AMPHITRYON:                          Oh, how can you
Freely commit this sin with a clear mind?

HERCULES: Then tell me now what you would have me do.

AMPHITRYON: I ask for nothing. Sorrow goes no further.
   Though you may be the only person who          1630
   Can spare my son's life, even you can't snatch
   That son away from me. I have escaped
   That last great fear. You cannot make me more
   Unhappy than I am. You only can
   Return my happiness. Make your decision
   Whatever way you will, but recognize
   You risk your reputation and your claim
   To innocence—for either you will live
   Or you will kill your father. Now my soul
   Stands trembling on my lips, weary with age,        1640
   Worn down with suffering, ready to depart.
   Does any son so grudge a father life?
   (*He takes his sword and points it to his chest*)
   I won't delay. I press the deadly blade
   Against my heart. And this, this crime, will serve
   As testament to Hercules' sanity.

HERCULES: Stop, father. Stop at once. Put down your hand.
   My resolution melts. A man must do
   His father's bidding. Add this task as well
   To Hercules' labors. Let us live.
   My father's fainting. Theseus, catch him!        1650
   My hands are too defiled to touch him now.

AMPHITRYON: But I will clasp those hands with joy, and they
   Will help me stand again. I'll hold them close
   Against my troubled heart, and feel them banish
   My every grief.

HERCULES:       What country shall I seek?
   Where shall I hide? What land will bury me?
   Can all the waters of the Nile or Don,
   The raging Tigris flooding Persia's shore,
   The savage Rhine, the golden Tagus roiled

With Spain's resplendent sand, wash clean these hands?    1660
If cold Crimea poured its icy sea,
If all great Neptune's ocean rinsed my hands,
The deep-set stains would cling incarnadine.
What country will receive me so unclean?
I don't know whether to turn east or west.
Known everywhere, I have no place of exile.
The world recoils from me. Even the stars
Twist sideways in their courses to avoid me,
And Helios would rather turn his face
To shine on Cerberus.

                O Theseus,                            1670
My loyal lord, find me some hiding place—
Remote, obscure. You've always been compassionate
In judging sinners. Show me mercy now
In recompense for aid I've given you.
Return me to the underworld of shadows.
And load me with the chains that once held you.
That place will shelter me. But even hell
Knows who I am.

THESEUS:         My country waits for you.
There Mars once cleansed his hands of bloody murder
And earned his sword again. This is the land          1680
That calls you, Hercules. And our path leads
To where the gods win pardon for their deeds.

# A CLOAK
# FOR HERCULES

*(HERCULES OETAEUS)*

Translated by Stephen Sandy

# INTRODUCTION

To all intents and purposes *Hercules Oetaeus* has not been available to a contemporary audience. There has been no good modern translation, though it bears the distinction of being the longest of surviving ancient dramatic texts and is the only Senecan drama with a happy ending. Perhaps because it is the longest by far of Seneca's tragedies, it has not been included in modern Seneca selections, such as E. F. Watling's Penguin Classics *Four Tragedies and Octavia*.

While smoothing (or curbing) some of the unrelenting forcefulness (and occasional repetition) of the text, I give a straightforward version. There is repetition. *Hercules Oetaeus* "is much longer than Seneca left it," as Moses Hadas says, "and the repeated rehearsals of Hercules' labors make tedious reading." I have pruned back repetitive passages that are doubtless later accretions and in any case mar the rhythm of the work. Seneca is difficult to translate. Latin is more compact than English and Seneca often especially concise, yet the translator must try to maintain the flow of ideas and dramatic action. The intellectual content, in fact, often outweighs the actions, for Seneca's are "closet dramas," written to be read or adapted, as T. S. Eliot notes, "for declamation before an imperial highbrow audience of crude sensibility but considerable sophistication in the ingenuities of language." Again as Eliot observes, "though Seneca is long-winded, he is not diffuse." Rather than do a modish and slangy version that would cut it back to something un-Senecan, I wanted actually to translate the text, to offer lay readers a version lucid and idiomatic yet relatively close to the Latin—and Senecan in tone, if possible—of this most voluble and least read of Seneca's dramas. At some times this goal was a cause for despair; at others, it gave delight—when I found here and there a stretch that seemed to sing

107

out for Englishing. And there are patches that surely might be included in an anthology of Latin lyric poetry but never have been, for want of a decent translation.

The first English translation was that by Studley (1566), included in Newton's *Tenne Tragedies* (1581), the influential Elizabethan Seneca reader. Studley's is one of the less readable versions in that collection. His translation is not only in inchoate fourteeners but is also almost a précis of the original. Succeeding translators, choosing to do the *Hercules Furens* rather than the much longer *Hercules Oetaeus* (with one late-seventeenth-century exception), neglected this drama until the turn-of-the-century translations of Ella Isabel Harris (verse) and Frank Justus Miller (prose). Harris's 1904 translation was still being used in Duckworth's ungainly *Complete Roman Drama* (1942). Her *Hercules On Oeta* is brave but Victorian work that makes small attempt to achieve the focus of readable English; it is Latinate, somehow prolix and cramped at once, and needlessly euphemistic. Much is lost. In any case, that translation is ninety years old. Of the same vintage is the Miller's Loeb Classical Library translation, which is devastatingly literal and accurate and rendered in language of a very stiff Edwardian cut. Harris was committed to blank verse, but she was not a poet; and she admits in her introduction, "the choruses should have been rendered in lyric form; and it was with some regret that the decision was reached that this task was beyond the translator's poetic power."

The contemporary reader may find this long and long-forgotten play of interest. To begin with, there are passages of poetry that are grandly operatic (Hercules afflicted by the robe soaked with the poison of Nessus; the building of the pyre; the final incineration of Hercules) or vibrantly lovely (the choral odes of the first four acts, and to a lesser extent the last). Moreover, there is an exuberant balance of structure, which knits the drama together in an impressive way: for example, Hercules is the object of the envious acrimony Juno feels for her husband Jove, whose numerous infidelities climaxed, at one juncture, in Hercules, the product of his union with Alcmena. This conflict mirrors the one at the core of the play, in which Hercules' love for Iole is the last straw in the rage his wife Deianira has long felt at her husband's innumerable infidelities. The death and transfiguration of Hercules are not only impressive scenes, colorful and memorable for the intensity of their imagery, but also remarkable as pagan parallels of Christian doctrine.

The play is presumed to have been written in the second half of the first century. Moses Hadas reminds us (*A History of Latin Literature*, 1952) that *Hercules Oetaeus* "is an extremely interesting document in the history of religion. The report of Hercules' last moments . . . comes to this: Hercules undergoes a *passion* on a pyre in order to become a savior of mankind; this is to be followed by a *resurrection* and an *apotheosis*. . . . Hercules speaks to his father in heaven and hears his reply: 'Lo! my father summons me, and opens his heaven: Father, I come' " (251).

The themes of the play suggest contemporary applications, parallels too obvious not to consider: the character types of philandering husband, irresponsible parent, and the abandoned wife seeking liberation from her bonds are central. Before he is established in Act IV as a stoic hero and a savior of the peoples of the earth, Hercules behaves like a youth in a giant's body, the powerful male who never outgrows adolescent strife, a pro football player on steroids. A psychological reading suggests a chronological adult who remains psychically a boy because he is forever ordered—defined—from outside. He always performs tasks for others; he defines himself in terms of his ability to do what others tell him to do. His compulsive need to prove his manhood through violent labor is matched by his role as a brutal Don Giovanni, seducing and raping an endless series of women with gruesome abandon; a man without decency, discretion, or humility.

If we think of Deianira as the loyal wife who is trying to secure her husband's fidelity, we may sense that the robe of Nessus represents the cure for Hercules. But it is a false cure—or Hercules cannot be fixed, except by death. For the well-meant cure has been rigged by one of the hero's victims. Deianira is the discarded female whose rage at being powerless leads her to retribution by (albeit unwittingly) doing away with her callous partner. Of course, such surmises oversimplify a complex matter, but they may serve not only to recall this source of Elizabethan and Jacobean tragedy but also to suggest aspects of contemporaneity to be found in the text. A salient aspect of the play is the picture of Hercules attacked by the "plague" of the poison which eats away his skin and bones, as if he had contracted AIDS and were suddenly prey to opportunistic infections.

Gordon Braden's excellent study of Seneca, *Renaissance Tragedy and the Senecan Tradition: Anger's Privilege* (1985), offers the best recent insight as to the scope and heft of *Hercules Oetaeus*. If the chief Senecan theme of these plays is, to use Braden's words, taking "a fantasy of individual autonomy beyond almost any kind of limit" (57), then *Hercules Oetaeus* offers a dialectical structure of two vaunting purposes meeting head-on. We see the opposition and interpenetration of two willed autonomies, of Hercules and Deianira, competing with and destroying each other. Braden asserts:

> The real momentum in Senecan tragedy leads . . . toward uncompromised individual power. In the wake of the apocalypse men discover what they are; and where the shaken survivors of the Greek stage can regain a sense of community in their helplessness, the victims of Seneca face their conquerors, not each other, and discover only the absoluteness of the power that has destroyed them. This power is absolute and immitigable because it is totally human, and in that knowledge the world is unimaginably bleak. . . . Left to its own mercy, the human race is its own damnation. (58)

Yet Hercules achieves a kind of salvation; he ascends to enter the kingdom of his father, Jove. He attains heaven, however, without any awareness or understanding of his crimes against Deianira, Iole, and others; and of course this gap between the protagonist's understanding and the dramatic structure is where, from our viewpoint, the play is most clearly flawed (or its text corrupt).

Hercules does not comprehend the forces which build the play around him. He celebrates his good deeds without recognition of his bad. His role as a redeemer of the oppressed—the Senecan theme of heroic salvation—is not offered in expiation of his crimes. Hercules is coldly made to absent himself forever from both his mayhem and his mercies. Thus, one view of his apotheosis might be that finally it is irrelevant to the primary plot of the drama, and the issues which its text proclaims are left unresolved.

Another view, a more embracing reading of the play, finds mankind bent irreversibly on doom, running headlong toward its damnation. Braden surmises that this "is the vision toward which Senecan tragedy naturally moves—a desolation especially harrowing because it is the self-willing destiny of so much that is basic and stirring in classical heroism. For that very reason the urge to mitigate or transcend that destiny is a powerful one; so much of value is at stake, and one wants to save a place for it in some version of an acceptable world. That, I think, is the motivation for *Hercules oetaeus*, the one Senecan tragedy with a happy ending, opening up the dead end of *Hercules furens*" (58). What we might view as a cosmic pardon for Hercules comes as a ration of amelioration, a hope for salvation and, for Seneca, an endurable way of looking at the world—if not quite positive yet not wholly negative. When Hercules has immolated himself on the pyre and risen to the realm of Jove, he appears to his mother, Alcmena (and the chorus). He admonishes them: "Why do you wish me with such weeping / to know the world of death? Stop it! Already my valor / has paved the way for me to the stars—and the gods themselves."

Quoting this climactic speech of Hercules, and speaking of *Hercules Oetaeus* as a whole, Braden concludes, "The deified Hercules, speaking from the clouds, has now achieved the goals that in *Hercules Furens* were the expression of his madness. Because of the Stoic resonance of the claims for his virtus, the play—put last in the codex etruscus—has been seen as the culminating event of the corpus, in which the heroic spirit finally emerges victorious after its worldly trials" (58).

I have had my way with the text; the extravagances and liberties are mine. I owe a debt to many readers, but especially to Wendell Clausen, Don Gifford, John Nims, and Virginia Scoville—enquiring friends, hearteners of the work.

Stephen Sandy

# A CLOAK FOR HERCULES

## CHARACTERS

HERCULES, son of Jove and Alcmena
DEIANIRA, wife of Hercules, daughter of Oeneus, king of Aetolia
HYLLUS, son of Hercules and Deianira
ALCMENA, mother of Hercules, daughter of the King of Mycenae
NURSE of Deianira, a sorceress
PHILOCTETES, friend of Hercules, son of Poeas
LICHAS, messenger of Deianira (mute part)
IOLE, daughter of Eurytus, king of Oechalia
CHORUS of Oechalian maidens, captives with Iole
CHORUS of Aetolian women, loyal to Deianira
CHORUS of men, attendants of Hercules

SCENE: *Hercules has completed many labors, performed for King Eurystheus, but in fact ordered by Juno, whose hate for Hercules is the agency which provokes his career. Among these labors, many were beneficial, by which Hercules delivered a person or a people; others were simply cruel, such as his most recent exploit, the destruction of Oechalia and slaughter of King Eurytus, all because the king would not hand over his daughter Iole.*

*The scene is Oechalia, soon after Hercules has destroyed it and rounded up the Oechalian maidens to transport them into slavery. The stage is bare save for a low-stepped plinth upstage center.*

113

ACT I

Scene 1

(CHORUS *of three or four young men, attendants in the retinue of Hercules, stand at attention stage right, outlined against a lighted backdrop. Near them but alone stands* LICHAS, *messenger of Deianira.* HERCULES *stands on the plinth, looking upward.*)

HERCULES: Father of gods, who hurls the thunderbolt around
      the globe, where suns dawn in the East or set in the West,
      reign on untroubled! I've made peace in your name throughout
      the land, to the very shores of the embracing sea.
      No need to thunder now! Sadistic kings lie vanquished
      and savage tyrants. For I—I have destroyed whatever
      deserved your punishment. But now, father above,
      is heaven denied me even now? Surely I proved
      myself worthy of you on every count; and Juno,
      my stepmother, assures me you are my true father.          10
      Why the delays? Are you afraid of me? Couldn't
      Atlas hold up the heavens with Hercules there too?
      Why, O parent, would you deny me a place in heaven?
      Surely Death returns me to you; and every evil thing
      that earth or sea or sky or the infernal world
      could put forth has submitted to my strength. No lion
      prowls the towns of Arcady now. The birds of Stymphalus
      are crushed; the Maenalian stag has fallen and is no more.
      The dragon died, drenching the golden grove with blood.
      The Hydra's strength is severed with its heads. I slaughtered  20
      the herd of Diomedes, fattened on the blood
      of his guests, and grabbed war loot from Thermodon. I
          witnessed
      the dead amid their silent lot. Returned with black

Cerberus, whom trembling day beheld and he
the sun. The Libyan Antaeus is nothing now; Busiris
collapsed before his altars. By my hand alone
did Geryon die; the bull as well, that scourge of tribes
by the hundred. Whatever the hostile earth has given birth to
is done for now. The wrath of the gods has come to nothing,
reduced by my right hand.
                                      If the earth has nothing more    30
—no beast or plague—to satisfy the rage of Juno
(which leaves me nothing more to do down here), I ask you,
join father with his son, and son with the constellation
he deserves! I do not ask for help; I'll find a way
to you. But if it is some rising crop of monsters
that's worrying you, never fear; whatever earth
can offer, I am here; I'm ready. Who else would handle
chance emergencies, or in the Argive cities
earn such hate from Juno? I am rich in honors.
Everyone sings my praise, from snowbound Scythians         40
to sunburned Indians and Africans. Bright sun,
bear witness! Wherever you shine, you've shone on me, yet I
pursued fresh victories beyond your reach. I've gone
beyond the sun and left day far behind. To me
Nature surrendered; earth herself could not keep pace
and dropped back first. Utter chaos and night waylaid me.
No one escapes from that; but *I* did, I got back
to this world; no gale-force tempest could sink the ship I sailed
    on.
How very tame Perseus' exploits were to mine!
(HERCULES *descends plinth and walks downstage to stand in pool*
    *of light which comes up as stage darkens. He speaks as if to*
    *himself.*)
Outer space is not enough now for his wife's                  50
hatred of me, but earth has no more ogres to send
against me. The beasts are finished! Hercules alone
stands in their stead. What ills, what crimes have I put down—
and all wholly unarmed! The things I had to do
I did with ease. And yet I spent no idle days.

I've even removed some creatures no one told me to!
Courage more resolute than Juno herself—sheer pluck
has kept me going.
                              But what good did it do to free
mankind from fear? The gods don't have a moment's peace.
And earth, now free, can see all manner of thing it feared          60
installed in heaven—and see this is the work of Juno.
That crab I finished off is now the Zodiacal Cancer;
the year as it turns will pass from Leo into Virgo;
the lion roars, and all the world is parched. Look how
those animals entered heaven first, preceding me;
though I won, I view my feats from here below! With Juno,
constellations go to the brutes and monsters first;
she thinks that such a heaven will frighten me off. Well,
think again! Let her fill up the cosmos with them—
and leave the sky laid waste more horribly than earth,                70
than Styx—a place shall still be given to Hercules!
After the wars, beasts, hell's own Cerberus, if I've
not earned a stellar home, may Sicily touch the shore
of Italy and join, one land, where I'll have made the seas
recede. If Jove calls back the waters—then let Corinth's
isthmus split, that ships may find fresh passage home
to Attica. Let earth be changed! Let rivers find
new beds! At least allow me to guard the gods; Jove
can shelve his thunderbolts while I am on the job.
Whether I am ordered to guard the North Pole or                        80
the equator, the gods may rest assured they will be safe.
Apollo deserved a temple at Delphi and a home
in heaven for slaying the Hydra—how many pythons in
that many-headed serpent were cut down! Bacchus
and Perseus both have joined the gods, but as for Bacchus,
what a paltry world the East was that he won! And what
a pitiful trophy for Perseus was the Gorgon's carcass!
Jove's son deserves, for all he's done, to join the gods.
I claim the skies I carried on my shoulders once!
(*Turns to attendants standing at attention. Lights go up.*)
But you, Lichas, companion of my labors,

(LICHAS *steps forward from the group*)
                                           report                    90
my triumphs. This state that Eurytus ruled is crushed, his
   home destroyed.
(*Exit* LICHAS *stage right. Hercules turns to the other attendants,
who face right and march off stage right, after the following
speech.*)
                        Quick now, lead off the herd for sacrifice
at Cenaean Jupiter's shrine, raised high above that shore
which surveys the Euboic sea, windswept by southerly gales.

(*Exit* HERCULES *stage left on his way to the headland to sacrifice to
Jove.* IOLE *and* CHORUS *of Oechalian maidens enter stage right.*)


Scene 2


CHORUS *of Oechalian maidens,* IOLE *among them:*
   He might as well have gods for kin
   Whose life and luck run side by side.
   But when he begins to pay off Death—
   Daily sorrows and pain dragging
   Him down—all thought of fortune sinks.

FIRST CHORISTER: Whoever does not fear the fates                    100
   Or that ferry across the final stream
   Won't give his limbs, already captive,
   To shackles. He won't be displayed,
   A trophy in the victor's parade.

SECOND CHORISTER: Life isn't hard, when a man is ready
   To die. Should his craft break up in a gale
   He does not try to mend it there,
   At sea, as if on land; he's ready
   For shipwreck, who's given up his life.

THIRD CHORISTER: But hunger and tears disfigure us,          110
    Our hair is fouled with the dirt of our
    Land; yet the flames that level our city
    Will never defeat us. The ones you're after,
    O Death, are full of laughter; you pass
    The wretched by. We're still alive!

FIRST CHORISTER: Yet now this tilled field soon will fall
    To wildwood, and from the temples' ruins
    Only poor filthy shacks will rise;
    Soon flocks will graze above the ashes
    Of Oechalia, hardly cold. Right                          120
    In our streets Thessalian shepherds practice,
    Rehearsing songs that tell our sorrows.

SECOND CHORISTER: In a few generations you'll seek in vain
    For where our country even was!
    Once I was blessed with a fruitful land
    But now I go to rocky Trachis
    Of the barren hills, bristling with thorns
    And woodlots even goats avoid.

THIRD CHORISTER: But if a better lot awaits
    Any of us, she'll have to go                             130
    Over the swift Inachus or dwell
    Secure behind the walls of Thebes
    Where the shallow Ismenus slowly runs,
    Where the mother of arrogant Hercules
    Was wed. That tale of the double night
    —Two nights without a day between—
    When the stars stayed out too long and he
    Was born: all that is lies, to think
    The evening star replaced the morning's,
    And the slow moon held back the sun!                     140

FIRST CHORISTER: Did craggy Scythia create him? Or
    Did Rhodope beget him to be
    A brawling Titan? Or sheer-cliffed Athos?

Did a Caspian beast or a tiger nurse him?
His limbs are proof against all wounds;
His flesh blunts iron, dulls the spear.

SECOND CHORISTER: His impregnable bulk breaks the sword
   And stones bounce off it. He scoffs at fate:
   With that impregnable body he
   Challenges death. —Scythian arrows,         150
   Sarmatian spears, or those sharpshooting
   Parthians out of the East who target
   Neighboring Arabs with perfect aim.

THIRD CHORISTER: Nothing can wound this superman.
   Single-handed he leveled the walls
   Of Oechalia. No one stands up
   To that brute! He only has to think
   Of conquering and it is done.

FIRST CHORISTER: Few fall from wounds he gives—to glimpse
   His fury is all it takes. Could         160
   The giants Briarius and Gyas,
   Inflated with pride, grabbing for heaven
   With slithering hands from their plinth of mountains:
   Could they stare him down?

CHORUS:                But calamity
   Brings advantages: no pain is left
   For us; for we, miserable we,
   Have seen great Hercules enraged.

IOLE: (*Ascends first or second step of plinth but not to top*)
   But I do not mourn because I grieve
   For the gods abandoned in the rubble
   Of fallen temples; or for home-fires         170
   Stamped out; nor the mass graves, fathers
   And sons heaved in together; corpses
   With gods; temple and tomb grown one.
   Another fate brings my tears; my

Calamity is unique. Which grief
Comes first? Which last? They all come first!
Earth did not bear me with the strength
To mourn these losses as they should be.
Change me, dear gods, to a stone that weeps
On the slopes of Sipylus, or put me                              180
Down on the banks of the Po, where woods
Ring with Phaethon's sisters' keening;
Or make me a siren on Sicilian rocks
And I'll bemoan the fate of Thessaly;
Or carry me to the Thracian forest,
Where I'll mourn like Procne bewailing her son
In the Ismarian shade! Find me
A guise that's fitting for my tears;
Let rocky Trachis echo with my cries.
Cyprian Myrrha is weeping still,                                 190
The wife of Ceyx is groaning yet
To have him back, and Niobe
Outlives herself. Philomela
Withdraws from human form yet still
Mourns for her son. Will my arms ever
Sprout feathers like these others? O
Happy, happy me if I
Could make my home in the woodland and,
Free as a bird in my native fields,
Carol my fate in quavering notes.                               200
Then fame would tell of Iole,
Who had become a bird.
                           I saw
My father's pitiful fate, I saw
Him lie, felled by that deadly club;
Saw him in pieces, chunks thrown here
And there, all through the place. If fate
Had decreed a grave for you, O father,
How great a search must there have been
To fill it!
                 Then, could I have stood
To watch your death, my brother, with cheeks                    210

Yet smooth; manhood not yet, my dear
Toxeus, flowing in your veins?
But how can I do the work of mourning
For you, dear parents, when helpful Death
Has put you at a safe remove?
My own fate claims my tears. Soon, soon
In bondage I will have to tend
Distaff and spindle for my mistress.
It was my devastating looks,
This shapely figure, that contrived                     220
My end; for these alone our house
Was doomed to fall, because my father
Denied me to Hercules. He was
Afraid to be kin to Hercules!
But now it is high time for me
To report to the mansion of my mistress.

CHORUS: It's madness for you to dwell on your
Family's noble state and your
Disaster. Why do it? Blot out
All thought of former circumstances;                    230
Happy is he who can survive
As king or slave, playing either role
Equally well, for he has wrested
The heft and strength from evil fortune
Who takes what comes dispassionately.

(Exit CHORUS *and* IOLE)


ACT II


(*The scene changes to Trachis. The lights go up, brightly illuminating downstage a drop painted with the Hellenistic façade of the palace of Hercules and Deianira.*)

Scene 1


(NURSE *enters by a double door in drop center stage*)

NURSE: O how bloody the anger is that starts
    women going, especially when the wife
    and the mistress lodge together under one roof;
    Scylla and Charybdis, roiling Sicilian waters,
    are no match; nor does any wild animal                    240
    cause more fear or caution.
                                For when we all
    beheld the beauty of this captive, Iole
    shining there like a summer's day, or star
    glittering in the unclouded sky of midnight,
    the wife of Hercules, turning aside, stood there,
    as a tiger with newborn cubs prepares to leap
    from her stronghold when danger threatens, or as the maenad
    invited to join the throng of the god who moves her
    bides her time, unsure which way to turn.
        So Deianira stood; then bolted, hysterical,            250
    through the house of Hercules—the whole house
    was hardly large enough to hold her rage.
    She rushes headlong this way, that way; comes
    to a standstill. All her sorrows are in her face;
    the last secret of her heart is out. Her mood
    keeps swinging; threats, then tears. That countenance
    cannot contain her wrath; her cheeks, now flushed,
    now pale; her grief informs each look she gives—
    she cries, implores; she moans.
                                Listen! The doors
    are opening. Look, she staggers forward, recounting      260
    in addled rant her secret, most intimate thoughts.

(*Enter* DEIANIRA *from stage left*)

DEIANIRA: O Juno, wife of Jove, wherever you
    may be in your heavenly domain, help me,

send a wild beast against that Hercules,
something to give me satisfaction. If any
unconquered serpent greater than the swamp
it comes from should appear, whatever is
that's worse than all the other monsters—grizzly,
horrible, grim—which Hercules would blanch
to turn his gaze on, let it steal forth from its                    270
unfathomable cave. Or if wild beasts
are out, then change my heart to something else,
anything else I can become, so long
as it's infernal. Grant me an image to fit
my burning anguish; I can't hold in this rage.
No need to go to the ends of earth and turn
things upside down or ask Pluto for evils.
Right here in my heart you'll find what you need, all
abominations that may terrorize him;
take this, my dagger, for your enmity.                              280
You have the power to ruin Hercules—
let me take part, use me however you
see fit. O goddess, don't hold back! Use me,
a maddened woman, command me to commit
any crime! Don't hesitate. Though you
may pause now, my wrath alone will carry the day.

NURSE: O calm yourself, dear child, hold back your heart's
agony; control this flaming passion, this grief.
Remember you are the wife of Hercules.

DEIANIRA: (*To center stage and stands before doors of palace*)
Do I want that captive Iole to give a brother                       290
to my sons? Shall a slave be daughter-in-law to Jove?
Fire and water do not mix; the laws
of nature cannot be changed. Nor will I go
unavenged! A plague greater than the Hydra
awaits you—the furor of a wife enraged!
The fires in Aetna's crater burning aren't
as hot as mine. Your conquests, Hercules,
my spirit will make conquests of as well.

No slave is going to take my marriage bed!
Till now I shrank from savage things unknown.                    300
But such plagues are no more, and in their place,
this hateful whore! King of the gods most high!
O bright sun! I stood by Hercules,
his wife; throughout his trials, I prayed. Is this
foul concubine the answer to my prayers?
For you heard my prayers, O gods, but for her sake,
not mine, has he come home again! O hell,
no vengeance can relieve this agony!
Suggest some punishment unprecedented,
unspeakable, some horrid terror even                    310
Juno in all her cruelty can learn from.
It was for me my husband did those things,
made Achelous shed his watery blood and then
grappled with him as a snake; and soon
(when he changed himself once more) as a raging bull
defeated him. In that one enemy
he killed a thousand beastly creatures.
                                              If I
no longer please you, then you shall not have *her*
to please you. For the day our marriage ends
will also be the day your life is over.                    320
                    Yet what's this now?
          My courage of a sudden
shrinks and withdraws its threats. Why does my miserable
grief subside?
                    —My anger now has cooled.
My madness is cured. And I am once again
the perfect wife, faithful and mute. Why can't I
add fuel to the fire now? What force is stamping
the flames out? Stay with me now, my passion; let's
move ahead together, no vows required!
Let Juno guide me now, all unaware!

NURSE: What are you planning now, demented one?                    330
Would you kill your husband, whose praises ring

across the earth, whose celebrity covers
the globe and reaches to heaven? Greece will rise
to punish such offense; your father's house
and the whole Aetolian clan will be the first
to be leveled. You will be stoned and burned
alive, since every country will back its savior.
Unaided, what punishment you'll take! You might
think to escape, but remember there's always his father,
Jove, with his thunderbolts. Now, now see                    340
how his menacing lightning crackles down, flashing
to kindle his sky-shaking thunder! Fear
even death, which you've been calling a safe
haven: you can't escape your Hercules,
for that is where Jove's brother Pluto rules.
On every side, poor woman, you find his divine
kin.

DEIANIRA:      It's a serious crime I'm planning, I
admit it. But affliction makes me do it.

NURSE:                                    You'll die.

DEIANIRA: Die, yes; but die the wife of Hercules.
No sun shall dawn on me a widow. The sun will rise          350
in the West; Indians grow pale in the midnight sun,
before those Thessalian women see *me* jilted!
I'll put out Iole's marriage lamps with my
own blood! He dies—or I do. Let him add
a wife to his heap of butchered animals;
count *me* among his famous labors!
                                    Still,
when I am dying, I'll throw myself on his bed.
It's sweet to savor the lower world as the woman
of Hercules; but not without vengeance! if
Iole is with child by Hercules,                             360
with my own hands I'll rip it from her womb:
I'll confront that whore in her bridal chamber. So what

if he kills me on his wedding day, so long
as I fall across Iole's corpse? Happy
is she who brings those down with her she hates.

NURSE: Why add fuel to the fire? And dote on this
extreme grief? Poor thing, your fears are groundless.
He did desire Iole, and he sought her
as a king's daughter, when her father yet
ruled his land. It's only now the princess                         370
has fallen to a slave's position. She's lost
her power. Her lowly status has canceled her
attraction! We love what we can't have and when
it's in our grasp, desire melts away.

DEIANIRA: O, but in him a fall from fortune kindles
hotter lust! For this very reason he wants her—
that she's lost her father's house, that her tresses
hang down unpinned by gems and gold. Perhaps
Hercules loves her for the plight she's in!
It is like him to fall in love with captive girls.                 380

NURSE: He loved Dardanian Priam's captive sister,
yes, but he gave her up; then add in all
the women, virgin or not, he loved besides—
roving drifter that he is! Indeed,
he raped the Arcadian maiden Auge while
she led the dance sacred to Pallas; but
he dropped her cold. Need I continue? Old flames
are legion. The Thespiades, a passing fancy;
then queen Omphale—head over heels in love
he sat beside her, helping to spin, twisting                       390
the moistened threads between his calloused fingers—
Omphale, for whom he shed his lion skin
and stood before her, her obedient slave,
his shaggy hair streaming with her rich oils:
he is always hot, but mildly, briefly so.

DEIANIRA: After playing the field, a lover often chooses
  one alone.

NURSE:                                   Now, will he take a slave
  and the child of his enemy instead of you?

DEIANIRA: As loveliness covers nature when spring comes,
  but when winter howls you see the bare unshapely          400
  limbs of trees, so does my beauty pass
  continually away. What once men saw in me
  is there no more, or weakens, day by day.
  Old age, or motherhood, has gnawed me clean.
  But see this girl is still a charmer. Her gauds
  are gone, she lives in squalor, yet her beauty
  gleams through her hardships. Misfortune has taken
  nothing from her but her high estate.
  Fear of her shakes me, nurse; this dread kills sleep.
  I was the famous wife, of universal                       410
  prominence, envied by women everywhere,
  the standard of any woman's prayers when she
  beseeched the gods for what she might become!
  Where will I find another like him, nurse?
  Or a father-in-law like Jove himself? Even
  Eurystheus, who has command of Hercules,
  would be a paltry match. It's nothing to be
  divorced by a prince, but she has truly fallen
  on evil times who loses Hercules.

NURSE: The children sometimes bring the husband back        420
  for love of family.

DEIANIRA:                       A child might well remove him
  from my bed—if it is Iole's child.

NURSE:                                        Meanwhile
  that slave girl's hauled in here as a gift to you!

DEIANIRA: The man you see going around, famous
   in every city, wielding his club, wearing
   that lion fur, takes from the high and mighty
   and gives to the poor in spirit; that eminence
   the whole world sings the praises of—he
   does not wander through the world to compete with Jove.
   He does not seek the glitter of glory, no;                       430
   he is looking for *someone to love!* He is chasing girls!
   He forces those who would deny him. He
   rampages through whole countries, and in their ruins
   hunts for brides. And this disgusting vice
   passes for virtue! Renowned Oechalia gave way;
   she stood at sunrise and by sunset fell,
   lust the only cause of the warfare. A father
   who withholds his daughter *should* feel dread; he'll kill
   the man who turns him down as son-in-law.
   Why then should I restrain these blameless hands              440
   until once more, as with Megara, feigning madness he
   picks up his bow and slaughters both his son
   and me. Thus Hercules gets rid of wives! It's his
   kind of divorce; and he never feels in the wrong,
   for his crimes look like Juno's to the world.
   What does my slow rage sleep for then? His sin
   must be outstripped. Why don't I make my move;
   strike while feelings run high, while outrage burns!

NURSE: Will you kill your husband?

DEIANIRA:                                    You mean this concubine's
   mate?

NURSE: Not Jove's offspring!

DEIANIRA:                              Yes, but Alcmena's, too.            450

NURSE: With a sword?

DEIANIRA:                    With a sword.

NURSE:                              And what if . . . ?

DEIANIRA:                              I'll find a way.

NURSE: What means such madness?

DEIANIRA:                              Such as my husband teaches.

NURSE: Not even Juno could destroy him; how will you?

DEIANIRA: Divine wrath makes men wretched, mortal wrath
   destroys them.

NURSE:                              Forget it, pitiful woman, and be
   afraid.

DEIANIRA:                     When you're not afraid of death, you have
   nothing to fear. It's good to take the sword in hand.

NURSE: The pain is greater than the wound, dear girl. Don't
   take it so hard. Give only as good as you get.

DEIANIRA: You think it's nothing for a wife to have a mistress     460
   to deal with? But nothing causes offense like this!

NURSE: Then is your love for famous Hercules dead now?

DEIANIRA: My love remains, dear nurse, believe me, deep
   in my heart; but to be enraged by one's own love
   brings heavy sorrow.

NURSE: (*circling* DEIANIRA)     Women hold on to their men
   by prayer, by tricks of magic. I made the trees
   leaf out in winter snow and jagged lightning
   freeze in its sizzling course. I've made heavy seas
   on a calm day and caused fresh springs to rise
   from desert rocks. I've opened wide hell's gates,     470
   bid spirits speak and Cerberus keep silent,

while midnight saw the sun, and day sank, toppled
by darkness. Earth and its waters, heaven and
Tartarus do my bidding. Nothing holds sway
before my chanting; we will break him! My spells
will find the way and cause him to bow down.

DEIANIRA: Where will I find a potion strong enough
to lay him low? Some herb from Pontus or the rocks
of Pindus? Does such a plant exist? Though the moon
through magic should land on earth, or winter witness          480
ripened grain and lightning stall—all through
your magic—though all be changed utterly
and the noon sun burn amid a crowd of stars,
he will not bend.

NURSE:                            Yet love has conquered even
the mighty . . .

DEIANIRA:              Perhaps he'll be conquered only by—
himself. And love will be his final labor!
But you, by all the gods, and by my dread,
keep secret what I'm planning. Hold your tongue.

NURSE: What are you plotting then?

DEIANIRA:                                          No blade. No flame . . .

NURSE: I can keep secrets: if silence itself does not          490
incriminate.

DEIANIRA:                    Come! And keep your eyes peeled.

NURSE: The coast is clear. No one is near.

DEIANIRA:                                          A distant
hidden closet of the palace guards my secret.
Where no sunlight ever sees it, waits a charm
for Hercules' devotion. I confess, it is

the pledge given by Nessus, whom Nephale bore
where Pindus Mountain and Othyrus touch the clouds.
When Achelous had done with changing shapes
and stood with broken horn, defeated, the victor,
Hercules, went off to Argos with me, his bride.                    500
By chance the River Evenus had burst
its banks along the plains where it meandered
to the sea. It was high enough in flood to reach
the treetops. The centaur Nessus, well versed, practiced
in fording torrents, proposed to take me over
for a price. Then, setting me up where the backbone joins
the horse to the man, he bore me into the stream,
breasting the swollen flood. Reckless Nessus
soon emerged from the waves, while Hercules
was straying yet, out in the middle, striding                      510
against the currents. When Nessus saw him still
in midstream, he whispered, "now you are my prize,
and you shall be my wife. The flood will keep
your man from rescuing you!" And, gripping me
in his arms as he carried me, he galloped off.
The currents didn't hold back Hercules
for long! "Treacherous ferryman," he cried, "if Ganges
and Hister should join their streams I would surmount them:
as I will overtake you in your flight."
His bow was swifter than his threats. The poisoned               520
arrow sped to the target; homed on its wound,
which seemed to open to receive the shaft,
affixing death there, ending his stymied flight.
Now groping blindly, in his right hand he caught
the poison seeping from the wound and poured it
in his hoof, which, with his desperate left hand, he'd
torn off and given me. His dying words
came then: "Lovers by this potion can be
made faithful, so magicians say; thus did
Mycale teach the Thessalian brides, the only                       530
sorceress the moon deserted the stars to follow.
You must give him clothing smeared," said he, "with this,
this bloody paste, if a hateful mistress should

invade your bed and your unfaithful husband
give one more daughter-in-law to thundering Jove.
Keep it from light and sealed in pitch-black darkness,
so the volatile blood retains its active powers."
Then silence overtook his speech, and the sleep
of death crept through his tired limbs.
        You now,
whose fealty admits you to my secret, go quick,    540
that the potion, daubed on his shining vestment, may
steal through his heart and limbs and silently seep
to the very marrow of his bones.

NURSE:        I rush
to obey, my child; and you, pray to invincible
Cupid, whose hand sends arrows with deadly aim.

(*Exit* NURSE)

DEIANIRA: By those on earth and sea and those above
who fear you; by Jove who brandishes Aetna's flame,
and by your vicious mother, Cupid, I
beseech you: send an arrow—not a lightweight
but a heavy one, and fresh, with your sure hand    550
and sure aim—dead at Hercules that he
may feel the force of love. Pull tight the bow
till both tips touch. Now fire such an arrow
as you shot at Jove when he dropped his thunder once
and as a greenhorned bull breasted the churning sea,
abducting Europa. Inject him with passion greater
than any; let him learn love for his wife. If Iole's
beauty lights his fire, quench it—and let him
drink deep of mine. You conquered violent Jove
often; often the king of the world below    560
who rules with dusky scepter that whole crowd
and the river they have crossed. And now, O god,
more severe than an angry stepmother, win this triumph
and single-handed conquer Hercules.

(*Enter* NURSE)

NURSE: The venom is ready, and a cloak that wearied the hands
    of all your maids to weave. Now mix the potion
    and let this cloak of Hercules drink in
    its virulence, and I'll add on my spells.
    (*They prepare the robe.* LICHAS *approaches.*)
    But here comes sedulous Lichas. Hide the dire
    smudge on the cloak, or our game is given away.      570

(*Enter* LICHAS *with* CHORUS *of Aetolian women*)

DEIANIRA: O Lichas, though loyalty is rarely found at court,
    you're ever faithful to your lord. Carry
    this clothing then, which our own hands have woven
    while he was wandering the earth or, fuddled with wine,
    embracing Lydian women, or courting Iole.
    (*aside*)
    And yet, with luck, I'll bend his uncouth heart
    my way. I deserve it, and merits have been known
    to conquer those who do us wrong.
    (*To Lichas*)
                         —Direct
    my husband, before he wears this cloak, to burn
    incense and, binding his gelid locks with leaves      580
    of silvery poplar, satisfy the gods.
    (LICHAS *approaches* DEIANIRA, *accepts the robe, and exits*)
    Now I'll proceed to the sanctuary of the palace
    and offer prayers to the mother of implacable love!
    (*To* CHORUS)
    And you, Calydonian maids, friends of my youth
    and father's house, grieve for this, my tearful fate.

(DEIANIRA *exits, followed by* NURSE)

Scene 2


CHORUS *of Aetolian women*:   O Deianira,
   Daughter of Oeneus, yes, we weep,
   Your adoring childhood friends, for this!

FIRST CHORISTER: We used to wade the river shallows,
   When the floods of spring had ebbed, with you;
   When the Achelous, becalmed, flowed softly                    590
   And the Lycormus no longer roiled
   Yellow with soil from its source. We'd go
   Seek out the altars of Pallas, join
   The maiden chorus, or bring forth
   The close-wrapped Bacchic implements
   Each third springtime, when summer raised
   The sun, and Ceres at Eleusis held
   The mysteries in her private hall.

CHORUS: Now too, whatever you fear, trust us,
   Most faithful when misfortune rules;                          600
   Take us along to share your fate.

SECOND CHORISTER: Though everyone throngs your halls, O kings
   Of the world, crowding through countless doors;
   Though when you go out, a populace
   Presses around you, in all of these
   Scarce one is a true friend. The fates
   Stand watch at the gilded gates and when
   They open, deceit and wary fraud
   Enter, and the concealed weapon.

THIRD CHORISTER: And if you venture among the people         610
   It's with envy at your side. Since each
   Day follows a treacherous night, kings wake
   Each dawn as if reborn. Men serve
   The king's power, not the king;
   The glitter of court is what excites them.

FOURTH CHORISTER: One man longs to be seen with the king;
    Lust for celebrity eats his heart out.
    Another would feed his hunger with gold,
    Though not the Ister's gem-rich acreage
    Would slake his thirst, nor Lydia, nor Spain,      620
    Where the Tagus glints with gold when the West
    Wind blows: not even if the Hebrus,
    The Hydaspes, or the Ganges watered
    His fields; for avarice—for avarice
    The entire earth is not enough.

FIRST CHORISTER: One waits on kings; he haunts the hearths
    Of kings: not that his ploughman, bent
    Forever at his plough, nor field hands
    Tilling his thousand fields may rest—
    But only that he may make a fortune      630
    To salt away.

SECOND CHORISTER:    Another man
    Courts kings that he may learn oppression,
    Ruining many, raising up none;
    He longs for power but to do wrong.

THIRD CHORISTER: How few die when they ought to die!
    And those the Cynthian moon found happy
    The next dawn's light finds miserable.
    It's rare to be happy and old at once!

FOURTH CHORISTER: A bed of sod is softer than a gown
    Of purple and brings deep slumber; but      640
    A palace cancels rest, and royal
    Bedclothes make for sleepless nights.
      O, if we could see into the heart
    Of the billionaire, what anxieties
    We'd find great fortune breeding there—
    Waves tossed by gale-force winds are calmer!

FIRST CHORISTER: The poor man's heart is carefree; though
　His cup is made of beechwood, he holds it
　With steady grip. He eats plain food
　And cheap, and faces no drawn sword.　　　　　　650
　The cup of gold holds bloody wine.

SECOND CHORISTER: The wife of a man of modest means
　Cannot wear pearls, nor gems of the East
　In her earrings; no lambswool double-dyed
　In Sidonian vats for her, nor silks
　From Asian leaves harvested under
　The sunny skies of China! Though
　She dyes the homespun her own hands wove
　With local plants, she has a marriage
　She can count on every night.　　　　　　660

THIRD CHORISTER: Revenge, with torch in hand, pursues
　The bride that fame's made popular,
　Nor is the poor man happy till
　He sees the fortunate brought low.
　Whoever leaves the middle of the road
　Will find the going tough!

FOURTH CHORISTER:　　　　　　When Phaethon
　Borrowed his father's chariot to make
　A day's sunlight and drove those wheels
　Astray among the stars unknown
　To sunlight, he crashed—and crashed the world;　　　670
　While Daedalus went straight on through
　The hub of the sky; he made a pleasing
　Landfall—no sea is known for him.
　But Icarus the boy ventured
　Beyond the birds in flight, looked down
　Upon his soaring father, flew
　Close to the sun—and gave his name
　To an unknown ocean.

FIRST CHORISTER:                     Pity for us,
  Disaster meets success half way.
  Let others get a reputation                              680
  For being grand and prosperous.

SECOND CHORISTER: I don't want any crowd to call
  Me powerful! My small craft
  Will keep near shore; let no gale drive
  *My* little vessel out to sea.
  Bad luck bypasses sheltered coves—
  Gives chase to ships on the high seas
  Whose wind-filled sails buffet the clouds.

(*Enter* DEIANIRA, *followed by* NURSE)

THIRD CHORISTER: Miserable woman, speak: what fresh
  reverse of fortune's wheel is this?                      690
  Though your lips are sealed, your countenance
  says everything you would conceal.


ACT III


Scene 1


(DEIANIRA, *stage right, proceeds to right of palace doors;* NURSE,
*stage left, proceeds to left of palace doors, through which the* CHO-
RUS *of Aetolian women has filed*)

DEIANIRA: A tremor shudders along my limbs; I have
  the shakes. My hair stands up on end; this fear
  clings to my spirit, the heart thumps wildly
  and my trembling liver pulses from jittery nerves,
  as when rough seas still churn, although the wind
  has died and the sky cleared up for a calm day;

just so my mind, weighed down with troubles earlier,
is still anxious. Once a god begins                              700
to bear down on the prosperous, he truly
goes at it. No great performance goes unpunished.
The high and the mighty come to no good end.

NURSE: What twist of fate has possessed you now, poor thing?

DEIANIRA: When I sent off that centaur-bloodied garment
and went dejected to my room, my heart
feared fraud; feared something, I knew not what. I thought
I'd run a test. That awful Nessus warned me
to keep that barbarous blood from fire and sun,
and this deceit itself predicted treachery.                     710
By chance, in a cloudless sky the blazing sun
was bringing on a scorching day—anxiety
even now hardly allows me to speak—
right out in the sun I tossed the blood-soaked pelt
we used to smear the cloak. The bloody stuff
shuddered and, heated by the sun's rays, burst
into flame! It's almost too monstrous to talk about!
As the East or warming southerly winds melt
the snows which glittering Mimas Mountain loses
in spring; or as the tossed waves crash out of              720
the Ionian sea against Leucadian rocks
and with a dying surge foam on the shore;
or as on sacred shrines the sprinkled frankincense
dissolves amid the flames of the altar; so
the skin all shriveled up and lost its fleece.
And while I am wondering at it there, what caused
my wonder—vanishes! In fact, the ground
it touched shudders itself and begins to foam,
and whatever the poison comes in contact with
begins to wither away!
(HYLLUS *approaches from stage right*)
                                    But here I see              730
my son come running. He looks terrified!

(*To* HYLLUS)
What news? Speak up!

HYLLUS:                                Run for your life! The farther
  you flee the better; on land or sea, among
  the stars, or in hell below, escape, mother,
  far from the troubles Hercules has found!

DEIANIRA: What great evil my heart forebodes, I cannot say!

HYLLUS: Triumphant Juno's still in charge; Juno
  will give you sanctuary. Go to her
  temple. Anywhere else is impossible.

DEIANIRA: What calamity drowns my innocence? Tell me!        740

HYLLUS: That splendor of the earth and the one protector
  the fates had given the world in place of Jove
  is gone, O mother. Through those muscled limbs
  of Hercules some plague, I know not what,
  is raging. And he who subdued monsters, he,
  he the victor, is mastered; is suffering; grieves.
  What more do you want to know?

DEIANIRA:                                The afflicted rush
  To listen to their troubles. Tell me, how
  does it look for our house? O family, O
  miserable household gods! Now I am widowed            750
  altogether; driven out now; now overcome.

HYLLUS: You do not grieve for Hercules alone;
  the whole world is cast down because he is,
  Mother. Don't think it's your distress alone.
  Every land is crying out against it;
  look, all will grieve together with one lament.
  The calamity you suffer is common to all,
  you but anticipate their grief. You mourn
  Hercules first, poor dear, but not alone.

DEIANIRA: But tell me, do, how near to death he lies.        760

HYLLUS: Death, whom he had once subdued in Death's
  own country, shuns him; and fate dares not admit
  so vile a wrong. Maybe Clotho dropped
  the distaff from her trembling hand and fears to finish
  spinning the fate of Hercules. What a day,
  unspeakable day! Shall it be the great man's last?

DEIANIRA: You say he's already gone to death and the shades,
  that luckless world? Can't I go first; outstrip
  his dying? Tell, if he has not perished yet.

HYLLUS: On every side the sea crashes against            770
  Euboea's beetling cliffs. Caphereus' crag
  splits open the Aegean—the south wind blows
  on one side, on the other the snow-filled north wind howls
  where the Strait of Eurypus sends its vagrant tides
  seven times to flood and ebb again, until
  sun drives his weary chariot into the sea.
  Here, on a lofty headland buffeted
  by thunderheads, a venerable temple
  to Cenaean Jove shines through the cloudy air.
      When all the votive cattle stood at the altars     780
  and gilt-horned bulls groaned throughout the grove,
  he stripped off the lion's skin all stained with gore,
  laid down his club, loosed quiver from his shoulder;
  then, gleaming in your cloak, his matted hair
  crowned with a wreath of poplar, kindled the altars.
  "Accept these offerings at your altar," he said,
  "and rightly claim them, father. Let the sacred
  fire burn brightly with plenty of incense, which
  the rich Arab who reveres the sun harvests
  from Saba's trees. Now earth and sea and sky            790
  are pacified; all beasts put down; and I
  return, the victor. Resign your thunderbolt!"
      In the middle of this prayer he moaned. Amazed
  at himself, he collapsed. Then a dreadful clamor

filled the air to heaven. As a bull, when the blade
sinks deep, would flee—bearing the wound and the axe
together—and fills the frightened temple with
enormous roaring; or as the rolling thunder
blankets the sky, so did he strike the stars
and sea with his cries; high Chalcis echoed him                    800
and all the Cyclades heard his bellowings.
Then Caphereus' cliff and all the forest's groves
returned the cries of Hercules.
                                        We saw
him weeping!
                        The men supposed his former madness
had returned. Then his servants got away.
But he—the flame twisting his face—went after
one among them all. He sought out Lichas.
With quivering hands Lichas gripped the altar:
and died from fright. He left little behind
for punishment! Now Hercules held up                               810
the shaking corpse and cried, "Is this the hand,
O fates, is this what did me in? Has Lichas
conquered Hercules? Behold more bloodshed;
now Hercules annihilates this Lichas!
This stains my record—that my final labor
be such a puny one." And he hurled the body
up to the stars, its blood spattering the clouds.
A Getan arrow speeds like that into the sky,
or one a Cretan archer shoots: yet not
so far as Lichas flew. The body fell in the sea,                   820
the skull dashed on a rock: one youth, twice dead.
        "But wait!" he said, "I have not lost my mind
to madness; this ill is worse than anger
or insanity: I am raving at myself."
He names his ruin. He rages, lacerates
his flesh, tears limb from very limb. The garment
seethes upon his wincing flesh. He tries
to throw it off. I see him unable to
do it! Trying to shed the thing, he rips
his limbs instead. The mantle grafts to that                       830

muscular physique. The toxin decomposes
the skin, and the fabric merges with it. The cause
of this awful scourge is not apparent, though
cause there is. Hardly enduring the pain
he lies down, drained, on the ground; now begs for water—
which doesn't help—and creeps shoreward, guided
by the booming surf. He pitches into the sea,
but a servant pulls the straying hero back.
Cruel fate! We had become, in strength, the equals
of Hercules.
                    Now a ship conveys him from                    840
Euoboea's shore, a light south wind drives on
the weight of Hercules. Breath leaves his body.
Night presses on his eyes.

DEIANIRA:                                  Why does my heart
skip a beat? Why this shock? The evil deed
is done. Jove wants the son back Juno took
and she must give the world back all she can.
A well-aimed sword will drive my body through.
So be it. Yet, should one so weak inflict
a pain so great? Sir, with your lightning bolts
destroy your criminal daughter as you would            850
a plague; with a flash such as you hurled at Phaethon;
send even the bolt you would have used against
the Hydra, had Hercules not been your son!
For I through Hercules have brought down nations.
But why ask the gods for weapons? Spare at least
his father! Hercules' wife should be ashamed
to sue for death—I'll do it myself! I'll die
by my own hand. I'll get a sword. Only
a sword then? Whatever weapon kills will do.
I'll leap from a cliff! I'll choose the peak of Oeta,     860
which dawns first touch; a fine spot to throw myself from.
The sharp outcrops below will tear me apart;
my bloody hands will grasp sharp rocks, my blood
will daub the whole stormy mountainside.
One death's a trifle. A trifle—yet still it can be long.

But I can't choose the weapon to do me in.
Oh, that the sword of Hercules was hanging
in my room! There would be steel for me to die with!
But is it sufficient that one strong hand should kill me?
The whole world should stone me: let every hand          870
be raised against me for killing the great man.
Now tyrant and monster may safely ravage the earth
and human sacrifice occur once more.
I've been a model for crime, exposed a populace
to evil kings and savage gods by slaying
the avenger. Don't spare me, Juno, sister
of Jove the thunder king! Just scatter flames
as he does, grab lightning from his hand and strike me!
Enormous honor and praise are taken from you,
Juno; I got there first by slaying your rival.          880

HYLLUS: Why drag our shaken family down? The crime,
    if there was one, was committed by mistake.
    He does no harm who harms unwillingly.

DEIANIRA: If you blame fate and pardon thus yourself,
    you're sure to go wrong. It's right I am condemned
    to die.

HYLLUS:                    He who wants to die longs to look guilty.

DEIANIRA: Only death can set the misguided right again.

HYLLUS: From sunshine fleeing . . .

DEIANIRA:                              the sun itself avoids me!

HYLLUS: Will you give up life?

DEIANIRA:                    I'm so depressed. Yes—to follow him.

HYLLUS: But he's alive; still breathing!

DEIANIRA:                        When it came about          890
   that he was beaten, Hercules began
   to die.

HYLLUS:          You'd cut your life off? Leave me behind?

DEIANIRA: She has lived long whose son must bury her.

HYLLUS: Don't go until he's gone.

DEIANIRA:                        It's usual enough          900
   for the chaste wife to go before.

HYLLUS:                        Poor mother,
   blame yourself and you convict yourself
   of crimes.

DEIANIRA:      The guilty can't commute their sentences.

HYLLUS: Many live whose only sin was of
   bad judgment, not commission. Who can blame
   his fate?

DEIANIRA:                  Whoever's met with an unjust fate.          910

HYLLUS: But he dispatched Megara with his arrows,
   slew his own sons as well, with spears from his
   frenzied hand. Three times a murderer
   of family—yet Hercules, who could not
   forgive his madness, forgave himself; he cleansed
   himself and washed his guilt away. Must you
   be in such a hurry to condemn yourself?

DEIANIRA: It is his ruin that will finish me.

HYLLUS: If I know Hercules, he'll be back, perhaps
   triumphant over his misfortune; and pain,          920
   surmounted, will submit to your Hercules.

DEIANIRA: It's reported that the plague has wasted his body.
The Hydra's venom has hollowed out his limbs.

HYLLUS: Do you think the poison of a serpent dead
could vanquish the one who conquered it alive?
He cut the Hydra down, although its teeth
were sunk deep in his flesh, he standing there
thigh-deep in the swamp, victorious, the venom
drooling down his limbs! Can Nessus' blood
prostrate the man who slew Nessus himself?                    930

DEIANIRA: It's no use to hold back one ordained to die.
Just so, I have been sentenced to flee the light—
whoever perishes with Hercules
has lived enough—

NURSE: (*Approaching*)   Look, by these gray hairs
and these breasts just like a mother's to you, I
implore you, forget the terrible promptings of
your fevered heart and these black thoughts of death!

DEIANIRA: —who may dissuade the hopeless from dying is
the unfeeling one! Sometimes death is punishment,
sometimes a gift; for many it means pardon.                  940

NURSE: Hold on, unlucky one, so he will know
the deed was not his wife's, but a mistake.

DEIANIRA: In hell I'll be vindicated; the gods of hell
will acquit the accused, though I condemn myself.
Let Pluto purify me. I'll stand on your banks,
a dismal shade without a memory,
O Lethe, and I'll embrace my husband there.
(*To herself*)
But you, Pluto, master of torment in
the dark kingdom, think up a suffering
—for this offense outweighs whatever crime                   950
anyone ever dared commit; Juno

herself would not rid the world of Hercules—
prepare some special punishment for me!
Let Sisyphus relax, I'll put my shoulder
to his stone; let the evasive waters flee
my lips, the deceiving currents Tantalus craved
taunt *my* thirst! Bind me to Ixion's rack, the wheel
revolving yet, on which the Thessalian king
suffers. Let greedy vultures eat my guts out!
One of Danaus' murdering daughters, sent                     960
below, is missing; make room for me, pale sisters,
I'll take her vacant place beside the cistern
of your punishment. —Or make me your comrade,
Medea; my crime is worse than both of yours;
and Procne too, I am your equal in crime.
You see a daughter in me, Althea; —mother!
Receive me, though yours are not such deeds as mine.
O faithful wives, who dwell in hallowed woods,
bar me from Elysium! But if any
has splashed herself with a husband's blood, forgot        970
her marriage vows, and stood there with dripping sword,
she'll see in my hands the work of hers—and praise it!
I well might join that club of wives, but they
would not want such a demon in their crowd.
Unconquered husband! The flesh is guilty but
my heart is innocent. Oh, I was taken in!
(*Turns to* HYLLUS)
That false brute, Nessus! Trying to save Hercules
from a whore I took him from myself. Enough
of life and daylight, that coyly lure us on
to sunlit miseries. The light is worthless                    980
without him! I'll pay the price for you, Hercules,
and give up life—or shall I save my life,
if you have strength, for your own hands to take?
Can you still shoot an arrow true, or does
your hand grow helpless to bend the bow? If you
can deal the blow, I'll wait. I'll wait till you
can shatter me as you did blameless Lichas.
Strew me from city to city, or hurl me to

some unknown planet! Slay me as you did
the beast of Arcady and all the rest.                    990
At least from them, dear husband, you returned
in triumph.

HYLLUS:          Stop, I beg you, mother! Accept
your fate. Mistakes are not the same as crimes.

DEIANIRA: Hyllus, if you would be a loving son,
Now kill your mother. Why does your hand tremble?
Why do you look away? This deed would be
filial piety. Why this cowardly delay?
This hand wrecked Hercules for you, destroyed him
who made you the grandson of Jove. I took
a glory greater than I gave you when                     1000
I brought you into the world. If you don't know
about villainy, I'll teach you. If you want,
bury your sword in my throat, or if you want
bury your sword in my womb; a mother's help
will give you courage. This great deed will not
be by your hand, but from my spirit, truly.
Are you afraid to obey, to stamp out monsters
as your father did? Get started! I forgive you this
impiety; the fates themselves will pardon you.
—But at my back I hear the Furies' lashes crack!        1010
(*To herself*)
Who's that, whose locks with vipers twist and braid,
whose foul wings quake about her scaly brows?
Why do you trail me, Megaera, with smoking torch?
Has the court of hell passed judgment even now?
It has—I see the prison gates gape wide!
I see an old man struggle with a boulder
on his back, bent double. See, where the stone hauled up
slowly begins to roll back down again!
Look, where Tisiphone stands, pale and awful;
she states her case: O spare your whips I beg you,       1020
Megaera; hold back the infernal flames;
it was a crime of love!

But what is this?
The earth shudders; the palace roofs cave in;
where did that dangerous mob come from? As one,
the whole world overruns me; on all sides
populations riot; all the world
demands its savior. Now spare me, nations! Where
can I go? Now death alone will grant safe haven.
By the flaming glare of the sun and by the gods
I swear: though I must die, I leave behind                    1030
Hercules, on earth, alive.

(*Exit* DEIANIRA)

HYLLUS:                              Oh no!
She's gone; completely distracted. She's finished. She
is bent on dying. Now it's time for me
to keep her from her rush toward death. Painful
duty of a son! If I avert
my mother's death, I wrong my father; if I
let him die, I wrong my mother. Evil besets me
either way. And yet I must prevent her
so she will not do such a wicked deed.

(*Exit* HYLLUS. *Enter* CHORUS *of Aetolian women through palace doors.*)

FIRST CHORISTER: When Orpheus, the happy son              1040
Of Calliope, strummed his lyre
Beneath the peaks of Rhodope,
He sang; and what he sang was true:
Nothing made will last eternally.

SECOND CHORISTER: His music stilled the mountain streams'
Loud tumult there; oblivious
To their wild flight the waters stopped,
Mid-air; and while the rivers paused,
Downstream the Thracians found their Hebrus
Dried up. The forest brought the birds;                    1050

THIRD CHORISTER: They came to rest on every limb,
  Or the song might make some roaming bird
  Wandering on the upper air
  Pause and, trimming its wings, descend.

FOURTH CHORISTER: Mount Athos tore its summit free
  And, gathering centaurs on the way,
  He came to stand next Rhodope,
  His snow cap melted by the song.

FIRST CHORISTER: The dryad left the refuge of
  Her oaks and hurried to the bard;                        1060
  Finding fresh dens at hand, the wild
  Animals came to hear his song.

SECOND CHORISTER: The African lion lay, all ears,
  Nearby the cattle, unafraid.
  Finding the wolf, deer did not bolt,
  And the snake crept from his hiding place,
  His poison out of mind for once.

THIRD CHORISTER: When he passed through the gates that led
  Below the world to the speechless dead
  and struck his grieving lyre, he                         1070
  Subdued the sullen gods of darkness
  And hell itself;

FOURTH CHORISTER:        he paid no mind
  To the Stygian lake the gods so love
  To swear by. The wheel of Ixion ground
  To a halt, its whirling overcome.

FIRST CHORISTER: And Tityus' liver healed, ignored
  By vultures enraptured with his song;
  Even the merciless stone gave up
  And helped old Sisyphus along.

SECOND CHORISTER: Tantalus lost his thirst, although          1080
  The waters rose; and had no need
  To reach for the apples now within
  His grasp. You heard as well, grim Charon:
  Your craft unguided crossed the Styx!

THIRD CHORISTER: Thus Orpheus with his dreaming song
  Subdued the gods of death; and so
  The sisters gave Eurydice
  More thread—extension of her fate.

FOURTH CHORISTER: But while forgetful Orpheus,
  Incredulous, looked back to see                            1090
  Eurydice restored to him—
  Now following in his tracks—he lost
  The reward his song had earned. Just when
  She would be born once more, she died.

FIRST CHORISTER: Then seeking relief in melody
  He sang in a weeping tempo to
  The Getan people:

SECOND CHORISTER:      "Even the gods
  Must obey their laws, as he who planned
  The seasons decreed four changes round
  The fleeting year; so it must be.                          1100
  The sisters spin fresh threads for no one,
  And all that's made, or shall be, dies."

THIRD CHORISTER: With Hercules' annihilation
  We should believe the Thracian prophet.
  A new day soon shall come for men,
  When southern skies will bury all
  From Libya to the farthest shores
  That Africans inhabit; so too
  Shall northern skies fall on whatever
  Exists beneath the pole where north                        1110
  Winds howl.

FOURTH CHORISTER:     Mankind will see the old
    Laws overturned; the frightened sun
    Shall plunge from the extinguished sky
    And snuff out day. The courts of heaven
    Shall sink; sunrise and sunset shall
    Go down with them.

FIRST CHORISTER:     One form of death
    Or another, and chaos, will destroy
    All of the gods; and in the end
    Death shall find its destiny
    In dying.

SECOND CHORISTER:     And what safe haven then                1120
    For mankind? Will Tartarus open its
    Doors to a wasted universe?
    Or is there room enough between
    Heaven and earth (too much perhaps?)
    For all the mischief of existence?

CHORUS: What space could possibly be large
    Enough to hold so great a doom—
    Or keep the gods? Such a place would hold
    Three realms: the underworld, the sea
    And land, the distant fields of stars.                    1130

THIRD CHORISTER:     But what immense commotion
    Strikes the astonished ear? It is—
    It is the sound of Hercules.

## ACT IV

### Scene 1

*(The backdrop of the palace rises, revealing the plinth upstage.*
CHORUS *of Hercules' attendants is at stage right.* HERCULES *enters
stage left.)*

HERCULES: Turn round your winded horses, bright sun; let loose
    the night!
  Let the day I die be canceled from the world's archive,
  and black clouds overcast the world—this day I die!—
  so Juno may not witness it.
  *(Ascends the plinth, raises his arms, and looks aloft)*
                    Now is the time,
  O father, to bring obscuring chaos back to smash
  the firmament from side to side and pull both poles
  apart. And do not spare the stars! For you are losing          1140
  Hercules, proud father. Now survey heaven, Jove,
  throughout, lest any Titan such as Gyas or
  Enceladus be hefting stones, or bodies, thinking
  rebellion. Now, now lordly Hades will swing wide
  the dark gates of his prison, loosen Saturn's chains,
  and deliver him to heaven. I, your son, dispensed
  your justice here on earth—did duty for your thunder
  and lightning—but I go back to the Styx; your enemies,
  fierce Enceladus and that gang of louts, will rise
  against you. My death, O parent, will cast in doubt your
    kingdom,                                                    1150
  even the air you breathe. Before the Titans sack
  heaven, father, bury me under the ruins of the world,
  destroy the skies that you will lose in any case.

FIRST CHORISTER: Your fears aren't idle, son of Jove.
  Soon now, Mount Pelion shall press
  On Ossa's height and Athos, piled
  On Pindus, poke its forest tops
  Among the stars. From there Typhoeus
  Shall rise above the cliffs, a giant,
  And send Mount Inarmine aloft                                    1160
  Out of the Tuscan plain.

SECOND CHORISTER:                    Not yet
  Defeated by your thunderbolt
  Enceladus shall raise the furnace
  Of Aetna and lance its flaming side;
  Already the kingdoms of the skies
  Decline, following your course.

HERCULES: I who have beaten death and braved the Styx and who
  returned with plunder straight through Lethe's stagnant swamp
  —the sun, spying me, all but fell from his chariot—
  I, whom the gods above, below, and on the earth               1170
  have reckoned with, I am dying! It was no sword,
  nor did Mount Othrys, stronghold of Titans, get me. No Titan
  with slavering mouth will bury me under some mountain!
  I am vanquished without a victor; and what is worse—insult
  to manliness!—my last day sees no harm extinguished.
  Oh me, I lose my life not doing any deed!
        Master of the world; and you gods, long spectators
  of my accomplishments; and the round earth itself!
  Have you decided that your Hercules must perish
  this way? Horrible shame for me! Fate most foul—              1180
  a woman will be known as the one responsible
  for Hercules' death. For whom then does he die? Oh me!
  If unyielding fate has said I die by woman's hand,
  if this is the last frayed thread unwinding from the spool
  of my destiny—better that Juno's hate had caused
  my downfall! But by what hand is *her* opponent crushed?
  A woman's! More shame for you, goddess! A mere woman
  has surpassed you! Till now you thought that only I outdid you,

but now you are outdone by two! Of rage like yours,
let heaven be ashamed! I shall have been a gift                    1190
to centaurs, such as Nessus; it would be better if
I still were fixed in place chained to unyielding rock
in the world of darkness. But still I hauled my spoil to daylight
from the Styx, and Death was stunned to witness Cerberus
my prize. Did I escape from bondage, and Death back down
at every point—only to meet at last this trivial doom?
Woe is me, how often I forsook a virtuous
death! What shall my title of honor be at last?

THIRD CHORISTER: See virtue with a view to fame
  Not flinching at the Lethean stream!                            1200

FIRST CHORISTER: He feels no pain at dying, but
  Only shame at the cause of it.

SECOND CHORISTER: He longs to end his last day crushed
  Under the bulging body of
  Some giant, to endure a Titan's
  Mountain-hefting weight, or die
  In the claws of some enraged wild beast.

THIRD CHORISTER: But after all your deeds, poor man,
  There are no more—no beast, no giant—
  No fitting agent, Hercules,                                     1210
  To cause your death, but you yourself.

HERCULES: (To himself) What scorpion out of the Sahara or what
    crab
  from a jungle pool burns in the marrow of my bones?
  My heart was strong and steady, now it bursts my lungs;
  my liver is being scraped dry; persistent fever saps
  my blood. First, this plague gnaws at the skin; from there
  it enters the body, ravages arms and legs; and next
  it gets into the joints and ribs, undoing as it goes
  each organ. I am in appalling pain, and it
  calmly eats and drinks away my body. It                         1220

holds a life-lease of even the marrow of my bones;
my bones, which lose their old rock-hard solidity
and, as they soften, bend; they fall together like
an imploded building. My muscular body shrivels
and turns to mush. Not even all my massive limbs
will satisfy this venom's relentless appetite.
How great must be the illness that Hercules calls great!
Shocking abomination! Look at me, cities, see
what's left of him, that Hercules who helped you so.
Can you tell this is your son, father, your Hercules?          1230
Did these once powerful arms pin that marauding beast,
The Nemean lion, and wring its massive neck? Are these
the hands that drew the bow and from the stars brought down
the Stymphalian birds, the hands that managed all those
    strenuous
achievements? Are these the shoulders that bore up the world?
Is this my tremendous build? The neck thick as a bull's?
My manhood's dead and buried, yet I am still above ground.
Poor man, how can I ask Jove now for a place in heaven?
    Whatever this poison is that festers in my guts
I pray it will leech away, stop suppurating, stop            1240
dosing me with its invisible injuries.
Where did it come from, out of the icy Black Sea waters
or the muddy Tethys? From Gibraltar, or Morocco
across the straits? O killing punishment, are you
some worm that lifts his filthy hooded head within me,
or some other evil thing unknown before, even
to me? Did you breed in the bloody mire of the Hydra
or did you drop like a bloated tick from the Stygian dog?
    You are all calamities yet none—I cannot meet you
face to face. Let me at least behold my killer:              1250
whatever plague, whatever creature you may be,
openly meet me! How did you take up residence
in the chambers of my bones? Look, my right hand's torn
the skin away, laid bare these pustulating coils
of viscera; and yet the germ of this lies deeper still!
O strong catastrophe, the equal of Hercules!
But why this grief? Why tears staining my cheeks? I never

was one to weep; no hurt has ever smeared my face
with tears, yet—shame on me!—at last I've learned to cry.
No one anywhere has ever witnessed Hercules                    1260
in tears; I've borne my hardships dry-eyed! My strength, which
    has
put down so many terrors, surrenders only to you,
my pestilence. You first brought tears to my eyes; my visage,
once more steady than rock, harder than tempered steel,
is going soft and helpless. Commander of the skies,
everyone here on earth has seen me sobbing and bawling,
yet greater torture for me is knowing that Juno sees!
But O, the fire comes once more and roasts my guts.
Oh where is the lightning bolt to deal the final blow?

(*He drops to his knees*)

FIRST CHORISTER: What cannot sorrows conquer? Once        1270
    Harder than Thracian mountain peaks
    And more composed than Parrhasian skies
    He has given in to bitter griefs.

SECOND CHORISTER: His head slumps down; he rolls his weight
    From side to side, and bravery
    Alone—sometimes—holds back his tears.

THIRD CHORISTER: Thus sun cannot melt glaciers down;
    However bright the rays it sends
    The radiance of the ice defies
    The torches of the scorching sun.                         1280

(*Chorus of Hercules' attendants exits stage right*)

HERCULES: (*Looking up*) Think of my sufferings now, father! Think
    of me!
    I never turned to you for help before, not even
    when the Hydra held me pinned with its many heads
    nor when I stood with Death beside the lake of hell,
    enveloped in the black of utter night. So many trials

and tyrants overcome, yet I relied on myself
and didn't look to you for help. My strong hands did
the work; not prayers. Now put me out of misery; just
one thunderbolt, I pray! Think of me as one
of the Titans invading your domain, if it will help.          1290
After all, I might have assaulted heaven myself,
but since I knew you were in fact my father, I
refrained from harm. Whether by nature cruel or
compassionate, father, I beg you, lay hands on me,
your offspring; dispatch me quickly and add to your good name.

    Or, if your hand is troubled to perform this deed,
from Aetna let loose the fiery Titans on me, giants
who carry mountains such as Pindus in their hands,
and I will be buried under one of their projectiles!
Or let Bellona burst the infernal prison bars          1300
and rush me with drawn sword; or send truculent Mars—
though he's my half brother, still he's Juno's son!
You too, Athena, my half sister, Jove's daughter,
aim your spear; and lastly, Juno, I implore you,
at least you'll have a spearpoint ready for my side
(though if it's you I still would perish at a woman's hand).
O, hated one, at last subduing, sated at last,
still gorging on revenge, what more could you ask? You see
Hercules, a suppliant on his knees, when no
corner of the world nor any beast has ever seen          1310
me beg. Now that I need a stepmother full of rage
and violence—now does your temper cool? Have you
    renounced
your hate? Will you spare me—now all I want is death?
O cities of the world and earth itself, is there
no one among you to deliver torch or weapon?
If you supply me with the arms I need, I will engage
that no region shall bring forth wild beasts when I
am gone, nor any corner of the world require my aid.
If evils come to life, may your avenger come
once more! Now, gang up on me, overpower me,          1320
stone me. An ungrateful world deserts me; forgets me.
O peoples of the earth, you would be suffering untold

calamities now had you not brought me into the world.
Deliver your advocate from his miseries!
This is the chance for you to pay me back for all
I did. And death will be the wages all shall earn!


Scene 2


(*Enter two of Hercules' attendants stage left, followed by* ALCMENA)

ALCMENA: Where shall the wretched mother of Hercules
    look next? Where is my son? Where? Where? See,
    on the ground there, if I can trust my eyes, it's him
    lying there in a fever and tossing, short of breath.    1330
    He moans. He's finished! Let me embrace you, one
    last time, dear son, and with my lips on yours
    draw in your spirit with your final breath.
    Take me in your arms! But where have they gone,
    your powerful limbs? What happened to that neck
    that held the stars in heaven up? Who left you
    like this, a shadow of your former self?

HERCULES: It's me you see all right, mother; Hercules,
    the—what should I call this?—the vile remains of the old me.
    Look at me, mother! Why do you turn away and hide    1340
    your face? Are you ashamed that I am called your son?

ALCMENA: Where in the world, where on earth did this
    unlikely monster come from? What dreadful thing
    has got hold of you? Who has demolished you?

HERCULES: By his wife's deceit, you witness Hercules laid low!

ALCMENA: What malice suffices to undo Hercules?

HERCULES: Call it what you will, mother—a woman's fury!

ALCMENA: And how did this poison infect your body?

HERCULES:                                  A garment
  envenomed by a woman's hands gave entrance to it.

ALCMENA: Where is this robe? I'm looking at naked limbs.    1350

HERCULES: It merged with my flesh!

ALCMENA:                             Whoever heard of such a
  plague!

HERCULES: Through all my entrails the Hydra, and a thousand
    wild
  creatures with it, rove! Believe me, mother, it burns
  hotter than Aetna erupting, or the scorching heat
  below the changeless sky of the equator's noon.
  O comrades, throw me into the sea, into the river—
  would the Hister itself be deep enough to cool me? Vast
  as it is, the ocean could not quench these flames; touching
  my agonies, the water would evaporate,
  all moisture fail. Why did you send me back to Jove,    1360
  O lord of hell? More fitting to have kept me with you!
  Return me to your shadows, show me the way to the ghosts
  of those I conquered on earth! Don't be afraid of me
  this time. Come, Death; fear not! I am prepared to die.

ALCMENA: Control yourself! At least hold back your tears.
  Show yourself unmoved even before
  such trials. Stop thinking about death
  and conquer the dead as you have done before!

HERCULES: If the wild Caucasus takes me bound in chains and
    makes
  a meal of me for the hungry birds in Scythia,    1370
  resounding with mournful cries, no cry would pass my lips.
  If those mobile cliffs of Symplegades shook their crags
  to close like pincers on me, I'd bear it all, defiant;

if I lay beneath Mount Pindus, with Haemus and Athos (rising
firm from the ocean) piled on top, and Mimas too,
off which the bolts of Jove glance harmlessly; mother,
if heaven itself fell on me and the chariot of the sun
rolled burning across my shoulders, no unworthy cry
would beat the spirit of Hercules down. Wild animals
by the thousand might spring on me and gore me; on
   one side                                                           1380
Stymphalian birds, on another the massive bull charging
with lowered head, all earthly scourges; even if Sinus
the giant should bend some tree and with it catapult me
into the air, scattering limbs across the sky,
still I'd not whimper. No animal, no weapon, nothing
that I could openly fight would draw one groan from me.

ALCMENA: Perhaps it is no woman's venom that sears
   your body, son, but that exhausting round
   of labors; it's work that's brought on this collapse
   and doubtless nourished some infection in you.          1390

HERCULES: (*Delirious*) Where is this sickness then? Where is it?
   Is there
something of evil in the world while I'm still here?
Hand me my bow—let it come against me—my
bare hands are enough. Come and get it! Come on!

(HERCULES *sinks down*)

ALCMENA: O woe is me! In his shocking pain he has
   taken leave of his senses.
   (*To attendants*)
                    Here now, remove
his bow and arrows, put them out of sight.
His flushed features threaten violent deeds.
(*Exit attendants with weapons, stage right*)
Now where shall an old woman find to hide?
This illness is madness, that and only that              1400
is doing this. —But why should I run or hide,

frantic as I am? Alcmena deserves
to die by a powerful hand, so let me perish
right now before some idle drifter takes me
or some low-life finishes me off.
   But look, he pants in coma, his straining chest
heaves with troubled breathing; with sleep affliction
binds up his drained limbs. Gods, help him! If,
to my misfortune, you have denied me him,
my star, my son, at least give back the world          1410
its liberator, I ask you that. Drive out
his illness, let Hercules regain his health!


Scene 3


(PHILOCTETES *has joined them. Enter* HYLLUS.)

HYLLUS: This day is filled with evils, and bitter light
   that finds Jove's daughter Deianira dead.
   Oh, she is dead! And Hercules lies dying.
   I, Jove's grandson, survive alone. My mother's
   wickedness is causing him to lose
   his life; and she was tricked into the crime.
   What aged senior looking back through all
   his years would have such heartaches to recount?          1420
   One day has done away with both my parents.
   Not to tempt fate, I won't recite details
   or mention other ills: it is enough
   to say farewell to Hercules, my father.

ALCMENA: Be quiet, son of illustrious Hercules
   and grandson of Alcmena, sad as you!
   Perhaps a good sleep will conquer grief.
   But look! Quiet deserts his drained spirit;
   pain calls his body back, and me to mourning.

HERCULES: (*Awakening, delirious*) What's this? Do I see Trachis
　　and its rocky cliffs?                                              1430
Or have I risen to the stars and left behind
mere mortals at last? Who readies heaven for me? You,
you, father, I see you now; and I see Juno too,
at peace at last. What heavenly words sound in my ears?
Juno is calling me her son! I see bright heaven's
palace gleaming, and the path worn by the flaming chariot
of the sun. I see the bed of night now; night's shadows
call me. What is this, though? What locks me out of heaven?
O father, who leads me from the stars? Just now the sun
blew on my face, and I was nearing heaven. But             1440
I see Trachis! What's got me back to earth again?
Just now Mount Oeta rose below me, the whole world
lay at my feet. I'd said farewell to pain, but it
has made me talk. —Yet I'll forbear. I must keep still!
(*To* HYLLUS)
Hyllus, son, you are your mother's wealth, her gift
to me. O, would that I could take my club to her;
smash the depraved life out of her, just as I clubbed
the Amazons to death along the snowy slopes
of Caucasus Mountain. —Dearest Megara . . . were you
　　not . . .
my wife when I went mad? Oh, hand me club and bow—  1450
I'll put this blot on my reputation, I'll pollute
my hand and let a woman be my final labor.

HYLLUS: Stop all that angry threatening, father. She
is gone! It is finished. The punishment
you sought to give her she has found herself.
My mother took her own life; she is dead.

HERCULES: The traitor! She deserved to perish at the hands
of Hercules infuriated! Lichas has lost
a confederate. I want to savage her lifeless body—
I'm that enraged. Why should even the cadaver          1460
be safe from my assault? Let wild beasts take their meal!

HYLLUS: She suffered more than him she caused to suffer.
Poor woman, you might have eased her pain somewhat.
She died by her own hand, weeping for you.
She paid a greater price than you had asked.
But you have not been felled by her deception,
nor by the villainy of a bloodstained wife.
Nessus, hit with your arrow, disgorging his life,
set up this trap. Your robe was smeared with blood
of Nessus, father, half man, half beast; Nessus        1470
who with your pain now pays you back for his.

HERCULES: That's it, then. It's all up with me, as well! My fate
is clear. This is my final day. The oracle
the sacred oak once told for me, confirmed by that
of Delphi on Parnassus, said: "One day you will
be vanquished by some someone you have vanquished; the end
that waits you after passing all those lands and seas
and worlds of darkness: to be slain by one you've slain."
No more complaint!
                          This end is right. It fits, that no one
alive could make this Hercules capitulate!        1480
Now I can choose a death that's worthy of me, something
unprecedented, shining, unforgettable.
This day will go down in history because of me. Go,
fell all the trees and stack Mount Oeta's forest up
in a pyre great enough for Hercules.
                          Over here,
my old companion, Philoctetes, son of Poeas!
Young man, perform this gruesome commission for me.
   Brighten
the broad daylight itself with Herculean flames!
         And now, I'll say a prayer for you, Hyllus; my last.
Foremost among the captives is a beauty; her looks        1490
show she has breeding, she's of the ruling class. Her name
is Iole, daughter of King Eurytus. Take her home;
with wedding torches lit, escort her to your bed.
A grimy, bloody conqueror, I took her from
her home, her country; then gave the miserable girl nothing

but Hercules; now even *he* is snatched from her.
Relieve her devastation, treat her well, that she
may care for Hercules' son, grandson of Jove. If she
has conceived a child by me, let it be born as yours.

     And you, dear honored mother, desist from wailing
  grief;                                                                                    1500
your son is living yet. By my heroic labors
I've shown that you are Jove's true wife, and Juno only
a mistress, a recreation. Whether the tale they tell
about the night I was conceived is true, or if
my father was only human—no matter: if it is
a lie about my parentage, still I *deserve*
to be Jove's son. I was an ornament of heaven;
in praise of Jove my mother bore me. In fact, though he
is Jove, he is delighted to be called my father.
Now mother, wipe your tears, and you shall hold your
  head                                                                                     1510
high among Greek mothers everywhere. What son
has Juno borne to compare with me, though she controls
the sky and was Jove's bride? Though she ruled heaven, yet
she envied you—wanted it said that Hercules
was hers.

     Now sun, you must go on alone for I,
your comrade, set out for Hades and the region of
the shades. Nevertheless, to the dark I'll take this fame,
that no plague anyone on earth could see defeated
Hercules, and those they could see—he has slain.

*(He walks off stage right slowly)*


Scene 4


*(Time passes. Enter* CHORUS *of Hercules' attendants from stage
right one by one in measured procession. Each carries a piece of*

*lumber, places it on or near the plinth, then turns to face the audience.)*

FIRST CHORISTER: Splendor of heaven, sun, at whose     1520
   First rays wan Hecate, queen of night,
   Unharnesses her chariot,
   Inform the Sabaeans far in the East,
   The Iberians in the West; tell those
   Enduring arctic nights and those
   Who cringe under your searing rays,
   That Hercules is heading for
   The eternal Shades;

SECOND CHORISTER:    he is approaching
   The kingdom Cerberus guards, that bourne
   From which he never will return.     1530

THIRD CHORISTER: May clouds obscure your shining; look
   On a world in tears with face gone pale
   And mists that catch around your head.
   Where on earth will you find, brave sun,
   Another such as Hercules
   To guide you?

FIRST CHORISTER:    Where will the poor world go
   For help if plague should rear its head
   And spread as if from venomous tongues
   Of a hundred angered snakes?

SECOND CHORISTER:    Or should
   Some boar disturb the quiet peoples     1540
   Of Arcadia in their ancient woodlands,

THIRD CHORISTER: Or tyrant such as Diomedes
   Splash human blood around the stables,

CHORUS: Who would the helpless people go to
   for help? The one the earth created

The equal of thundering Jove lies down,
Like Everyman, to die. Throughout
The world let cries of grief resound
And women with their hair down thrash
Their arms; lock every temple but Juno's,                    1550
For she alone is not distraught.

FIRST CHORISTER: You're bound for Lethe and the shore
Of Styx; no craft will bring you back;
You're headed for the grieving Shades
Where once you triumphed over Death;
Not this time! —you, all skin and bones,
Limp face downcast on neck gone limp.

SECOND CHORISTER: Yet you shall not reside among
The lesser dead but lodge with such
As Aeacus or that Cretan pair                                1560
—Minos and Rhadamanthus, twins—
A judge of men, the whip of tyrants.

THIRD CHORISTER: Power, show mercy to the helpless!
It's to your credit you did not draw
Your sword when you held sway; thus you,
When fate would menace, kept the peace.

FIRST CHORISTER: Such courage rates a place among
The stars; arctic or tropic zone,
Which region shall you occupy?
What piece of heaven will you anchor?                        1570
No part off limits to Hercules!

SECOND CHORISTER: But let Jove seat you far enough
From the fierce lion and fiery crab
Or those astonished stars will shudder
And forget their natural laws.

THIRD CHORISTER:                          So long
As flowers bloom in spring's first warmth

Or winter shakes the leaves from trees
Or summer draws them on again,
So long as autumn's fruits give way
And fall before the retreating year,                    1580
Never shall time diminish your fame
In this world.

CHORUS:                     You shall be one with sunlight
And the stars. Fields of grain shall rise
From the well of the sea, the crashing surf

FIRST CHORISTER: Sound soft, and the snowy bear shall come
Down from the stars to the water's edge,
Before the peoples of the world
Neglect to extol you with their praise.

SECOND CHORISTER:      To you, Jove, father of all things,
Miserable supplicants we pray:                         1590
Keep plague and ogre from being born
and make the poor world safe from fear
Of savage dictators.

THIRD CHORISTER:        Let no one
Dominate at court who counts
It glory to use force; if some
Threat comes again to terrorize
The nations, we beseech you, send
Abandoned earth a champion!

FIRST CHORISTER: Now listen: the heavens echo! Look there,
He mourns; the father of Hercules                      1600
Is mourning!

SECOND CHORISTER:      Or might it be the cries
Of the gods, or the voice of Juno frightened?
Does she run at the sight of Hercules?

THIRD CHORISTER: Does Atlas waver under this
    Fresh weight, or is it that the shades
    In hell are shaken, groaning to see him,
    The scourge of the infernal regions,
    Throw off his chains and go?

FIRST CHORISTER:                                    I was wrong!
    Look there, it's Poeas' son who comes
    With beaming face, and on his shoulder                    1610
    Those illustrious arrows jostling
    In the quiver everyone knows. See,
    It is an heir of Hercules!

## ACT V

### Scene 1

(*On stage is the* CHORUS *of attendants to Hercules. Enter* PHILOC-
TETES.)

SECOND CHORISTER: Speak up, young man, tell us how Hercules
    died.

THIRD CHORISTER: Pray tell what was the expression on his face
    at the last moment?

PHILOCTETES:                                    Like none you ever saw.

FIRST CHORISTER: He met the flames in a carefree frame of
    mind?

PHILOCTETES: The flames were nothing to him, he made that
    clear.

Has anything on earth been left unconquered
by Hercules? Think of it—all things were conquered.        1620

SECOND CHORISTER: Could he be brave while he was burning
    then?

PHILOCTETES: The one foe he'd not conquered, flame, is
    mastered;
it's one with the other wildnesses he vanquished.
Braving the fire is one of his labors now.

THIRD CHORISTER: Pray tell us how he overthrew the fire.

PHILOCTETES: When his mourning followers on Oeta began
    to cut the sacred forest down, one hand
    canceled the beech tree's shade; its whole trunk lay
    sliced off at the base; another felled a pine
    that towered skyward; he called it down, out            1630
    of the clouds, and as it crashed it shook the earth
    and brought down lesser timber in its path.
    A wide-crowned oak, like that oracular one
    that spoke Chaonia's portents, stood, the limbs
    so thick and wide no sunlight touched its den
    of shade. It moaned at all the blows it took.
    It broke the wedges; did not budge; it dulled
    the flailing axe blades, too soft for such dense grain.
    When, tottering at last, the oak began
    falling, it brought great ruin in its wake;             1640
    the place grew pale in the sun's immediate rays;
    the birds, evicted from their branches, flew
    distraught in the unaccustomed spaces; made
    their cries in the empty silence, seeking nests.
    All trees were felled. Not even the age of the oaks,
    those immemorial monarchs, could induce
    terrible hands wielding the steel to spare
    the sacred groves. The woodland, cut clean, piled up.
    Too small a pyre still for Hercules,
    skyward the tree trunks stacked in layers rose,          1650

the flammable pine, pitch-filled, the iron oak,
the stubby holly. And poplar wood helped too,
whose leaves had made many a chaplet for his brow.
    But like a great lion, wounded, roaring with pain
in the African bush, he dragged himself along.
You'd not expect him to hurry to the flames!
When he got there and surveyed the finished pyre,
he had the look of someone gazing at the stars,
not fires on earth. When he climbed up the pyre,
the lumber cracked under his weight. He called then          1660
for bow and arrows, saying, "Take these, son
of Poeas, the farewell gift of Hercules.
The Hydra felt these arrows, as did all
the other foes I brought down from afar.
Young man of happy courage, you'll always kill
the enemy with these! Or if you want—for instance—
a bird in the clouds, this arrow will pursue it
unerringly and bring it down. It works
every time—this weapon will never fail,
for the bow is finely tuned and keeps the arrow          1670
right on target; once shot the arrow seeks
its quarry out infallibly.
                              In return,
to set the fire is all I ask of you:
light the last torch for me! No one but me,"
he added, "has ever used this club, so throw it
on the fire. I'd give you this also, but only
I can swing it, so let this be the one
weapon that stays with me." Then he called for
the Nemean lion skin. That trophy would be
the bed between his body and the flames.          1680
    Everyone groaned, and mourning filled their eyes
with tears. His mother, beside herself with grief,
ripped off her clothes and beat her body, sobbing,
crying out against the gods, and Jove himself.
The whole place echoed with a woman's cries!
Then Hercules said, "Mother, quiet down.
Don't cry, you are disgracing me. Juno

will see you weeping and be pleased. Mother,
compose yourself, for it is criminal
to beat the breasts and womb of her who bore me."          1690
    Soon, growling loudly, like the dog of hell
when he led it around the towns of Greece, triumphant
over Hades, he lay his body down
on the pyre. What conquering hero ever stood
more gladly in his own parade? What dictator
ever laid down the law with such a face?
Even our weeping ceased, he was so calm;
and the shock of seeing him perish left *us* calm.
Shame even checked Alcmena; the woman fell
silent, worthy mother of her son at last.                 1700

FIRST CHORISTER: Did he invoke the gods as he was dying?

SECOND CHORISTER: Was not Jove asked to hear his prayers?

PHILOCTETES:                              He lay there
at peace with himself, looking to heaven, intently
casting his gaze about for signs of Jove.
With outstretched hand, he said, "Wherever you are,
father, watching me now, receive this soul
in heaven, since wherever the sun is shining—
on Scythian steppes or desert waste—my praise
is sung, because it shines on a crime-free world.
I have no fear of death's infernal regions,                1710
the gloomy realm of Jove's dark brother Pluto:
but I am ashamed to go in death where I
have been a conqueror in life. Now part
the clouds so all the gods will see me burn;
deny me a place in heaven if you will,
but first you must—if this voice of grief can force you—
acknowledge me your son. Let this day prove me
worthy of the stars. All that's been done
means nothing now; today my father will
damn Hercules or bring him to the light."                  1720
    When he had said all this he asked for fire.

"Up here! Bring up the Oetean torch, comrade,
show Juno that I can bear the flames. Do you
shrink from such a deed? Does your hand shake?
Give back my quiver, you helpless, harmless coward!
Is this the hand to bend that bow? Show me
some spirit; pick it up. Don't blanch, but set
your face like mine! Poor fellow, think of me!
—But look, my father appears! He beckons! Father,
I'm coming!" Then his look was changed. I trembled          1730
but applied the blazing pine. The flames leapt back,
the brands would not ignite or touch his limbs;
but he embraced them. You heard no voice, but the fire
appeared to groan itself. Oh heart of steel:
Typhon himself lying there would have cried out!
    But out of the blazing inferno now, half burned
and mutilated, he rose and looked around,
defiant. "Now you," he said, "are truly the mother
of Hercules to stand like this beside
my pyre—and fit for me to be mourned thus."          1740
    Within the towering flames and searing steam
he stands, unmoved, unshaken, not moving his limbs
that twist while they are burning. He stands there
admonishing, cheering us on. He gives
heart to every follower. You'd say
he desired to burn. The crowd stands stupefied,
scarcely thinking the flames are real, so mild
his brow, so great his majesty.
                                    He did
not hurry, but when he thought he'd shown enough
valor, he drew the burning beams together          1750
and climbed among them where the flames burned most.
He stared the flames down, yet even when his beard
shone bright with fire, and the leaping tongues of flame
glittered at his head, his eyes were open.
    But what is this? I am looking at one weeping
clutching the urn of Hercules to her heart,
her ashen hair flying, mourning her son.

Scene 2


(*On stage are* PHILOCTETES *and* CHORUSES *of Aetolian women and*
*attendants of Hercules.* ALCMENA *enters running, stage left, carry-*
*ing an urn of ashes.*)

ALCMENA: Be fearful of the fates, O gods! To what
   few ashes is Hercules reduced! To this,
   to this that giant body's shriveled! O sun,                    1760
   how great a thing has come to nothing! Woe
   is me, this old woman's breast will hold him,
   it's sepulchre enough for Hercules! Look,
   he scarcely fills the urn! How light a weight
   for me he is who once carried the heavens
   on his shoulders. Once you went to the farthest parts
   of hell, my son, whence you returned—and when
   will you cross over the Styx again? Forget
   returning with spoils, or Theseus, who owed you
   his liberation! But when will you come, just you?             1770
   Can the weight of the whole world hold down your ghost
   or the dog of Tartarus restrain you? I wonder
   when you'll break down the gate of Taenarus,
   that entrance to the lower world. Or shall
   your mother go there and, applying to Death,
   present herself at the mouth of hell? You take
   the trip to the land below, and it's the last one
   you'll take.
   (*To herself*)
                Now why do I waste the day in tears?
   How does this miserable life keep going on?
   Why cling to sunlight? How can I bear another               1780
   Hercules for Jove? No one like him
   will call me mother, call me his Alcmena!
     How happy you are, my Theban husband! Too happy
   mortal, for you went down to Hades when
   our son still lived! Perhaps the infernal ones
   stood back, because they thought you were the father

of Hercules—how could they know? Oh where
shall an old crone go, despised in every land
however barbaric! Oh, I am wretched!
All the sons of fathers Hercules murdered                          1790
will now be after me—with revenge in their hearts
and tears in their eyes. If young Antaeus or
Busiris, or any of the others, finds me
I will be led in chains as plunder, sold
for a slave. Or maybe angry Juno wants
to punish me with the full force of her
resentment for being his mother. Now Hercules
is dead and gone and she can rest assured
I, her rival, survive: what punishments
would she consign me to! My son has made                          1800
my womb something to fear.
                                        Where shall I go?
What locale, what part of the world, what country
would take this refugee? There is no place
to hide for a mother familiar everywhere
through him. So I could go home to my own
country, my miserable family. But
Eurystheus rules Argos. Or head for Thebes,
my husband's home, and seek our marriage bed—
where once I found infatuated Jove.
How happy I'd have been, too greatly happy                        1810
if I had felt only his thunderbolt!
I wish that foetus had been torn from me
before it came to term as Hercules!
        But now the time has come, I have the chance
to see him rival Jove for praise; and now
I can take the measure of what fate takes from me.
(*Addresses both* CHORUSES)
Will those he helped forget him? Nobody's grateful
anymore. Cleon perhaps, or maybe
those Arcadian folk? Or all those lands
known far and wide for what he did for them,                       1820
Here a bloody tyrant vanquished, there
a monster?

(*Addresses the urn she carries*)
    If the world is grateful as it should be,
I'd find safe haven among all peoples on earth.
Shall I go to Thrace or the people of the Hebrus?
Those countries also were saved by your good deeds.
  And where shall an old unlucky woman find
a tomb for you? All countries should be bidding, vying
for your grave. Any people and every temple
should be asking for your remains. Then who'll demand
to take this urn, this burden, off my hands?    1830
What mausoleum, son, would be sufficient
for you? The entire world should be your grave
and your fame be the inscription on the tomb.
  Why should I be afraid? I hold the ashes
of Hercules! This relic will be my fortress;
even your ghost will terrify a king.

PHILOCTETES: You son deserves these timely tears, but cry
 no more, mother of eminent Hercules.
 Do not grieve for him in clamorous prayer,
 he does not need the work of mourning done    1840
 whose courage changed the course of fate. His valor
 lives forever—and forbids our tears.

ALCMENA: Shall a mother calm her grief because her one
 champion is gone?

PHILOCTETES:    You're not alone in grief
 when earth and oceans, and the splendid sun
 observing them from his chariot, mourn too.

ALCMENA: (*To herself, distracted; looking down, supporting
  herself on the plinth where she reclines*)
 O worthless mother! In this one son how many
 children have I lost? I didn't have
 a principality but might have given
 many. I was the only mother on earth    1850
 who did not pray! I asked the gods for nothing

while my son lived. For what might not the ardor
of Hercules give me? What merely mortal
mother has such a son? I think of one
mother who stood, deprived of all her children,
alone and hardening to stone—O
Niobe, grieving for your many children!
But how many flocks like hers would my offspring
be equal to? Till now there's been no measure
great enough for the grief of mothers. But                    1860
you can cease now, all mothers who, transfixed
by chronic woe, are weighed down by despair
so deep you turn to stone. Give way before
the all-embracing welter of my sorrow!
　　　Now I shall beat my breast with grieving fists,
now let me find a tempo for my woe.
Can one decrepit pitiful old lady
express a loss so great as this? Though soon
the whole world will join with me, yet I
shall raise exhausted arms in lamentation                    1870
and sing of grief to make the gods feel jealous
and coax mankind to join in mourning him.

(ALCMENA *sings and slowly dances while from time to time the* CHO-
RUSES *join her*)

　　　Weep for the son of powerful Jove
　　　And Alcmena; come all, join in. It took
　　　Two nights—for the day between was eclipsed—
　　　To beget the marvelous boy: and something
　　　Greater than voided light is lost!
　　　Gather as one and mourn him, all
　　　You whose bloodthirsty dictators he
　　　Forced to give up their gory weapons                    1880
　　　And enter dwellings beyond the Styx.

FIRST AETOLIAN WOMAN:
　　　Let all the world render its tears

For such accomplishments and echo
Laments;

SECOND AETOLIAN WOMAN:
                    let Crete in the cobalt sea,
Land dear to thundering Jove, lament him,
Its folk in hundreds flailing their arms!

FIRST ATTENDANT:
          Now Cretans, loud priests of Cybele,
Clang your swords like cymbals now
(fitting to mourn that hero with arms)!

SECOND ATTENDANT:
Now say farewell with a proper wake,                    1890
For Hercules has fallen, a man,
O Crete, no less than Jove himself.

CHORUS *of Aetolian women:*
Weep, Arcadians, race that lived
Before the moon was born to the sky,
Weep now, for Hercules is dead.
Parthenian and Nemean hills
Will sound, and Maenalus shall echo
Their lamentation. The boar's remains
Strewing your fields require sighs
For mighty Hercules; just so                            1900
Those monstrous birds whose endless wings
Blanked out the sky encountered his arrows;

CHORUS *of attendants:*
And many another feat as well,
As when he fed the wicked king
Diomedes to that rogue's horses,
The steeds that ate Bistonia's youth.
Bistonian mothers, weep for him;
Because of him your sons are born
No more to be fodder in a barn.

ALCMENA: Weep now, you nations he delivered                1910
　　　From evils, lovely Argos and
　　　The lands Antaeus and Geryon ravaged!
　　　Despondent peoples, weep with me;
　　　Let the sea from one horizon to
　　　The other echo with your cries.
　　　　　And you, companionable gods
　　　On the arc of wheeling heaven, weep
　　　For the fate of Hercules, for he
　　　Once bore your universe, the sky,
　　　Upon his back while Atlas, whose lot               1920
　　　It was to hold that star-world up,
　　　Reposed. Where now your dome, great Jove;
　　　Where is the promised mansion of heaven?

FIRST AETOLIAN WOMAN:
　　　Hercules, mortal of course, is dead;
　　　Indeed, he is ashes now.

SECOND AETOLIAN WOMAN:          Often
　　　He'd save you the labor of hurling
　　　Your lightning bolts—how often he
　　　Punished wrongdoing for you!

ALCMENA:                          At least
　　　Think of Alcmena now as Semele;
　　　Consume me with your radiant fire!               1930
　　　And now, have you found a place, my son,
　　　In Elysium, where nature calls
　　　All mortal folk? Or since you stole
　　　The dog that guards the gates of Hades,
　　　Does Styx prevent you, and the fates
　　　Delay you at those very gates?
　　　　　Now does confusion reign, O son,
　　　In the country of the shadows? Is
　　　The boatman steering his dinghy out
　　　In flight; do Thessalian centaurs bolt,           1940
　　　Trampling those astonished shades?

And the Hydra, terrified, pull all
His seething heads below the waters—
All fearing you, my son?
                          O fool,
Fool, I am fooled; frantic, insane!
Spirit or shadow, none fears you now:

THIRD ATTENDANT:
That awesome yellow mane you skinned
From the Argolic lion no longer
Protects your arm nor does its jaw
With ferocious teeth fence round your brows.          1950

FIRST ATTENDANT:
You made the quiver a gift, and now
A weaker hand will aim the arrows.

ALCMENA: You go unarmed, defenseless, son,
To journey there among the shades
With whom you shall remain forever.

HERCULES: (*Heard over the sound system; loud but distant,
perhaps through an echo chamber*)
I occupy domains of the starry firmament. At last
I have entered heaven. Why do you wish me with such
    weeping
to know the world of Death? Stop it! Already my valor
has paved the way for me to the stars—and the gods
    themselves.

ALCMENA: Where is that sound coming from? What voice      1960
is that, forbidding my cries? Now I know
the infernal world has been overcome. From the Styx
have you made your way to me once more, O son,
broken away from gory Death again?
The fates are powerless to hold you back.
Even Pluto could not head you off and fears
for his own power. Surely I saw you placed

on the tree trunks roaring in furious flames that raged
skyward alarmingly. You were cremated! Why
didn't you go to the bottomless pit? Tell me                          1970
what the ghosts of the departed feared in you.
Was even your ghost too terrifying for Pluto?

(*Vast image of* HERCULES' *head and shoulders projected dimly on
scrim upstage*)

HERCULES: The stagnant pools of the grumbling Styx did not hold
    me.
Nor did that little craft ferry my shade across.
Mother, desist from mourning now. I have seen the last
of the dead. Whatever was part of you in me and mortal
the now extinguished blaze refined away. That portion
my father gave has gone to heaven; the part of me
that's yours and human was given to the flames.                      1980
So make an end of crying as for a worthless son.
Tears are for the base and shameful. Virtue aims
for the stars, and fear looks deathward. O mother, from the
    stars
Hercules, in person, live, addresses you.
But now it is fitting that I return to the sphere above.
Hercules has vanquished the infernal world once more.

ALCMENA: (*Looking upstage where the image projected on the
    scrim is fading out*)
Stay for a minute! Stay . . .
                  He's vanished.
                          He's gone!
He is carried to the stars. Have I been tricked
or do I only imagine I saw my son?
My wretched heart cannot believe it.                                 1990
But you are divine, the heavens keep you
eternally. I do believe this victory.
    Now I'll go on to Thebes and sing
of the further god bestowed upon their temples.

CHORUSES *of Aetolian women and attendants of Hercules:*
 To the shades of the Stygian region
 Virtue is never consigned. The brave
 Survive. Nor will the savage fates
 Force you across the Lethean stream
 But on the final day and life's
 Last hour glory will clear a path                     2000
 To heaven.
                    And you, great conqueror
 Of wildnesses and strong peacemaker
 Of the world, be with us; now and as
 Before, watch over this world of ours,
 And if some unexampled threat
 With brutish face should make us shake
 Once more in terror, strike him down
 With invincible thunderbolts more strongly
 Hurled than ever your father could have hurled.

# OCTAVIA

Translated by Kelly Cherry

# INTRODUCTION

Russians had roped a wire noose around the neck of the statue of Feliks Etmundovich Dzerzhinsky—founder of the Cheka, the secret police, "father of the KGB"—and were hauling the statue, huge in the Stalinist so-called heroic mode, away. It weighed fourteen tons. It apparently had swung wildly in the air and then listed to one side, a hanged man.

The statue had stood in front of the KGB headquarters—the Lubyanka—in Moscow. Now it looked as if it was about to fall, like all the rest of the Soviet Union.

Eventually even government officials got into the act, engineering a way to remove the statue without disrupting the operations of the subway station directly beneath. Cranes carried the statue to a waiting flatbed truck.

The workers had nothing to use but their chains. In Vilnius, a monolithic Lenin, horizontally attached to rigging, seemed to fly through the air on its way to the trash heap.

Thus did the Romans topple the statues of Nero and Poppaea. "They're so lifelike, these statues," the people cry in *Octavia*. "Let's smash them on the ground." And this they do, as the messenger dutifully reports: "Every statue of Poppaea that was put up, smooth marble or shining bronze, has fallen, knocked down by the hands of the mob and smashed repeatedly with iron crowbars. After they've pulled the sections down by ropes, they drag them off one by one, stomp on them, and grind them underfoot, deep into the mud. These barbaric deeds are accompanied by words that I hesitate to repeat." The crowd in Moscow painted a certain word around the base of Dzerzhinsky's statue: *executioner*.

Thus do empires collapse literally to dust, the symbols of them

185

smashing to wonderfully unsymbolic smithereens at the people's feet.

Do I make too much of this correspondence? I'm not alone in calling attention to it. The *New York Times* informs us that Edvard Radzinsky has written a play, produced in Moscow, titled *The Theater in the Time of Nero and Seneca*, which he describes as being "about intellectuals living under a repressive regime."

That the Soviet Union should have reached its conclusion (we hope it has reached its conclusion) while I was translating a play about the fall of the Roman Empire was, for me, not merely a coincidence but a gratifying and interesting irony. Years before, I had been engaged to marry a citizen of Latvia, one of the Baltic countries occupied by the Soviet army and forcibly annexed to the union in 1940, when the choice—an incomprehensible word in this connection, *choice*—was between rule by Hitler and rule by Stalin. As if economics is a centrifuge, the center of the union had spun and spun—but it was spinning its wheels—until these formerly free nations were flung into freedom once more. (But I have to say, here, that accounts in the *New York Times* and elsewhere seemed to assume that Baltic citizens had begun their fight to reclaim their independence less than two years earlier, in March 1990, when Lithuania asserted the restored sovereignty of its state by unanimous parliamentary vote, whereas in fact there were those in all three states who had worked toward this aim for decades.)

This, then, was how, that week in August 1991, I translated Seneca: with network television on, the radio turned simultaneously to National Public Radio, the telephone ready to take calls from a friend who had CNN, newspapers on the floor, my Latin books and papers spread around me on the bed, and my heart in my mouth.

What would Seneca have said about the events transpiring in the Soviet Union? It was not difficult to imagine him as a talking head, holding forth on *Nightline* or *The MacNeil/Lehrer NewsHour*.

Would Seneca have confined himself to the sententious remarks of a—say—Princeton prof? Or a free-lancing Kissinger? Yet the Seneca here, in *Octavia*, is capable of, must have been capable of, awareness of others' perceptions of him, and unafraid to state them. Self-protective he is, conservative to a fault, but he could not survive as well or as long as he does without discerning, and calculating for, the young emperor's adolescent contempt for an old man.

Scholars suggest, of course, that Seneca could not have written this play in which he is one of his own characters. There may eventually be incontrovertible proof, documentary or textual. I rather think, though, that for now, anyway, the evidence for this thesis is at least partly biased by a belief that writers of an earlier age are never so ironic or playful as writers of the current age.

In Michael Grant's translation of the *Annals*, Tacitus refers to Seneca's "pleasant talent" for speechwriting and points out that "Nero was the first ruler to need borrowed eloquence." Seneca the speechwriter might have been at home in modern America, a bureaucrat for the party in power or an overpaid professor on more or less permanent leave from teaching. Tacitus says that Agrippina, angered by her son Nero's defection from her tutelage in favor of Seneca's (because Seneca smiled on Nero's affair with Acte, a slave girl), denounced Seneca as "that deportee with the professorial voice."

In *Octavia* Nero appears, at times, to be merely hormonally inflamed the way teenagers always are, but Tacitus reminds us that "[a] number of contemporary writers assert that for a considerable time previously Nero had corrupted" Britannicus, the half brother he arranges to be poisoned. Incest and child abuse. There is in this play a disarming note of intimacy that can seem to reduce Nero's actions to those of a boy being a boy. But what we have, really, is an emperor being an emperor, assassinating his mother, his brother, and anyone else who dares to get in the way of what he perceives as his due.

Perhaps the young Octavia is the main source of this sense of intimacy. Although she's often self-righteous and self-pitying, her circumstances so clearly justify her that the reader, or audience, forgives her. (But we also can't help assenting, even if guiltily, to Nero's longing for love, even if he has confused love with lust, and to his idealization of love as a refuge from the dangers of his position.) Tacitus says of Octavia that "young though she was, [she] had learnt to hide sorrow, affection, every feeling." And how *does* one love the man who has pretty much wiped out one's family?

Conventionally this play would have been rendered primarily in iambic pentameter, with a shorter line for the choruses. I found iambic pentameter, with its regularity, its singing extension, which I otherwise love, too controlled, maybe too public, to convey this drama's intimate character. Nobly born the central personae may be, but their personalities tumble off the page in a tangled heap of emotions. They are so psychologically defined that every one of them possesses an irrefutable logic, and the result is a kind of Shakespearean sympathy with points of view that are at variance with one another, that Shakespearean genius for seeing a thing from all its angles. Not that Seneca was in that class, but may I propose that what Shakespeare learned from classical drama was more than plot, was what made Shakespeare even more than a great poet. Made him Shakespeare.

I rendered most of the sexual women in verse: Octavia in a loose, four-stress line; Agrippina in the free verse of an anathematic hysteria that turns, finally, as so much in this play does, on itself; the two allusively erotic recitations of the chorus of women in sonnets, as if their voices flowered like roses in the wilderness of text. Octavia's chorus is another loose four-beat line, echoing her in their allegiance. The nurses are guidance counselors, prosy with pedagogy. Poppaea is in prose—I don't know why. Something about her anxiety, the way her desire for contrition arises from fear for her fate. She is a modernist figure, haunted by bad conscience, the dreams of "a mysterious, subconscious intelligence." The men are all prose.

A Menippean sort of solution.

I made these decisions, but I would not want to elevate them into principles. If I adhered to any principle, it was to an idea of metaphor. Wherever I could, I followed metaphors inherent in the author's Latin language, as if tracing an underground river through the text.

Another principle was not to worry about anachronisms. As I have said, part of the interest of this play, this historical drama, lies in its parallels to a later world.

A third principle, for me, was to stay within the bounds of the established text. I admit I would have liked to rewrite the play. I'd have done this and that, except then the play would have been mine, I think, not Seneca's or the reputed Seneca's. Translation is a constant denial of temptation, this way. Possibly the translator achieves purity of soul by being willing to compromise! What an odd process, a poet thinks. But I have found it an enlightening one.

The poet and translator Willis Barnstone, whose books include *With Borges on an Ordinary Evening in Buenos Aires,* told me a story: He and Borges were in a taxi on their way to the University of Chicago in spring 1980. The question of where everyone was from came up. Barnstone identified himself as being from Indiana and explained that Borges was from Argentina. "Hey, buddy," said the taxi driver, "*I* was in Europe too."

"When was that?" Barnstone asked.

It had been during the Second World War. Barnstone asked the taxi driver if he had seen any action. And what it was like, the action. The taxi driver didn't want to talk about it. "I don't think about war, about all those things of the past," said the taxi driver, "because memory is hell."

Elated, Borges seized Barnstone's wrist. "Why, those words could have been written by Seneca!" he exclaimed.

I have thought I might have liked to translate the taxi driver.

The Duckworth edition (1942) of Seneca's plays, including the translation of *Octavia* by Frank Justus Miller, announces, "The *Octavia* enjoys a unique distinction, for it is the only *fabula praetexta,* or Roman historical play, which has survived to our day." Detailing the ways in which the play is indeed Senecan, the Introduction to that edition nevertheless adjudges that "it seems extremely doubtful if Seneca is the author of the play. . . . It is not impossible that Seneca wrote the play, which could have been published after his death, and, presumably, after the death of Nero. But it seems preferable to assume, as do most scholars, that the *Octavia* was composed soon after Nero's death by a dramatist who had been an eye-witness of the events described, and who, in his portrayal of the pitiful fate of Octavia, imitated the technique and structure of Senecan tragedy."

This argument has a persuasive Ockhamistic elegance but may be set aside briefly to let us see what it misses: the extraordinary bleakness at the devastated heart of a play in which antagonist and protagonist, joined inextricably in a life-and-death struggle, do not even encounter each other on stage. What an irony! What a deep, deep cynicism underscores the very existence of this play. If, here as elsewhere in Seneca, questions of how to rule—What is the right relation between emperor and people? *Whose* justice shall prevail?— if these questions appear to provide the philosophical substance, something else, also, is going on. For the question of how to rule, in a historical drama, has already been settled by how the emperor *did* rule: any answers are hypothetical, and useless. And the author, whoever he may have been, knows this. And this knowledge changes everything.

The always marvelously perspicuous Moses Hadas described Stoicism as an "evangelical" project devolving into a notion about how to live. To the Senecan Stoic, Hadas suggests, pain cannot be painful (not even the pain of memory), because all things happen for the good of the whole. I think *I* want to suggest that in this observation may lie the strongest argument to be made for *Octavia*'s having been written by a later hand.

For—let us repeat—the author knows how history has happened, or is going to happen, and the play reflects this knowledge in its despair. At the end of the play, we see the future foreclosing on itself. We see the text, which has already claimed its right to comment on itself, dissolve itself, like a parliamentary government. It is as if there is no longer any question of the good of the whole: as we have said, in a historical drama, history has answered many questions. And it is as if Stoicism has unwound itself even further, becoming a notion about how one *has* lived. How has one lived? Has it not always been exactly like this: *things end, and then they go on, having already ended?* That, I suggest, is the true temper of this author's mind. We live, are living, after the fact. We are, or know we soon will be, post-empire, post-modern, post-everything. Octavia cannot save herself, because she has already been destroyed. She was destroyed from the beginning, from the moment her history began to unfold. This is what *fate* means. Everything that can happen to her has been foretold—*fatum*, an utterance—and the foretelling has sealed what can happen to her. "*Do not pray,*" she chastises herself, "*To gods who have no use for you!*"

But the domestic drama of *Octavia*, as *fabula praetexta*, is an emblematic acting-out of the transaction between individual histories and history, between the self and the state. Octavia is the repository of the people's hopes. She represents themselves to themselves. Their future is hers, and if Nero cleaves to her, and if she bears sons, "the world may rejoice / And Rome's glory endure." But the dissolution of her marriage has been yoked by history to the dissolution of the empire, and all fall down.

Once upon a time, I was married—to an American—and my husband and I thought that if we had a daughter we might name her Octavia. As it turned out, we had no child, no daughter named Octavia. I may have come to this play, in part at least, to search for a daughter named Octavia. I thought this even as I worked on it. And watched Latvia becoming free again.

It was an occasion for rejoicing. But it was also an occasion for wondering why the past had had to happen exactly the way that it did. History!

History is a cannibal, cutting off its own arms and legs to devour them. It is Cronos, the god of time, swallowing his own children. In the Introduction to the Loeb edition (1917) of *Octavia*, much is made of Roman drama's debt to Greek tragedy, but not quite enough of the way in which this particular play negates itself.

A parent devouring his own children is *deconstruction with a vengeance*. To us, in our dilettantish days of theoretical preciosity, this is the harshest truth: a text that, I submit, chooses to obliterate its own tradition. If Seneca is not his own character, the real author—the Loeb nominates Maternus—may be said to have devoured Seneca. If Seneca is his own character, the text has, in a sense, consumed him. The play closes with a brutal image: other peoples offer only strangers as sacrifices to the gods, but Romans—this *civilized* people, these people who think of themselves as, alone among the peoples of the world, *not being barbarian*—kill their own citizens. *[C]ivis gaudet Roma cruore.* "Rome's delight is in her children's blood," says the Loeb. Our metered Duckworth has it: "But Rome delights to see her children bleed." In the parlance of today we would, surely, say, *Rome eats her own.*

To avoid slang, which tends to trivialize meaning, and at the same time to express the philosophical underpinning of these words, I passed up the vividness of the metaphor of cannibalism for the richness of another metaphor that alludes to Cronos: "Thus Time itself is in exile." With these last words, the play rounds on itself and writes itself *out* of existence. There is no history, then, because history ended when the world ended, and for Romans, that was when Rome declined and fell. Self-negation, the complete dismissal of everything, of oneself and the world. This is a play that consigns its audience to irrelevance, a text that suicides. It *is* a suicide. We feel, at the end, the way we feel at the death of anyone we knew well. Grief, rage, terror, despair—all of these feelings that the play, the play, understands cannot resurrect one life, ever.

Kelly Cherry

# OCTAVIA

## CHARACTERS

OCTAVIA, stepsister and wife of Nero
OCTAVIA'S NURSE
CHORUS of Romans, sympathetic with Octavia
SENECA, former tutor to Nero and later one of his counselors
NERO, emperor of Rome
PREFECT of Roman soldiers
GHOST OF AGRIPPINA, mother of Nero, slain by him
POPPAEA'S NURSE
POPPAEA, mistress and, afterward, wife of Nero
CHORUS of women, attached to the interests of the court and
   sympathetic with Poppaea
MESSENGER

SCENE: *The palace of Nero, emperor of Rome,* A.D. *62*

## ACT I

### Scene 1

OCTAVIA: Now dawn chases the trespassing stars
   Out of the sky, the sun climbs up
   A ladder of radiance, carrying daylight
   To the world once again. *You*

*Carry on, too, Octavia:*
*Weighed down by despair, pick up*
*Your familiar refrain and out-cry*
*The sea-birds and the nighting-wails.*
*Your burden's heavier than theirs.*
O Mother, for whom I grieve first,                                    10
Foremost, and forever, if sound's
The shadow of silence, hear my dark
Words, down among the shaded dark.
If only I'd not lived to see
Your face wadded up like a rag, blood on it
Like a red dye! That stain! Since then
I hate the light more than the dark.
"Day" now means "endurance"—of
A stepmother's cruelty, even enmity.
Because of this woman, my marriage was made          20
Not in heaven but in hell.
It was she who caused your death, O Father
Who—it seems like yesterday—
Caesared the world as far away
As Britain, that land's first Roman
Leader. Oh, Father, you were brought down
And buried by your own wife's plots,
And I and your house are captive to a tyrant.

(*Exits to her chamber.* OCTAVIA'S NURSE *enters.*)


Scene 2


OCTAVIA'S NURSE: Anyone who's dazzled by the superficial shine and
   splendor of success should observe how suddenly destiny has
   overtaken the house of Claudius, which was until recently all-
   powerful. Claudius's rule embraced the whole world! Even the
   ocean submitted to him, seduced by his ships. Well, he who first

conquered the British, he who traversed foreign seas with his stupendous ships, he who moved untouched among barbarians and tempests was destroyed by his *wife's* wickedness. And then *she* was killed by her son—who had already poisoned his own stepbrother! The son's stepsister and wife—and I speak of *one* woman, a doubly unfortunate woman—grieves, and cannot conceal her bitterness at being made subservient to her angry, abusive husband. Each time, she insists on refusing him, and this inflames him with incestuous desire even though their hatred's mutual. A vicious cycle, to say the least! I try to console her, but it's no use; her injured pride prevents her from taking my advice, and she refuses to temper her attitude. Instead, her sense of hurt and need to settle scores keep getting stronger. Oh, I'm afraid of what she may do! May the gods keep her from it!

Scene 3

OCTAVIA: (*From within her chamber*)
Though I recall your misfortune,
Sad Electra, mine is unmatched.
*You* could shed the tears you had
For your father, could avenge                                    60
His death—with your brother, your brother
Whom your love had rescued, your faith
Defended. But I— I am afraid
To mourn openly the parents so cruelly
Taken from me, or my brother,
My one hope, my brief solace.
And now I am left with no companion
But my own misery, a shadow
Of a noble name, a shadow
Of silence.                                                      70

OCTAVIA'S NURSE: Listen! I hear my unhappy Octavia. Come now, has age slowed me so much that I can't go to her?

(*Heads for the chamber but is met by* OCTAVIA, *entering*)

OCTAVIA: Be tolerant of my tears, dear nurse,
Trustworthy witness of my grief.

OCTAVIA'S NURSE: When will you be done with your grieving, poor
child?

OCTAVIA: The day I die and go down to the shaded
Dark.

OCTAVIA'S NURSE: I pray that day's far off!                          80

OCTAVIA: Destiny and not your prayers
Determines the course of my life now.

OCTAVIA'S NURSE: In time God will ease your sorrows; you must stay
calm and win your husband over, placating him the way a clever
woman can always placate a man.

OCTAVIA: I'd sooner subdue a fierce lion,
  A wild tiger, than the heart
Of that savage tyrant. He hates all who are fine,
Despising gods and mortals alike;                                   90
Yet he cannot even seize for himself
The fortunate fate criminally conferred on him
By his unnatural mother; ungrateful,
Considering himself belittled by this
God-*damned* gift of an empire, he repaid
Her with death. Ah, but it's her name
That survives.

OCTAVIA'S NURSE: Control your anger! Take back your rash words!

OCTAVIA: Though I'll endure what must be endured
Nothing will put a period to my pain                                100
Except my departure to the place of darkness.
With my mother slain, my father

Stolen from me, robbed of my brother,
Weighed down by grief, both envied and hated
By my husband, who has made me subservient to
My own slave, I take no pleasure
In *daylight*. My heart pounds, not from fear
Of death but from fear that my good name,
Too, may be taken from me, and so long
As that accusation is not among                                    110
The crimes I must suffer, death will be
My *delight*—because to gaze into the face
Of a tyrant, a face that may be said
To be *tumescent* with anger toward me,
And kiss my enemy; to have to fear
The smallest nod of his head, a submission
My aching heart cannot countenance
Now that he's murdered my brother, whose throne
He occupies while rejoicing in having
Accomplished the unspeakable—this, this                            120
Is a fate far *worse* than death.
                                        How often
My brother's sad shade appears before me,
When tiredness has overtaken me
And sleep closed my tear-weary eyes!
Now he arms himself with smoke-black torches
And, shaking, hurls them at his stepbrother;
And now, still trembling, he takes refuge with me
In my chamber. His enemy pursues him
And, even while the boy clings to me,                              130
Thrusts his sword violently through
Both our bodies. And then I wake
In fear and trembling, and grief and fear
Return to my heart. Add to all this
An arrogant little something tricked out like a queen
With our family's jewels, for whom as a gift
The son set his own mother asail on a ship
Bound for death. When she had survived
The terrible shipwreck and the sea,
He—in a rage even greater than                                    140

The raging sea's—killed her with a sword:
What hope have I, if he could do a crime
As horrible as that? My victorious rival,
His concubine, besieges my chamber,
Burns with hatred for me, and demands
The head of his lawful wife as the reward
For her adultery. O my father,
Come forth from the place of darkness and
Bring help to your daughter who calls on you.
Or rip open the earth and reveal                              150
That abyss, so that I might
Fling myself down into it!

OCTAVIA'S NURSE: You are calling on your father's shade in vain, poor
girl, in vain. One who in life could prefer another's son to his own
and incestuously and sinfully marry his own niece is not going to
show concern for his children now that he is among the dead.

From that narrative seed has sprung a generation of crimes,
so many tragic plots—murder, treachery, lust for power, desire
for rank. Your own fiancé was sacrificed to your father's marriage,
because, married to you, he might have become too powerful.
Such an abominable act! Silanus, charged with a crime he did not
commit, was bound over to a woman as a *wedding gift*, a sacrificial
offering, and the ancestral gods were blasphemed by his blood.
Then—oh, God!—this monster, Nero, invades the conquered
palace and by his mother's conniving is made the emperor's son-
in-law *and* son. And he is a perverse young man with a genius for
wickedness, whose predilections his mother encouraged, forcing
you to marry him against your will. Heady with her success, your
mother-in-law, your *stepmother*, dared to reach for the highest
position in the world. Who could possibly recite the numerous
crimes, the wicked ambitions, the false flatteries of this woman
who would do anything to claw her way to the top?

Ultimately, Goodness herself became frightened—like a
young woman unprotected in a dangerous place—and fled, and
the power of Evil took over the vacated palace. Evil defiled the
household gods with occult rites and, with an insane abandon,
broke all the laws of nature and God. A wife poisoned her husband

and was murdered soon after by her son. You too, Britannicus, you poor boy, are dead, to be mourned by us always. So recently the bright light of the world, the foundation of a noble house, and now—oh, God—no more than the lightness of ashes and the darkness of a restless shade! Even your stepmother wept over you when she laid out your body to be burned on the pyre and when your face and form, angelic as a god's, were consumed by the funeral fire.

OCTAVIA: He'd better do away with me too,
If he doesn't want to be brought down by me.

OCTAVIA'S NURSE: Nature's not given you the strength for that.

OCTAVIA: Anguish, anger, sorrow, sheer misery,
Grief will provide it.

OCTAVIA'S NURSE: It would be smarter for you to subdue your unfeeling husband by yielding to him.

OCTAVIA: So he can give back to me my brother,
Whom he *stole*, as it were, from life?

OCTAVIA'S NURSE: So you yourself may remain unharmed! So one day you can raise up your father's fallen house with sons of your own.

OCTAVIA: The royal house *is* expecting
Another son—but not mine! As for me,
I am already caught in the net
That snared my poor brother.

OCTAVIA'S NURSE: Take courage from the people's immense love for you.

OCTAVIA: That thought makes me feel better but
Does not change things.

OCTAVIA'S NURSE: The power of the people is considerable.

OCTAVIA: The emperor's is greater.

OCTAVIA'S NURSE: He will respect his wife.

OCTAVIA: His mistress won't let him.

OCTAVIA'S NURSE: Surely no one pays any attention to her.

OCTAVIA: But she's "dear" to my—*her*—husband.

OCTAVIA'S NURSE: She's not his wife yet.

OCTAVIA: She will be soon, as well as a mother.

OCTAVIA'S NURSE: The passion of youth burns fiercely at first but quickly dies down to a mere flicker of flame; adulterous love never lasts for long. But the love of a faithful wife endures forever. Meanwhile, she who first dared to defile your marriage bed, though a slave who has for some time enslaved your husband, is already, herself, afraid—

OCTAVIA: (*Interrupting*) She's definitely found a way to rise
Above her station.

OCTAVIA'S NURSE: —restrained, keeping a low profile. And there are other telltale signs that give away her anxiety. Cupid, a false and unfaithful god—about as faithful as a bird of passage—will betray even her. Though she's pretty enough (and knows it), her triumph will be short-lived.

    The queen of the gods herself went through what you are going through, when the king of the heavens and father of the gods transfigured himself into all the forms of being, now putting on swans' wings, now outfitting himself with the horns of a Sidonian bull, and now again raining down in a shower of gold: The stars of Leda shine in the sky; there's Bacchus, at home on his father's Olympus; as a god, Alcides possesses Hebe and no longer fears

Juno's wrath—once her sworn enemy, he's now her son-in-law.
Yet clever kowtowing and keeping her anger in check won the day
for Her Highness. No longer worried that there could be a rival,
Her Highness, Juno, manages to keep the Thundering One in her
celestial bed; Jupiter no longer sneaks out from the heavenly
court, captivated by mortal beauty. You too, on earth a second
Juno, sister and wife to an Augustus, must master—or say,
*mistress*—your own deep unhappiness.

OCTAVIA: The savage seas will marry the stars
   —And fire wed water; heaven, hell;
   The sweet light, darkness; daylight, the night
   Sweet with dew—before I, haunted
   Forever by my brother's death,
   Can comprehend my scurrilous husband's
   Inhuman heart. If only the king
   Of heavenly kingdoms, who so often threatens
   The world with lethal thunderbolts                               230
   And throws the fear of God in us
   With pale fires and dark portents,
   Would strike down this prince—an *upstart,*
   By comparison, a prince of hubris—with
   The fire next time. We have seen in the sky
   A flame-throwing radiance, a comet, its hair
   Ominously loosened, where methodical Boötes,
   Numb with Arctic chill, wheels
   His wagon through an endless night,
   And so the air itself is poisoned                                240
   By the sickening breath of a sick leader,
   And the stars threaten undreamt-of disasters
   For the nations ruled by this godless leader.
   Not even Typhon, whom a vengeful Mother
   Earth bore to spite Jove, was such an infectious agent.
   This pestilence worse than Typhon, this enemy
   Of gods and mortals, has driven out
   The holy spirits from their shrines,
   The citizens from their country; he has stolen
   From his brother the breath of life                              250

And spilled his mother's blood—and he still sees
The light of *day*, still lives and draws
His noxious breath! O Father, exalted,
On high—why do you, with your imperious hand,
Hurl your thunderbolts so uselessly, so randomly?
Why, given such a deserving target,
Is your right hand held back? If only
He might be made to pay for his crimes,
This *bastard* Nero, son of Domitius,
This tyrant of a world yoked to him like an ox
Whose course dirties Augustus's name,
As the wagon-driver's ox soils sky.

OCTAVIA'S NURSE: I grant you, he's not good enough for you; but my
child, it's *no* good trying to fight fate—or city hall—because you
might make a violent husband act out his violence. Maybe some
god will appear on—or in—the scene to avenge you, and happy
days come again!

OCTAVIA: For so long has the anger of gods
Hounded this house, beginning when
Obsessive desire seized my unhappy mother
And she, though married, in a state of mad                     260
Foolishness married another man illegally,
Forgetting her children, forgetting her husband.
An avenging fury, hair loosened and streaming
Like a comet, slithery with snakes,
Crawled into that bed from hell, drenching
The torches of the bigamous wedding processional
In blood; she made the emperor burn
With the desire to murder my mother;
My poor mother fell—oh, *God*—
And, dead by a sword, plunged
A sword of endless suffering
Into me. Her husband and son,                                  270
Too, died with her, more or less,
And our house had fallen.

OCTAVIA'S NURSE: You mustn't upset yourself again by weeping. And
 you don't want to disturb your father's shade; he's suffered enough
 for his desperate deed.

(OCTAVIA *and* NURSE *exit to the palace*)


Scene 4


(CHORUS OF ROMANS *enters*)

CHORUS OF ROMANS: What's this we hear? Oh, let it be false!
 And may people not repeat it so often
 That they begin to believe what they've heard!
 And may no new wife join the emperor in his chamber!
 And may his bride, Claudius's child, retain
 Her rightful position! And may she bear sons,
 Hostages to *good* fortune, that the world may rejoice
 And Rome's glory endure everlastingly!                          280
 Her Highness Juno's sweet lot in life's
 *Her* brother's bedroom; why should the sister-
 And-wife of Augustus be turned out
 From her patrimonial court? Oh, what good, to her,
 Are her faith, her father-proclaimed-a-god,
 Her faithfulness and untarnished purity?
 Since his death, we too have forgotten,
 Utterly, our leader, and betray his child
 Out of abject fear. Our forefathers were *true*
 Romans, and, in them, the heart of Mars                         290
 Beat. From this city, they cast out
 All overreaching kings, and, Virginia,
 They avenged you well—you, slain by your father
 That you might not suffer the yoke of slavery,
 That you might not be spoiled, a spoil of war.
 A tragic war avenged you, too,
 The daughter of Lucretius, slain,

Poor girl, by your own hand,
To escape being outraged by a brutal tyrant.
A penalty was paid for the unspeakable crime          300
Committed, with her husband, by Tullia, who
Drove her wild chariot over her father's corpse
And then, still enraged, refused to bury it.

This age has also seen a *son*
Commit a crime of like magnitude,
When our leader, having trapped his mother
By a trick, shipped her out to sea—
A funeral ship on the Tyrrhenian Sea.
Strictly following orders, the sailors
Pull speedily out of the peaceful port,               310
The sea resounding with the blows of the oars.
The ship sails far out, into deep water,
Where the hull, overwhelmed, gives way and opens
Like a gaping mouth and drinks in the sea,
Sinking. A great chorus of crying,
In which can be heard the soprano cries of women,
Starts up, reaching to the stars.
They see death in front of them.
Each tries to save himself or herself;
Some, stripped of clothing, cling                     320
To planks from the wrecked ship as if to surf
On the high sea, while others swim
For shore; most of them are drowned.
Nero's mother tears at her garments
And tears out her hair and weeps, frightened.

In the end, all hope of rescue
Gone, filled with both anger and despair,
She cries, "My son, is this how you repay me
For all I gave you? Oh, I deserve this,
I confess: Fool that I am—                             330
For giving you life, for giving you light
And an empire and the name of Caesar—I deserve
This ship. Look up out of Acheron,

That world below the world, O
My husband, and satisfy yourself
That I have gotten just what I deserve;
I caused your death, poor man, and authorized
That of your son, and look, *just*
As I deserve, I am dragged down,
Unburied, coffined in the merciless sea,                          340
To your shade."
                              As she speaks,
The water washes her words away,
And she goes under, and then surfaces,
Frantically beating back the sea
With her hands, but soon, exhausted,
Gives up. There are still some subjects
Whose secret loyalty can overcome
The paralyzing fear of death;
There are many who dare to come
To the aid of their mistress, and when                            350
The sea saps her strength, they pull for her,
And as she swims by—though barely able to—
They pull her out. But what good
Did it do you, Agrippina,
To escape the violence of the stormy sea?
You are going to die by the sword of your own son,
A crime future generations
Will hardly be able to believe.
That monster of a son rages like the sea
And weeps that his mother, saved from the sea,                    360
Lives; and adds insult to injury,
*Injury* to injury.
Determined on his poor mother's death,
He stops at nothing. His hit-man, dispatched,
Carries out his orders; with a knife
He carves open his mistress's chest.
The wretched woman, dying, begs
This minister of *injustice* to bury his sword
In her womb: "It's *this* organ," she insists,
"*This* organ that gave birth to such a monster,                  370

That must be pierced by the sword!" After
These last words, spoken with a sigh,
She finally gave up the ghost, which fled
Like a refugee, out of the country of her body
Through the gate of the savage wound.


ACT II


Scene 1


(SENECA *enters. He is alone on the stage.*)

SENECA: Why me? When I was content with my lot! Why has Fortune, that lady who has her way with everyone, that charming but
duplicitous lady who always gets what—or whom—she wants,
raised *me* to these heights? That I might fall the farther from this
proud pinnacle? That I might have a *good view* of everything that
can go wrong? I was better off in hiding, out of reach of the long
arm of *envy,* in the seaside Corsican hills. There, free and master
of my own fate, I had time to meditate upon my favorite ideas at
leisure.

　　Oh, what joy it is, a joy unsurpassed by anything else
wrought by Nature, maker of this immense artwork, to look up at
the heavens, the sacred chariot of the sun and the wheeling of
the stars, and the sun's turn and return, and the moon Phoebe,
which the wandering stars surround, and the far-flung shining
beauty of the glorious sky! If it is true this universe is aging, the
whole of it breaking back down to a dark chaos, then the day is
coming, a judgment day for the world, that will bury sinning
mankind under the wreckage of heaven; and then, born-again and
better, the world may bring forth once more an uncompromised
race such as she produced in her youth, when Saturn ruled. In
those early days, that virgin, Justice, a goddess of commanding
power, who, along with Faith, had been sent down from heaven to
earth, ruled the human race with a light hand. The nations knew

no wars, no threatening blasts of the trumpet, no occupying forces, nor were they obliged to fortress their cities with a wall: the entrance was open to all, everything was available to everyone; and Mother Earth herself proffered her nourishing breast, a mother happy and safe among such obedient children.

But another race, which proved less gentle, arose, and then a third race, skillful in new ways but still god-fearing. Presently, there came a more ambitious race, which dared to hunt wild animals in the field, to fish in the deep seas (whether with a weighted net or a fishing rod), to trap birds, to keep wild dogs on a leash, to force wild oxen to accept the yoke, and to plow the virgin earth, which, outraged, withdrew her bounty deeper into her private places. But that sodomizing generation intruded even into the bowels of the earth, excavating—let's be blunt—shitloads of iron and gold. And soon after that, it armed soldiers. Defining boundaries, it established kingdoms, built new cities, defended its own homes or, intent on the spoils of war, threateningly lay siege to another's.

Neglected, the virgin Justice fled from earth and from the savage ways of man, from hands bloodied with carnage, becoming the brightest star in the sky. And throughout the world, lust for war, and hunger for gold, spread unchecked. Extravagance, which is the greatest evil, arose, a seductive contagion that acquired strength and force over time, and through self-perpetuating error.

These vices, accumulating for a long time, through many ages, abound in us; a heavy age weighs upon us, in which evil rules, godlessness runs rampant, lust triumphs over love; and extravagance, victorious, has for a long time now with greedy hands plundered the world's vast wealth—in order to squander it.

But look, here comes Nero, in a hurry and looking positively furious. I shudder to think what news he brings.


Scene 2


(NERO *enters; a* PREFECT *follows*)

NERO: Do as I've ordered. Send someone to bring me the heads of Plautus and Sulla.

PREFECT: It's no sooner said than done. I leave for the camp immediately. (*Exit*)

SENECA: One should think twice before turning against one's allies.

NERO: It's easy to look after the rights of others when you don't have to worry about looking after yourself.

SENECA: A first-rate cure for fear is clemency.

NERO: The most important thing any leader does is rid his country of its enemies.

SENECA: A finer way for a leader to protect the citizens is by ruling as the father of his country.

NERO: (*Aside*) The old woman should be instructing young boys.

SENECA: Rather, it's headstrong adolescents who need guidance.

NERO: I think that at my age I know what I need to know.

SENECA: (*Acidly*) May your actions always please the gods.

NERO: I'd be a right fool to fear the gods when I myself create them.

SENECA: Fear more that you have power as great as that.

NERO: My position makes everything possible for me.

SENECA: You should believe in your good fortune a little less. She's a capricious goddess.

NERO: You'd have to be stupid not to realize that power is meant to be used.

SENECA: May I suggest that it's commendable to do what one ought, not what one may.

NERO: May I suggest that the public runs right over anyone who's passive.

SENECA: It *crushes* the leader it *hates*.

NERO: The sword protects the leader.

SENECA: Loyalty does the job better.

NERO: A Caesar should be feared.

SENECA: Still more, loved.

NERO: It's essential to keep the people in fear—

SENECA: People perceive whatever is compelled of them as a burden.

NERO: —and they'd better obey my laws.

SENECA: Let these be just laws—

NERO: I'll decide for myself what's just.

SENECA: —which a consensus may ratify.

NERO: Respect for the sword will ratify them.

SENECA: God help us!

NERO: Shall I let them go on trying to assassinate me? One day, I'll suddenly find myself overthrown—not to mention unavenged and despised. Exile hasn't broken Plautus and Sulla. Their endless talk of revolution infects their comrades with their own heinous ambition. Which is, after all, to murder me.—Thus even in their absence they enjoy in this city a huge popularity that nurtures their hopes. I say let a sword do away with all those I suspect of being my enemies—and that includes my bitch of a wife. She can drop—yes, drop!—dead. Let her drop all the way down, down to the shades, on the heels of the brother she so adores. Whatever rises must fall. *Who*ever rises must go down.

SENECA: To be noble means to be a moral beacon for great men. To be noble is to tend to the interests of one's native land, to spare the downtrodden and abstain from bloodshed. It is noble to be slow to anger, noble to bring tranquility to the world, *peace in our time.* This is the height of moral excellence; this is the way to immortality. In just this way, that first Augustus, the father of his country, became a god in the heavens and in the temples. All the same, Fortune toyed with him for a long time first, on both land and sea, war's dangerous strokes of chance and mischance knocking him about until he overwhelmed his father's foes. But to *you* she has surrendered herself without a struggle, making you head of state over all the world. Factional hatreds, overcome, have concluded in a harmony of fealty; the Senate, the knights smile on you; and in accordance with an overwhelming plebiscite and the decision of the leaders you are the guarantor of peace, the arbiter of human destinies, elected to rule the world as if you were already a god, "the father of the country." Rome entrusts her citizens to you and begs you to rule in the spirit of this epithet.

NERO: It's by the law of divine right that Rome, and the Senate, are subject to my will. It's divine right, and *fear*, that decree that entreaties and professions of inferiority must be uttered by lips that would rather not say them: fear makes all men yes-men. And you want me to "protect the citizens"! To spare those citizens who are a nuisance to the emperor and the country, conspirators swollen with self-importance—what kind of stupidity is this, when one may with one word sentence to death those he suspects? Brutus drew his sword to murder his leader, the very man to whom he had pledged allegiance; Caesar, invincible in battle, a conqueror of nations, on the top rung of the ladder of success— next to Jove himself—was brought down by the nefarious conspir-

acy of *citizens*. What fountains of her own blood did Rome, run
through by so many swords, see then! The deified Augustus, who
(you say) got into heaven by being pious, how many nobles did *he*
execute, young men and old all over the world—scattered when
they fled their own homes in mortal fear of the Second Triumvi-
rate? All on the proscription lists, all on the death squad lists!
Grieving fathers saw the heads of the slain set out on the rostra but
dared not weep or wail for their dead sons, while the forum stank
of foul decay, and blood ran thickly down the decomposing faces,
those faces making a kind of un-music, clotting into silence. Nor
did this put an end to either the bloodshed or blood: the grim
plains of Philippi were to feed vultures and wild beasts for a long
time, and the Sicilian sea swallowed up ships in retreat, stacked
decks of men regularly trying to escape. The whole world was
convulsed by these contending forces. Epileptoid empire! With
his ships readied for flight, the great commander Marcus An-
tonius, defeated in battle, took himself off to the Nile, where he
was doomed to perish, and in short enough order. So for a second
time incestuous Egypt—Octavia is only my stepsister, after all,
but Cleopatra really did marry her brother—drank the blood of a
Roman leader; now the tide washes over his unstable shade.
There, truly, the long civil war, that sin against the state, is
buried. At last the victor, Octavius, wearied, sheathed his sword,
which was blunt as a club from the savage blows it had dealt, and
from then on held his position by—*fear*. Safe in the embrace, as it
were, of the arms of loyal guards, he grew old, and in the end,
after his death, through the profound piety of his son, Tiberius,
was made a god, consecrated and enshrined in the temple. The
temple of stars will be waiting for me, too, if I first destroy with a
pitiless sword whoever is hostile to me and then build my house
on the solid foundation of a deserving son.

SENECA: Octavia, the daughter of the god Claudius, and the beauty
(for beauty must be more than skin deep) of her elevated family . . . Octavia, who *is*, like Juno (*nota bene:* also the wife of a god),
married to her brother . . . Octavia will fill your halls with little
godlings.

NERO: Her whore of a mother raises doubts about her own legitimacy, and besides, she has never loved me.

SENECA: A young wife hides her passion out of modesty.

NERO: Right, this is what I told myself, even though it was clear that
she hated me. But enough's enough. I'm hurt and angry, and I've
resolved to make her sorry. *And* I've found a wife who by both
birth and beauty is worthy of my bed. Venus, Juno, Minerva
would all have to yield pride of place to this woman!

SENECA: Good behavior and wifely loyalty, virtue, modesty are what
a husband should look for. Only these, the treasures of mind and
soul, endure, unchanging, eternal; beauty's flower dies a little
every day.

NERO: All these praiseworthy attributes God has conferred on one
woman—and she was born to be mine.

SENECA: Don't be so naive. Love never lasts. It has no more staying
power than beauty's flower.

NERO: What? You can say this about a god whom even the caesar of
lightning cannot resist? About the absolute *tyrant* of heaven, the
god whose power extends through the measureless seas to the
realm of Dis and compels *other* gods to come down out of the sky
—to chase the skirts of mortal women?

SENECA: It is a fatal mistake to make Love out to be an irresistible
god—winging here and there, armed with bow and arrows,
equipped with a blazing torch—and a *classic* mistake to account
him a son of Venus and Vulcan. Love is a wonderful invention of
the mind and a sweet passion of the soul; it is born of youth,
fostered by easy living among comfortable circumstances, and if
you cease to cater to it, it grows sickly and quickly dies, its power
gone.

NERO: Well, *I* reckon love to be the chief reason for living, because it's the source of pleasure. Love *never* dies, inasmuch as it's how the human race perpetuates itself—and it tames wild beasts too. May this god carry a torch for me—a wedding torch!—and lead Poppaea by its light into my bed.

SENECA: The sadness that the people feel at the prospect of this marriage can scarcely be borne. And it's wrong, besides.

NERO: Am I alone to be forbidden to do what everyone else may do?

SENECA: The state always makes its greatest demands on its leaders.

NERO: I'd be curious to know whether a little forceful persuasion could convince the state to rethink its position in this matter.

SENECA: It would be so much better if, for the sake of peace, you were to accede to the will of your people.

NERO: Something's rotten in Rome, when the populace rules the king.

SENECA: When their petitions count for nothing, the people have a right to express their dissatisfaction.

NERO: Is it just of them to try to bring about by force what they've not gotten by request?

SENECA: To keep refusing the people is unjust.

NERO: For them to dictate to a prince is an outrage.

SENECA: He should make the first move toward conciliation.

NERO: But they'll say he's given in.

SENECA: Who cares? Talk's nothing.

NERO: Maybe so, but it ruins plenty of fellows.

SENECA: It can't make a sow's ear out of a purse.

NERO: But it does its dirty work anyway.

SENECA: It will be hushed up easily enough. Think of your distinguished stepfather, think of the youthfulness, the goodness, the devotion of your wife, and change your mind about marrying Poppaea.

NERO: Enough already! Stop beating this dead horse, Seneca. I'll do what I choose to do, whether you approve or not. And, considering that she is carrying in her womb my promise to the future and a part of me, it's clear that *Poppaea's* is the petition I've put off responding to for too long. Why not make tomorrow the wedding day?

(*Exit* NERO *and* SENECA)


ACT III


Scene 1


(GHOST OF AGRIPPINA *enters, bearing a flaming torch*)

GHOST OF AGRIPPINA: I've come forth from Tartarus
   through a tear
   (or say: a *tear*)
   in the earth, and I bear

   in my bloodstained right hand
   a Stygian torch, with which to light
   an illegal marriage rite:

Poppaea can wed my son with this black fire                      600
that his mother's setting-right right hand
will metamorphose into their funeral pyre!

For I'm still unavenged, and always,
like a ghost chasing a ghost,
the memory of how I was wrongly slain
haunts me; it stays, stays, stays

with me, among the shades,
darkening my own.

I gave everything—and received in return
a short cruise on a ship for a fool,                             610
and that night during which I was made to mourn

my own death; I'd have wept for my companions' murder,
too, and for my son's cold-hearted crime—
no time,

no time for *these* tears; instead, a second crime
was added to the first, another kind of marriage:
rescued from the sea, I was struck down by the sword.

A fine, imperial reward!
I swam in my own blood.
Now that was an unholy flood.                                    620

Yet even my death failed to extinguish my son's hatred.
That dog of a tyrant (and I know who's the bitch here)
blasphemes my name, wants to make unsacred
my reputation; he knocks down statue after statue of me
and obliterates the inscriptions. He's broadcast this decree
throughout the entire world—the world
my unwitting love handed over, like a toy
or a game, to a callow boy.

It serves me right
(or say: right *handily*),                                    630
this unending grief, this still unkilled pain.

(*She sees her husband's ghost*)

Ghost chasing a ghost . . .
my dead husband, the afterword of him,
comes after me, shadows my shade,
like an assassin (if you could kill the dead).
You could say he's a mere shadow of his former self.

Oh, the man completely slays me,
the way he brings me face to face with this amusing fact:
Rome is not yet burning, but *he* is in flames
and he blames me.                                             640
Blames me for both his death
and his son's, and for just about everything that went on
     *entr'acte*.

Well, don't worry, my husband-on-fire-for-revenge.
You'll have the real murderer in your *hands* soon.
I've made plans for him—

an appropriate disaster, plenty of pain,
followed by a humiliating attempt to flee
and then torture that'll surpass even Tantalus's thirst,
Sisyphus's hard labor, Tityus's agony
(two eagles devour his liver, which grows large again with
     the moon, and so the eagles come again to gnaw at it and
     gnaw at it)                                              650
and that Ixion feels, ruined on the rack, wheel of misfortune.
He can build marble palaces with proud gold roofs,
stand armed guards at the door,
the whole world, exhausted by his rape of it, glad to be poor,
can give up its riches to him,
supplicating Parthians can entreat him for mercy,
and more kingdoms can bring him more riches,

the day and hour will still come when he will have to pay for his
    felonies
with his own guilty soul. Deserted and undone,
stripped of everything, he will offer up his throat to his
    enemies. Who'll slice it like a baker's bun.        660

Oh God, what's the point of my struggles, my prayers?

My mad son, has your insanity, like Icarus's, carried you
so far out of the world that even my anger,
the unsayable anger of one who has died by matricide,
is no more than a torch on the shore that will flare
briefly and then—
disappear into the darkness of its own nonbeing?
If so, remember the other shore, the other torch,
and ambition's swift slide down air.

If only, before I brought you into the light of day    670
and embraced you with a mother's kindness,
wild beasts had ripped out my womb!

You'd have died without sin, without the knowledge of evil,
innocent—and mine;
by my side for eternity, you'd observe, in the quiet corners of
    the after*world*
(this epilogue to everything),
your fathers and forefathers, the famous men
whom now shame and grief
(two devouring eagles)
will abide with forever    680
because of you, my monster of a son,
because of me, who brought into being the like of you.

But why do I put off going down to Tartarus,
I, a failure as a stepmother, as a mother, as a wife—
a woman who gave life to *death*,
a woman who is her family's curse?

Scene 2


(*The day after Nero has divorced Octavia and married Poppaea.*
OCTAVIA *enters and speaks to the grieving* CHORUS OF ROMANS.)

OCTAVIA: (*To* CHORUS) On this citywide holiday,
  Which *I* would call anything but holy,
  Hold back your tears, my friends, my people,
  For your great love and concern for me                    690
  Might wake the emperor's sharp wrath,
  And then I'd be a source of suffering
  To you.
                  This is not the first wound
  My heart's felt; I've known worse.
  This day will put an end to my troubles,
  Even if by death; hurray
  For that much. I'll not again be forced
  To look on my husband's face, nor,
  Like a slave, slave away at love
  In a bed I hate to get into.                               700
  I'll be Augustus's sister, *not*
  His wife. If only I can be spared
  Torture, a terrifying death—
  *Poor, silly girl, can you*
  *Yet hope for this, remembering*
  *The crimes your cruel husband's committed?*
  *He's let you live this long precisely*
  *So you can die on his wedding day,*
  *A wedding present, like dear Silanus,*
  *An astrologically favored offering!*                      710
  *But why do you keep looking back*
  *At your father's house, and crying?*
  *Get ready to leave this roof, to quit*
  *For good the prince's Palace of Blood.*

CHORUS OF ROMANS: Look! The day but dimly foreseen,
  But so often forecast, has dawned:

Octavia, the daughter of Claudius,
Has been driven by Nero out
Of her own house, which,
Already, Poppaea occupies                         720
Triumphantly, while we do nothing,
Frightened—even our feelings—into submission.
Where's our collective Roman courage,
Which, once upon a time, defeated
Famous generals, ruled by law
This country subject to no other,
Granted authority to worthy citizens,
Legislated war and peace,
Civilized barbarians,
Imprisoned captive kings, now?                    730
Look! Everywhere we turn
We're confronted by the offensive sight
Of Poppaea's image conjoined to Nero's!
They're so lifelike, these statues—
Let's smash them on the ground, and drag
*Her* down off "Her Highness's" couch
And then with merciless spears attack
The emperor's palace and set it on fire.

(CHORUS *exits*)


### ACT IV


### Scene 1


(POPPAEA *and* POPPAEA'S NURSE *enter.* POPPAEA *appears dis-traught.*)

POPPAEA'S NURSE: Where are you going, trembling all over like that, when you should be in your husband's bed, child? Why do you want to be alone? And such a troubled look on your face! Why are you crying? After all, this is the day we prayed for: having captivated him by your beauty, you are now married to your Caesar. Venus, the mother of love, the greatest god, has handed him over to you like a prisoner—though *Seneca* sneered at such bonds. Oh, how perfectly queenly you were, reclining on the dais in the palace hall! When you made the offering of the incense to the gods and sprinkled the sacred shrines with fine wine, your head covered with a filmy flame-colored scarf, the Senate gazed in astonishment at your beauty. And the prince himself, a colossus amid the cheering crowd, walked beside you, his face and bearing full of his joy and pride in you. This is just like the way Peleus took for his bride the goddess Thetis, who'd emerged from the ocean's foam, and to whose marriage, all agree, the gods, including every god of the sea, came in celebration. What has suddenly changed the look on your face? Tell me why you look white as a ghost, why you are in tears.

POPPAEA: Oh, Nurse, I'm confused and anxious because of an awful nightmare I had last night that still upsets me. You see, after the joyful day had surrendered to dark's stars, and the sky to night, I fell asleep in Nero's arms; but this sweet slumber was cut short. For there seemed to be a crowd of mourners thronging my marriage chamber: Roman matrons, with their hair in wild disarray, weeping and wailing. And amid frequent, frightening trumpet blasts, my husband's mother, Agrippina, making mad threats, brandished a blood-spattered torch. Terrified, I followed her, when suddenly the earth yawned open beneath me, in a huge chasm. Down through this chasm I plunged, and there before me, to my astonishment, I saw, as on earth, my marriage bed and I lay down on it in utter exhaustion. Then I saw my former husband, Crispinus, and my son, Rufrius Crispinus, approaching, attended by an entourage. Crispinus hurried to take me in his arms, to kiss me after so long a separation, when Nero suddenly burst into the room and buried his savage sword in Crispinus's throat. At this point my fear was so great it woke me; I was shaking all over and my heart beat wildly. I was too frightened even to cry out, but now your affectionate concern has helped me to find my voice again.

Oh dear, what is it that the spirits of the dead are threatening me with? What does it mean that I saw my former husband being murdered?

POPPAEA'S NURSE: Whatever you think hardest about during the day, a mysterious, subconscious intelligence, quick as a fox, calls up while you sleep. Does it surprise you that you saw your former husband and marriage bed while you slept in your new husband's arms? But will you let mere apparitions—of hands beating breasts and of women with uncombed hair—bother you on a day of joy? Those mournful Roman matrons—it was Octavia's divorce they were upset about, that's why they were here in her father's house, here in her brother's house. That torch you followed, the one Agrippina carried to light the way, is an omen that you'll be called Augusta, a distinguished name burnished even more brightly by others' envy of it. Your bed in the lower world promises that you'll live happily ever after. That your prince *buried* his sword in Crispinus's throat means he'll wage no wars but sheathe his sword in peace. Cheer up, count your blessings, I beg you. Stop worrying and go back to bed.

POPPAEA: No, I am determined to visit the shrines and sacred altars and offer sacrifices to the holy gods so these night terrors will stop troubling my sleep, and my enemies can sleep uneasy instead. Pray for me and implore the gods above to let nothing horrible happen to change the way things are.

(*Poppaea and her nurse exit*)

Scene 2

(CHORUS OF WOMEN *enters*)

CHORUS OF WOMEN: If what they say about the greatest god
    Is true, and he once took the shape of a swan

To love lovely Leda and, disguised again,
This time as a bull, was able to wed
Europa, eloping with her—he would surely skip
Out on the stars themselves to live with you,
Poppaea, for you are prettier than she who
Lay down to lay down, or Danae in gold, knee-deep.
Sparta can boast about Helen, and so can Paris,               770
Since he stole her—Poppaea will put in the shade
Even her for whom a war was made
(And a poem a little longer than this).
    But who is this fellow, headed our way as if death
    Were after him? What'll he say when he catches his
        breath?

## Scene 3

(MESSENGER *enters*)

MESSENGER: Whatever guards are here are ordered to defend the
    palace, which is being threatened by a mob. Look over there—
    the captains, recognizing the urgency of the situation, are calling
    up ranks to defend the city. Yet the masses are so riled that even
    this doesn't scare them away. They just keep getting more and
    more ornery.

CHORUS OF WOMEN: What has them worked up like this?

MESSENGER: They're crazy about Octavia and incensed about how
    she's been treated. And, carried away by these sentiments,
    they're swarming all over the place, ready to do just about any-
    thing.

CHORUS OF WOMEN: Tell us what they might, or mean, to do!

MESSENGER: They intend to give back to Octavia her father's house
and husband's bed—the part of the empire she's got coming to
her.

CHORUS OF WOMEN: The things Poppaea, as his wife, now shares
with Nero!

MESSENGER: It's this fixation on Octavia that has them fired up and is
driving them straight into an orgy of recklessness. Every statue of
Poppaea that was put up, smooth marble or shining bronze, has
fallen, knocked down by the hands of the mob and smashed repeatedly with iron crowbars. After they've pulled the sections
down by ropes, they drag them off one by one, stomp on them,
and grind them underfoot, deep into the mud. These barbaric
deeds are accompanied by words that I hesitate to repeat. They're
going to surround the emperor's house with a ring of fire if he
doesn't give in to them and hand over his new bride and return
Octavia's house to her. I'm off now to make sure the prince himself
knows of the citizens' uprising, as the prefect ordered me to.

(MESSENGER *exits*)


Scene 4


CHORUS OF WOMEN:
                              A Torch Song
        What do you people think that you are doing?
        It's no good—you can't beat back the flames
        Of passion, or burn it down with these flames
        Of your own. Cupid's been known to singe                    810
        Jove himself, now and again. Annoy
        The well-, uh, wing-hung god, or get in his way
        And we can promise you he'll make you pay.
        He's quick-tempered, unruly, a bit of a bad boy.
        A scorched-earth policy? Why, it was this god who

Got Achilles going, wiped out the Greeks—
And Agamemnon—this god, who overthrew
Priam and turned the Hellespont into a place for antiques.
We hate to think of how the earth might move
If Nero and his woman are *not* allowed to love.

(*They exit*)

ACT V

Scene 1

(NERO *enters*)

NERO: Clearly, my soldiers are too slow to use their swords and I myself have been too *much* kinder and gentler than my ancestors, considering the so-called "civil" disobedience I've had to deal with. Otherwise, rivers of their own blood would have put out the fires the "civilians" started. Otherwise, believe me, a very sad Rome would stink to high heaven with dead "civilians"—Rome, that gave rise to such men as these, these *un-civilians.*

But Octavia, on whose behalf the city turns against me in rage—a woman I know enough always to look over my shoulder at—*will* die. Will finally make me happy by dying! With her blood she'll extinguish my anger, if not any fire.

But just her death is not enough of a punishment for her followers—it lets them off too easy. This incredible insurrection deserves something even worse than death. Right, so let Rome burn! Let the city's roofs collapse in flames! I'll fight fire with fire! Let fire and a life in ruins destroy the culpable, the populace— they'll know demeaning poverty, severe hunger, grief, grief, grief! The mass of people has grown arrogant, encouraged by the high standard of living in my time; in its ingratitude, it can neither comprehend my clemency nor be content with peace. Instead, it is here swept along by the audacity of discontent and there is carried along by its own recklessness—both ways, straight to the brink. It must be held in check by suffering, made to bear a heavy yoke forever, so that it will never attempt anything like this again, never lift its collective head even to look at Poppaea, my sainted wife. When it's been brought under control by fear of punishment, it will be taught to obey every nod of its *emperor's* head.

But I see that the man whose exceptional loyalty and proven trustworthiness have made him the captain of my royal guards is here.

## Scene 2

(PREFECT *enters*)

PREFECT: I'm here to report that the people's uprising has been put down. Getting rid of a few key players did the trick.

NERO: And this is enough? This is how a soldier has obeyed his leader? *Put down?* This is the vengeance I'm entitled to?

PREFECT: The ringleaders, the traitors who were responsible for the rebellion, are dead.

NERO: But the mob itself, that dared to try to burn down my house, to dictate to me—the emperor!—that dared to drag my empress literally from our marriage bed, to violate her, insofar as they had an opportunity to, with their dirty hands and insolent threats— what about them? Have they not gotten what they have coming?

PREFECT: Is *emotional* pain going to set the terms of punishment for your citizens?

NERO: It's going to set terms that will go down in history.

PREFECT: A punishment so great that not even our power can stop history from recording it?

NERO: The very first person who's going to get it is the one who deserves it the most.

PREFECT: Say who you mean. I'll take care of it immediately.

NERO: I mean Octavia. Bring me her head.

PREFECT: How can I? I'm paralyzed by the sheer horror of this suggestion, numb with it.

NERO: You hesitate to obey?

PREFECT: Why do you question my loyalty?

NERO: Because you spare my enemy.

PREFECT: You call a *woman* your enemy?

NERO: If she's guilty of crimes against the state.

PREFECT: What is she guilty of?

NERO: Revolution.

PREFECT: Who's powerful enough to manipulate the people in this way?

NERO: The one who was able to stir them up.

PREFECT: That could not be just anybody, I think.

NERO: It'd be a woman to whom nature has given a devious mind inclined to evil, a heart ready, willing, and able to work against me.

PREFECT: But nature did not give her the power—

NERO: Precisely in order that she should not be unconquerable. Precisely in order that fear or torture might break her tenuous strength. As it will now, will crush this woman who has so long deserved to die. Better late than never.

Enough advice and prayers! Obey my royal decree: she is to be taken by ship to some remote shore and there she's to be slain, that my heart may finally stop pounding with fear.

(NERO *and* PREFECT *exit*)

## Scene 3

(CHORUS OF ROMANS *enters*)

CHORUS OF ROMANS: Oh, to so many, the approbation
   Of the public has proved to be
   Like a breeze on the open sea
   That, having borne the vessels it favors           880
   Far out, dies down, leaving them
   Dangerously stranded in deep water!
   Thus the unhappy mother of the Gracchi
   Wept for her sons, whose noble birth,
   Famous eloquence and devotion to Rome,
   Moral courage, legal expertise
   Could not keep them from being destroyed
   By the citizens' great love and overwhelming favor.
   You, too, Livius, were handed over
   By fortune to a similar fate,           890
   Unprotected by your position or family.
   This fresh grief makes it impossible for us
   To recall more examples. The citizens can now see
   The woman to whom, they just decreed,
   Her father's house and her stepbrother's bed
   Should be restored, dragged out, in tears,
   To punishment and death.

                   It is a fortunate poverty,
To be content to remain unknown
Beneath an unassuming roof:
Famous homes are frequently shaken                900
By storms, or overturned by fortune.


## Scene 4


(OCTAVIA *is dragged onstage roughly by the* PALACE GUARDS)

OCTAVIA: Where are you taking me? To what exile
  (If, perhaps, the tyrant—or his queen,
  Her heart softened and made sympathetic
  By my infinity of tribulations—
  Is ready to let me live)? Somewhere!
  Oh, but if she—the queen, the *queen*—
  Is getting ready to crown, as it were, my trials
  With death, why must she be so cruel
  As to begrudge me the right to die in my home?      910
  But now, all hope of rescue's gone—
  *Poor Octavia!* For I can see
  My stepbrother's ship, the one on which
  His poor mother was once set to sea,
  And now his sister, abandoned by him,
  Turned out from his bedroom, shall sail away
  On that same ship. Goodness
  Is no longer valued now, and
  The gods are dead. A harsh vengeance
  Rules in the world. Who can weep          920
  For me, who is *good* enough?
  What nightingale can cry out
  (For music can cry) as well as I,
  Or translate into night-wails
  The lamentations of a woman?
  If only I had the wings of a bird!

Flying swiftly far away
From stern assemblages of men,
From a merciless execution,
I might find a perch on a bough                                    930
In a secluded glade, alone,
And pour forth from my plaintive throat
A song of sorrow.

CHORUS OF ROMANS: We the people are ruled by fate.
    Not one of us—who are all mere mortals—
    Is guaranteed a steady course
    Through life: each day, anxiously awaited,
    Arrives bearing changes, like a Greek
    Bearing gifts. Take Misery's comfort
    In the thought of royal women                                  940
    Who suffered as much as or more than you.

    And you, the first Agrippina,
    You are the first Agrippina
    We must name, Tiberius's daughter-
    In-law, a wife to a Caesar, whose name
    Was like a light to all the world,
    The mother of so many sons,
    So many pledges of peace, and yet
    In time you would endure exile,
    Violence and insulting chains,                                 950
    Your friends' deaths—and the grievous sadness
    You felt—and finally your own,
    A long, drawn-out, agonizing death.
    Blessed with her husband, Drusus, and sons,
    Livia succumbed to evil ways
    And was punished. Julia suffered
    Her mother's fate; the time came when,
    Though no one accused her of any crime,
    She was slain by the sword anyway.
    What couldn't your mother do, once                             960
    Upon a time? Dear to her husband,
    Secure in her son, Britannicus,

She ruled the palace of the emperor.
Yet she, too, was subjected to a slave
And died by the sword of a merciless soldier.
What of her who could have hoped
For the highest throne, the majestic mother
Of Nero? Was she not first violated
By the sailors who would kill her,
And then, slain by the sword, didn't she                    970
Lie unburied for a long time,
The victim of her unnatural son?


OCTAVIA: And now the tyrant dispatches me
To the place of darkness, where I will be
A *flicker of dark,* let's say, an un-
Being, a darkness among darknesses,
Impossible to see and the sound of silence.
Why do I try to delay the inevitable?
Be done with it—and me!—you
To whom fortune has delivered me.                           980
I pray to God—*but are you crazy,*
*Octavia? Do not pray*
*To gods who have no use for you!*
I call on Tartarus and on
The gods of that dark realm, the goddesses
Who chase the wicked down, and you,
The shade of my father, to bring down
The tyrant—bring him all the way down,
To the death and punishment he deserves.

(*To* PALACE GUARDS)

I am not afraid to die.                                     990
Put in the oars, unfurl the sails,
And let the pilot make for the shores
Of Pandataria, of death!
(OCTAVIA *exits with* PALACE GUARDS)

CHORUS OF ROMANS: May breezes gentle as the touch
   Of her hand, like the breezes
   That once ferried Iphigenia
   On a light cloud from the altar
   Of a vindictive Diana,
   Hold this young woman in the palm
   Of their going, softly blowing her ship        1000
   Far from the awful punishment
   Meant for her, to the temple
   At Trivia. More merciful
   Than Rome is Aulis; more merciful
   Than Rome, the foreign land of Turin.
   In those places the gods are content
   With the blood of strangers, while
   Rome's delight is in the blood
   Of her children, the innocent and good.
   Thus Time itself is in exile.        1010

# THE PHOENICIAN
# WOMEN

## (PHOENISSAE)

Translated by David R. Slavitt

# INTRODUCTION

What have we here? Is it a play? Are there perhaps two scenes, from two different plays, that have come together in a scriptorium somewhere? Are we allowed to suppose that Seneca, in his acute, perfectly well-founded *Weltschmerz*, began to doubt the very idea of the well-made artifact, the poem or play that represents for us some ideal or at least coherent and rational existence? Is it conceivable that he might have been drawn to the fragment as a more plausible and accurately mimetic figuring of the discontinuities and opacities of what we call "real" life?

Anything is conceivable, and we can do what we like with these texts, because the texts do not change after all. There they are, in the Latin, and often with their English prose meanings *en face*.

My challenge, or say my opportunity, was to do something with these two fragments. As a co-editor of the series, I decided that I could allow myself a degree of latitude and imagine a play, a collage of texts perhaps. Or, better, think of it as an arbitrary union of the kind we sometimes see in museums in which a curator sticks this head on that torso to impersonate a sculpture, and for some years or decades—until a younger art historian comes along with a new reading—it stands there pleasing us. What do we feel, in such instances? Annoyance that we have been fooled? Resentment that a statue from which we have taken pleasure has been not only deconstructed but destroyed?

Much of what I might have said about the play I have put into the mouth of Seneca—or the figure "Seneca" whom I have introduced into the prose choral interlude, which is, let me confess at once, entirely my own invention. I could add a line or two about how there are precedents for the material of this play in *The Seven Against Thebes* of Aeschylus and *Oedipus at Colonus* of Sophocles, as well as *The Phoenician Women* of Euripides, to which "Seneca" and the Choragos make reference; but that would be either obvious or boring, depending on whether the reader already knew it or not.

More to the point, I think, this is an opportunity for at least a brief observation about what I think I'm doing in this most problematic business of "translation." I do believe these fragments, and particularly the first, to be valuable and stately pieces of Senecan tragic poetry. They have a convincing emotion and a resonant if somewhat florid diction. To react to that, to try to convey that, to be faithful not to the text, or even to the author's intention, but to the possibilities he saw, that is the great game. One must try to yield to the same blandishment as initially attracted and engaged the author, whispering the equivalents in whatever language one can contrive, to get the readers or members of the audience to respond to that complex of emotional and aesthetic cues arising from the action on the page or on the stage.

This is a tall order. Some would call it arrogance—and they would of course be correct—for the translator, by this light, must arrogate to himself the authorial privileges of manipulation and substitution. As fiction is a series of lies that amount to the truth, so translation is a string of tricks that arrive at last at something like fidelity. In Latin poetry, where there was a clear suggestion of what we now think of as voice or persona, this is not so bizarre or farfetched an enterprise. One can, with only a little grandiosity, begin to get the sense of a poet's address and tessitura, the characteristic Senecan, or Virgilian, or Ovidian mode, and like some vaudevillian doing a Presley or a Crosby or a Jolson imitation, convey not only a risible similitude, but—at an appropriate moment in the number— make it good, get something of the real quality and excellence of the original, and make them gasp—just a little—out there in their seats.

If I have managed that much in a few passages, I should be quite content. These fragments are very good, good enough, after all, so that even my Jolson imitation may serve some pedagogical and artistic function, suggesting, however inadequately, what kind of splendid voice was once speaking.

David R. Slavitt

# THE PHOENICIAN WOMEN

## CHARACTERS

OEDIPUS, until recently, king of Thebes
ANTIGONE, daughter of Oedipus, also half sister, and his
  companion in his suffering
JOCASTA, wife and mother of Oedipus
POLYNICES and ETEOCLES, sons of Oedipus and rivals for the
  Theban throne
MESSENGERS

And in the interpolation:
CHORAGOS, a character representing the audience
SENECA, the playwright, who is also adviser to Nero, emperor of
  Rome

SCENE: *A wild slope of Mount Cithaeron.* OEDIPUS *enters, led by*
ANTIGONE. *They are tired and pause to rest.*

OEDIPUS: (*To* ANTIGONE)
  Guide, nurse, crutch . . . What a daughter you are,
  worth the enormous trouble of your begetting!
  Leave me, I pray, or rather command, for prayer
  doesn't sit well in my mouth. I am accursed
  as no man ever was before. Go, go,
  let me stumble and grope my way to find
  that elusive step for which my soul and soles
  are tingling with desire. I see the darkness
  and wish to hear and feel it also—the great
  nothing. The light I am blind to finds me out.          10

Let go my hand; leave it to better employment.
My own Cithaeron calls me, its rugged crags
eager to finish that job of work they began
a lifetime ago. My life should have ended then
in these wild defiles. To these same slopes Actaeon
came with his hounds, beheld the naked goddess,
was turned into a stag, and felt their rough
embrace as they mauled and tore his flesh to prove
him merely mortal. To these foothills Agave
led the way for her sister-priestesses,                          20
and together in their enthusiastic revels
they tore apart her darling son and, shrieking,
held the head aloft on a sacred wand.
On these same slopes, the untamed bull ran raging,
dragging what at first was Dirce, and then
was what she had been, and by and by became
anonymous mere meat—and Zetus smiled
as he followed the bloody track and watched the swift
declension of his revenge. To those high cliffs
that tower over the sea and make the knees                       30
melt with their giddy height poor Ino came,
fleeing before Athamas's fury and leapt,
her babe in her arms, into the insubstantial
air and the waiting rocks and water below.
Compared to mine, their fates were gentle, sweet,
and enviable, for I survived that death
my father contrived for me, to endure much worse—
a lifetime's pain, and bitter shame, and griefs
unmatched in all the world. To these sweet woods
I now return to claim that favor of mercy                        40
the fates snatched from the grasp of my infant fists.
My proper place is here. Now am I home
among true kin—cruelty, savagery, blood,
fierce when they kill, and more fierce when they spare,
as some cats will for a time, the lives of their prey.
      Let my hand go! My father summons
his son, and I come. His blood calls out to mine.
My love for you is all that holds me back.

I detest my life. It sticks in my soul's craw
I want only to vomit out its poison.                                        50

ANTIGONE: No power in the world could tear me from you,
neither human nor divine. I cling
to what I love. Let my poor brothers quarrel
over the spoils of our noble house. Its richest
treasure I keep to myself—my own dear father.
Eteocles on the throne and Polynices
encamped at the gates wrangle over trifles.
Wealth and power are toys of children when love
is weighed against them. Jupiter's thunderbolts
could not loosen my grip on your hand. Not even                             60
you may forbid me. Go where you will, I'll guide
your unwilling feet—to mountain crest or plain,
along familiar paths or through wild brambles,
at the edges of dizzying cliffs where death gapes
far below. I'll walk with you even there,
and still, with hand in hand, we'll plunge together,
or I'll go first, my eyes to direct your feet,
your will to direct my eyes. Whatever you choose,
that shall content and delight me. I shall demand
nothing, oppose nothing—not even death,                                     70
if that is what you desire. Live or perish,
I follow and obey, as the parts of your body
perform what your mind decrees, your muscle and bone.
Only feel their strength, which is your own.
Take heart from the burdens you've borne and even the shame.
There comes at last defiance, a kind of pride
in not having been crushed. Hold your head high,
the king not merely of Thebes but of grief itself.
To give in to your woes would be to die.

OEDIPUS: In a sinful house, whence comes this sport of virtue?  80
That I should produce a loving child is madness.
Surely the gods mock me. Nature is playing
jokes. Rivers as soon will flow uphill,
and Apollo's torch usher in the gloom of night.

The cream of the jest will be my elevation
to sanctity, my foulness somehow transformed
to holiness by the love of this wide-eyed girl.
Do I weep or laugh? My eyes have no tears left
and want only one thing now—that my poor father's
death may be avenged at last by my own.                        90
You mean well, girl, but you only increase my pain,
for I am a corpse that yearns for the cover of earth.
My shadow stains the road; I offend the sun.
To kill someone who wishes to live is evil;
it is just as bad to keep a person alive
whose desire it is to die. I count it worse,
the pain of despair being worse than any death.
For your love's sake, and pity's, let me go.
No longer sovereign of Thebes, I am yet master
of my own life and death. Companion and friend,            100
give me my sword, that famous weapon I held
when I killed my father. Put it into my hand,
to use on myself, to use on my sons, to cut
in a blind frenzy at foulness that's everywhere!
My soul is on fire—build me a funeral pyre
on which I can fling myself, to embrace the cleansing
flames that will set me free. I can taste the ashes.
Or lead me to that cliff you spoke of. The blue
water below will wash away my sins,
tumbling in the brine corruptible flesh                    110
until there is only the white brightness of bone.
On such a cliff the Sphinx once sat and glowered,
and there I showed how smart I was with an answer
to her child's riddle. With the fates' much harder riddle
I performed less well, until, with many hints,
I groaned out my heartbroken reply. Lead me
to that stone seat where I shall sit and amaze
the passers-by, until one comes enraged
or disgusted enough to fling my feeble ruin
over the edge. But mothers will put to their children       120
my deplorable riddle, the worst the world has ever

propounded—and they all will know the answer.
*He was his own grandfather's son-in-law;*
*his father's rival; his sons' and daughters' brother;*
*his brothers' father. At one astonishing moment,*
*the grandmother brought forth to her husband children,*
*and to herself grandchildren. Who was he?*
They'll giggle of course, as children will, at the joke,
which is what they make of the monstrous. Master of riddles,
I couldn't master this one. In all Thebes,                        130
I was the last to guess the dismal answer.
O my daughter, what can you say to console,
to enhearten this battered hulk you lead about
like a dancing bear? Your gentle words would be welcome
to any heart, but mine is utterly dead,
a dull and heavy stone in a stupid chest
that continues to breathe. No night is dark enough
for me to hide in. Deep Tartarus itself
will recoil, I have no doubt, when I arrive
in something like the greeting I've grown used to            140
here in this life. You could not protect me from that
and cannot keep from me the release I seek,
for Death is everywhere. The gods in their wisdom
have arranged the affairs of men so that one may rob
a person of his life but not of his death.
Swords and nooses abound, and cliffs and ravines,
and venomous adders lurking in deadly plants.
To the hall of the dead, they say a thousand doors
gape in grisly welcome. I will enter,
by one or another, or let it enter me,                           150
for no part of my body is free from taint.
All is corruption, my fingers and hands, my blood,
my manhood and my heart. They all cry out
for mortal blows. My eyes that have wept red gore
blink in the expectation of new assaults.
I stand before my father that he may choose
what is the proper penalty and atonement.
Wherever you are, signal to me your will.
I am a novice yet of griefs and pains.

Decree whatever further sacrifices                                    160
my crimes require and I shall perform them all,
turning my bloodied hand upon myself.
Your hatred for me cannot exceed my own
self-loathing. Come to my aid and guide
my all but nerveless hand, and I shall strike
again, and deeper, having botched before
what ought to have been a final obliteration
not merely of sight but of life itself.
After the boldness with which I had sinned, my timid
attempt upon myself was contemptible, mean,                           170
and childish. I am filled with shame to think
by how far short I fell. Beyond the orbs
of the eyes there was the brain which should have been
obliterated. There was the world I wanted
to uncreate. Oblivion I wanted,
or the world's original chaos, that primal murk
in which my lust and savagery could hide.
The sockets were the door. I brought myself
up to the threshold but then fell back, a coward.
Now, in disgust and rage, I am ready to cross.                        180

ANTIGONE: O great of soul, I beg you, father, consider!
Listen to me, your wretched loving daughter.
Those thunderstorms of the passions are all behind you,
as distant as the grandeur of your throne.
We look down as a pair of soaring birds
on tiny creatures we know to be men and women,
animated by joys and sorrows we scarcely
credit now, indifferent as we are
and safe—for there is safety *in extremis.*
Beyond all hope and fear, not even the gods                           190
can affect you further. You have borne their utmost
and lived. You have survived, despising death's
easy evasion. That burden would have crushed
an ordinary man. You threw away
the blessing men desire and have endured
more than what men fear in their worst nightmares.

Your prize is a great detachment: you may look down
purged, perfected, purified, your heart
hardened to shining diamond and disconnected
from all those ties that trammel men: your throne,                    200
your palace, native city, mother, sons,
and even the light of day are all forgone
if not forgotten. What death can take away
you have let go already. What can its darkness
hold out for you in threat or promise of freedom
that your life has not already given? Having lost
all, you have lost all taint and blemish. The murmur
of castle and court has given way to the silence
of temple and tomb, with the long songs of the wind
as reverent descant. What can you imagine                             210
from death that can tempt you further? That great quiet
is in your heart already. Only listen,
attend to the wisdom you have so dearly bought,
the grand indifference that I have tried to learn
from you and with you, for your sake and my own.

OEDIPUS: I flee myself. And consciousness. I flee
my hands, my crimes, the sky, the gods, the earth
my feet offend, the air my breathing fouls,
sweet water the touch of my cursed lips
pollutes. I flee the limitless disgust                                220
I feel for my existence. The world's good order
I have defied, defiled. The one gift left
within my power would be to undo the offense
and erase myself from the slate of the universe.
The tenderest words of men and women affront
my ears when I hear them: parent, brother, child
set me apart as the monstrous one. I long
for utter silence, blank as the perfect darkness
I've drawn about me like a shroud. But guilt
can ravel that. It's consciousness I hate                             230
and want to be rid of at last.
                              And you, my daughter,
I want to be rid of you, for you remind me

what I have done and am, being who you are
and what you are to me. You mean no harm,
but the harm is done, is there. Your gentle voice
indicts, your caring touch burns like a brand,
and I turn away in loathing from what I love.
I cannot hide from my own unspeakable evil,
have peeled away the outer leaves of my life—
kingdom, parents, children, my famous wit,                    240
even my senses—but what remains offends
nevertheless: the onion's tears. Of these,
I have also stripped myself to the mere idea,
which is hateful still. For pity's sake, begone!
There is nothing for you to say. I will not listen.
I am like a stretched cord that vibrates response
to the sound of one note only—that of my fate
which all along awaited me. An infant,
I was doomed already. My first cry was that one
baleful note. Or before then, in the womb,                    250
I terrified my parents, who knew from the omens
that what I brought was disaster, disgrace, a ruin
like none that had gone before. Other children have died
at birth, or even before, but the taint of sin
has not attached to these. I was born guilty,
set out on the mountainside and left to the mercy
of savage beasts and Cithaeron's birds of prey,
thirsty for my blood. And death itself
disdained me, turned away as if in horror
of what I was fated to do, or as if to dare                   260
such terrible things to come to pass in the world.
Would the brat survive, would he commit those awful
crimes that had been foretold for him? He would!
I did. Like a puppet, I acted out the grotesque
guignol plot I could not escape, the strings
working my hands and feet and mind and heart
as if it were a natural thing for a son
to creep into his father's bed with his hands
still red with that father's blood and there,
as reward for the one offense commit a worse.                 270

It was nothing to kill my father—or nothing much,
compared to what followed, unnatural, affronting
nature itself. My very penance turned
to further and worse crime—I flung away
my father's scepter as if it were burning hot,
and what was the result? My sons are fighting,
a pair of curs greedy for one bone
and ready to kill. Eteocles refuses
to honor their agreement, and Polynices
brings his Argive host to Thebes to shed                        280
the blood of his native city. The widows, the orphans,
the maimed soldiers, the raped maidens and matrons
will hate those two but put the blame on me,
the begetter of all their troubles. Thebes is sick
of me and my house; the city I love hates me,
as it ought to do, and as I do myself.
All that I ever loved or touched, I've ruined.

ANTIGONE: But father, think! If you need a reason to live,
consider what you have just said. Who can better
talk to those two to restrain them? A father's command    290
may yet avert the threat of war. Your word
must resonate with authority. They'll listen—
to father, brother, king, and holy man.
That death you crave for yourself will be widespread.

OEDIPUS: Why would they listen to me? They are both of them
mad,
power-mad, the blood-lust up, accursed.
They are my sons, brought into this world
by evil and for evil. They outdo one another
in wickedness. They surpass even myself,
for they are beyond shame. Their passions drive them      300
headlong toward whatever goal their greed
and lust present. They are monstrous sons of a monster.
Their destiny is another reason for me
to want to die, in order that I may avoid
the further guilts they will bring upon my house

and on my head. Destruction seems a kind
alternative. Daughter, no, daughter, don't.
Don't fall to your knees, do not grasp mine, do not
weep with gentle tears to seek my further
pain. I am resolved. My quarrel with fate                              310
is easily resolved. I can walk away,
simply refuse to participate any further,
and decline to be. The only ray in the bleak
ruin of my existence has been yourself.
From moment to moment, the single thing preventing
my suicide has been the comfort that you
have always offered, that understanding love
I would not otherwise believe existed.
For you alone I have drawn my painful breaths.

(A MESSENGER *enters and bows*)

MESSENGER: I greet you great lord, and bring you news
      of Thebes                                                        320
    which calls you to her aid. Brother and brother
    brandish their weapons and threaten deadly battle.
    Only you can prevent the slaughter. We beg you,
    return home to separate your sons
    and impose as a father can, and as a king,
    a peace between them. For piety's sake we plead,
    do us this last great service, Oedipus.

OEDIPUS: What are you asking? Whom are you asking? Prevent
    crimes, sins, outrages? Has something happened
    to alter my appearance? I am no teacher                            330
    of piety and justice. I am a sinner:
    blood and guilt are my métier. I applaud
    their dreadful continuation of my sad story.
    They are my sons, my boys, chips off the old
    sacrificial altar, red with gore.
    I urge them on. Let them commit offenses
    to dwarf my own. Let them inscribe their names
    in the annals of evil in such huge letters that mine

will hardly occasion remark. Our noble house
is famous for this. Let them prove their mettle,                340
their high birth. The gods have their eyes upon us,
and what we do astonishes mankind.
I take a perverse pride. Let them spill their
blood and everyone else's. Let them bring down
our house in spectacular ruin, and let them know
as I have, the cold comfort of extreme
despair.

ANTIGONE:                    Father, restrain yourself. You play
with grief. My brothers need you, Thebes does. Go
and tell them to give over their vain ambitions.

OEDIPUS: I am no gentle sage! What is this nonsense?            350
I am enraged! A bitter, desperate man,
full of grief's blackness and that of hate
and cannot tell where one gives way to the other.
It's all black—the universe is the darkness
I stare at every moment! Let Polynices
rush upon Eteocles, and let them erase
a part of what I imposed upon the revolted
earth. Let outrage compound outrage. A brother
kills a brother? Better, give your mother
a sword and let her shed the too rich blood           360
of children and grandchildren. I'll hide in a cave
and wait to hear what happens and howl. And howl.

(*They freeze into a kind of tableau vivant. Two figures appear.*
SENECA *is dressed in a toga; the other, the* CHORAGOS, *is in contemporary clothing and carries a program of the performance. The
lights go down on the tableau to allow* OEDIPUS, ANTIGONE, *and the*
MESSENGER *to exit.*)

CHORAGOS: I beg your pardon. This is *The Phoenissae? The Phoenician Women?*

SENECA: Yes, yes. That's right. You have a problem? A question?

CHORAGOS: A question, yes. The Phoenician women . . . Who are they? Where are they? Have I missed something?

SENECA: No, no. You haven't missed anything.

CHORAGOS: They will be appearing later on, then, these Phoenicians?

SENECA: Ah, no. I'm afraid not. There aren't any Phoenicians. It's a kind of joke, actually.

CHORAGOS: A joke? But this is a tragedy! Why are you making jokes?

SENECA: Why not? What else is there to do, in the face of outrageous pain? One weeps, yes, but weeping exhausts itself. There are no more tears. And in the emptiness that follows, there can be some relief, some release in hollow laughter.

CHORAGOS: I still don't understand. What is funny about Phoenician women?

SENECA: It's their absence that's entertaining. The allusion is to Euripides' play which has that title. The material is roughly the same, in the next scene of this play—with Eteocles, Polynices, Jocasta, and Antigone discussing Theban politics. In Euripides' version, a chorus of Phoenician women happens by. They are on their way to Delphi. They listen to the wranglings and recriminations and wring their hands in some combination of sorrow and dismay. It is from their presence that Euripides takes his title, and from his that I take mine.

CHORAGOS: Even though you have omitted their chorus?

SENECA: Even though—or even because. My assumption is that a perceptive and attentive audience can determine for itself the appropriate emotional attitude to take to what is happening. Sorrow, dismay, or even disgust . . .

CHORAGOS: Disgust?

SENECA: I feel that sometimes. These characters are eloquent enough so that we ought to be able to assume a certain degree of intelligence. And that would in turn suggest that they might contrive to behave better—but they don't, of course. They can't. They just stand there and endure, acting out the same tawdry and stupid plot with no possible evasion or escape. Nothing they do can lessen the disasters that await them with each new performance of each new version. Nothing helps. They are beyond my help or yours. No matter how attractive or clever, or rhetorically inventive I make them, they stand there like cattle waiting for the sacrificial blade to fall. It's disgusting. The mind turns away— perhaps to make jokes. As the Phoenician women would say, if I were to trot them out onstage, "It really is too bad."

CHORAGOS: I see, I think. You're saying that we are all Phoenician women, observers, even sympathetic observers, but with our own duties and destinies to see to.

SENECA: If you like. But I am included in this "we" of yours. We are all in this together, audience, playwright . . . even the actors. The story is old, is there, like a mountain, and each ascent is a new one with its own risks and its own rewards.

CHORAGOS: That's very nice.

SENECA: Thank you. On this particular excursion, my interest, as guide, is to display certain striking views. Other routes and approaches offer other tableaux—as for instance the death of Oedipus in Sophocles' version. Or his apotheosis. Christians like it because it is familiar and reassuring, but it changes nothing. The curse of Thyestes upon the house of Laius continues its most baleful series of effects.

CHORAGOS: Can you just pick and choose that way? Is that fair?

SENECA: I can. I have. And the question of fairness—or of how we bear unfairness and injustice—is a legitimate one, but too close to the heart of this evening's business for me to allow myself any comment.

CHORAGOS: You poets are often suddenly reticent that way. Voluble, but then abruptly shy. Like bright children.

SENECA: That's very nice.

CHORAGOS: Thank you. You won't give even a hint?

SENECA: I'll say . . . I'll say that the finished work of art somehow troubles me. For this kind of material—pain, loss, outrage, the defeat of our illusions and of mankind's boasts and pretensions, the fragment seems peculiarly appropriate. The shard. The interrupted gesture. Think of the evening's proceedings as an equivalent of the still-standing columns of the wreck of some temple. Sophocles' building is in a remarkable state of preservation. Euripides' play, *The Phoenician Women,* is rather a wreck, a mishmash, with inconsistencies and interpolations. That was one of its chief attractions for me, actually. I felt sorry for it. My work is an ersatz ruin, an homage, and, in its way, also a joke.

CHORAGOS: I see. Thank you.

(*A bell rings*)

We'd better take our seats. The second part is about to begin.

SENECA: Yes. This is in Thebes. Whatever has happened to Oedipus—death or transfiguration—has happened. He's gone, at any rate. And Antigone has returned to her mother and to Thebes. In Euripides' version, Jocasta has not killed herself but has gone into deep mourning. One may try to imagine the feelings with which she hears of the death of Oedipus, her child, her husband, and the father of her children. . . . One may try. I have. And have failed. Her expression remains impassive altogether.

But her sons, Eteocles and Polynices, are making war; and, in the press of events and in the face of danger to her city and her children, she has been forced back into the public arena. Even though Oedipus is gone, she cannot indulge the feelings with which she received this news—grief, or relief, or some combination.

(SENECA *turns and watches as* JOCASTA *enters. He bows to her and exits.*)

JOCASTA: How lucky was Agave, who hacked her own
    son into pieces. This was divine madness,
    a mystery on which the youth had intruded,
    and what she did was violent but not
    lewd and wanton. I think of her with envy.
    I have borne worse guilt, and it comes back
    to threaten Thebes, my blood crying out for blood.
    I hate what they do, but love them nonetheless—       370
    Polynices, outside the gates in arms,
    and Eteocles here, so stubborn and unjust.
    I love them both and cannot even imagine
    what outcome to pray for. Three long years
    have come and gone while Polynices wandered,
    an exile from his city: I wept for him,
    wished him well, and rejoiced to hear that at last
    his fortunes had improved. Received in Argos
    with honor, he found favor there, and married
    King Adrastus' daughter. I gave thanks,       380
    but now he comes, Adrastus' creature, with all
    the might of the seven allies, to assert
    his right to the Theban throne. Whom can I bless
    without cursing the other? Whom can I pray for?
    Each side appears the weaker, and unjust,
    and calls out to my heart all the more loudly.

(MESSENGER *enters in haste*)

MESSENGER: My lady, the battle lines are drawn. The trumpets
    blare forth baleful challenges. We can see
    the standard-bearers of seven kings, and the field
    is a swarm of men in armor. As they march                          390
    they raise the dust like clouds—or the smoke of fires
    not yet showing their flames. The day is dark
    as if the eye of heaven were turned away,
    and the horses hoofs, churning the turf, add
    to the thick haze in which spearpoints and standards
    glint in menace, thirsty for blood and glory.
    Battle flags flap in the wind, proclaiming
    the great names come here to raven upon us. Help us!
    Intercede, as only you can. Prevent
    the ruin of all our lives and the city's fall                      400
    in this unholy conflict of brothers. Their wounds
    their own mother's words can prevent or cure.

ANTIGONE: Hurry mother! There still is time and the chance
    to intercede. Neither will lift his hand
    to strike at you. Stand between them and stop
    this war or threaten to be the first to die.

JOCASTA: I will. I'll go. And eagerly. I shall set
    my life as of no account between the two
    opposing sides. And any wound must fall
    upon me first. No impious crime shall issue                        410
    from my own issue, nor will I suffer either
    to sin while I look on. I'll strike the second blow
    to kill myself in answer to the first.

ANTIGONE: I fear worse than anything I can imagine.
    The opposing armies close upon one another
    slowly but inexorably. My tears,
    blurring their order, anticipate the tumult
    that is sure to come. I beg you, mother, stop them.

MESSENGER: The chiefs are shouting. The margin between them
    closes.

JOCASTA: I am borne along like a bird in a gale; the winds    420
    of fate that buoy me up can dash me down.
    I cannot control my actions. Like a Harpy
    I go to the battlefield to do what I can,
    not knowing what that is, and not believing
    that anything I may do can come to good.
    Nevertheless, I go to make the attempt.

(*She exits*)

MESSENGER: (*Looking after her*)
    She goes, a vessel tossed on the ocean's waves
    and driven by raging winds. She goes like a star
    dislodged somehow from the firmament and streaking
    across the heavens, leaving its fiery trail    430
    to startle us with awful portent. She goes
    like a mad woman, and who can watch her progress
    and not feel his heart crack and mind give way?
    On both sides now they've stopped, amazed, embarrassed,
    appalled by what they see: a tottering lady
    picking her way across the uneven field.
    They freeze, their sharp swords raised but immobile now,
    and a hush falls on the hosts of both sides. Peace?
    Not yet, but the thought of it surely, and the thought
    gives rise to a glimmer of hope. How can it not?    440
    She tears at her hair and kneels before her children,
    and the tears run down her cheeks and theirs as well.

(*Across the stage,* JOCASTA *kneels between her two hostile sons,*
POLYNICES *and* ETEOCLES)

JOCASTA: At me! Take aim at me, point your sharp blades
    at me, you from Argos and you from Thebes.
    Townsman and foe, brother against his brother . . .
    I cannot endure it. Show me that rough mercy

to close my eyes to what a mother's nightmares
could not envision. Tear me limb from limb.
You are both sprung from my body—do it this last
courtesy, I implore you. We are steeped in sin,                    450
but ignorant sin, the curse of our forebears.
This is knowing, willing, meditated
evil, and I forbid it. We must face our fate
but need not conspire against ourselves or connive
in our own damnations. Neither of you is monstrous
or so far fallen as to be deaf to the plea
of your own mother. I tell you the simple truth,
that I must be the target of any blow
from either side. Your father killed his father:
will you surpass his crime and kill your mother?                   460
To whom should I speak? Whom should I embrace,
implore, beg? If this war is to happen
both of you must reject my supplications.
I love you both, the one who has been absent,
and the other who must go if the arrangement
holds. To see you thus together, touch
you both at once, I may never do again.
(*She turns to* POLYNICES)
Come to my arms, my son. You have endured
the bitterness of exile. You are home,
and you see your mother again. Put up your sword.                  470
Bury the sharp spearpoint in the earth. Take off
the helmet that hides the face I love. You are safe,
for I shall be your shield, my aged body
protecting yours, so that any drop of blood
that spills will be mine. What else have I to live for
except my children and their welfare? Listen,
and trust in the love we feel for one another.

POLYNICES: (*He removes his helmet and lays down his shield*)
   I distrust love and nature itself. If a brother
   betrays his brother, what worth can there be
   in a mother's promise?

JOCASTA:                    You break my heart. Put on          480
the helmet and take your shield again while your brother
disarms himself.
(*She turns to* ETEOCLES)
                    Put down your sword
who are the cause of this sad business. Peace,
a truce, the return of reason—these things I ask
and you must be disarmed even to listen.
You fear him? As he fears you? You refuse?
Are you not ashamed? What kind of son are you
to me, or brother to him? What kind of world
is this? Wild beasts behave in a seemlier way,
show more restraint. You wish to govern men,          490
but nothing governs you! Is there no limit
to brute force, to ambition, to greed? Is there nothing
noble in your soul I can appeal to?
Assume for the moment that your distrust is right,
that danger lurks, that a hostile brother stands
ready to wound—would you not much rather
receive such a blow than give it? Flesh is nothing;
spirit and honor are precious. Look to them!
In sorrow I have mourned these years for your father.
Would you have me envy his blindness now? Must I          500
watch a son attack a son?
(ETEOCLES *sheathes his sword*)
                    Bless you, my child.
Your sword is sheathed. Your deadly spear is lowered.
(*To* POLYNICES)
And will you also yield to prayers? Or tears?
Once more I look upon that face I've longed
to see again, to touch. The poor outcast
is home again. In the palace of my grief,
I have kept a room for you—that I did not
lead you as any mother wants to do
to your bridal chamber. I did not deck the hall
or light the torches. I brought no wedding gift.          510
Bitter tears I shed at these offenses
to both of us. Another king protects you,

and other gods than those of Thebes. Exiled
for no fault of yours, you have roamed the earth
and found a home—for which no man could blame you.
But to come back as an enemy? Your bride's
father is no friend to us. Our house
marries badly—your father did, and you
have done as poorly, making the city suffer.
It is our fate, but the gods are not relentless,                                   520
and we may stop our hands in mid-air, balk,
refuse to serve their dark designs. We can!
I have prayed to see you again, although I knew
the deplorable cost you might impose on us.
It was a risk and yet I delighted in it,
as one may thrill to stand high on a cliff
and feel one's knees turn weak with the altitude.
I have feared for you all these years; must I now
fear you? You can give the word and your host
may yet withdraw. This is a dreadful crime                                         530
for brother to threaten brother, for one to spill
the blood we share more intimately than any
family that ever lived. I rage!
It makes me mad to think of—and pinch myself
as if to wake from a nightmare, but there is no
relief, and no escape, except through your own
decency and honor. Spare the city!
I beg you, by my womb that carried you.
In the name of your sister's love, in the name of your father,
the saddest man I know, whose name is pain,                                        540
relent. Give up your quarrel. Do not press
your reasonable claim. Learn from his anguish,
and try to live so as not to despise yourself,
which is what must happen if you persist in this
impossible business. Look out at that plain
where men at arms stand ready to kill your townsmen,
set fire to our houses, take us captive,
and lead us away in chains. Is this what you want?
The household gods we try to protect are yours,
as this city you threaten is your own fatherland.                                  550

What madness is this, reckless and cruel, that turns
a savage face to what you ought to cherish
as dearly as your life? Assume that you win,
what can you achieve? What city is left
for you to rule, with the crops in the fields all trampled,
and the people homeless, cowering in their caves,
sick, starving, and hating you for the ruin
you have brought them? What could it matter which
of the two of you is king if there's no kingdom?
These walls Amphion built will you now breach                        560
and tear back down to rubble? No hand set
these sacred stones; they leapt into place, enchanted,
dancing to the lyre's magic music,
a miracle—will you undo their charm,
enter the city, face your father's friends,
and choose from the maidens and matrons of your neighbors
household slaves and concubines for your rude
soldiers' prizes? And will you as the king
watch and listen with equanimity
as the weeping women are led away in fetters,                         570
cursing your name and our accursèd house?
Will I lead that procession, your own mother,
a captive of your madness, my hands bound
behind my back, my hair blotting my tears.
Blood and fire are everywhere about us!
What does it mean to rule if not to maintain
safety, justice, and reason—as well as one can?
One makes the attempt at least. Are you so full
of hatred as to be blind and deaf, so set
on revenge that you delight in death and destruction?                580
What kind of man is that to wield a scepter's
power? I cannot imagine what a disaster
your reign would be! Listen to me, your mother!
Come to your senses! Remember who you are!
Surely you must see what is right to do.

POLYNICES: What is right? For me to yield? To wander
  in exile again, as a suppliant and stranger?

Why should I be the one to suffer my brother's
injustice? For his breach of faith, let him
depart. Without a blow on either side,                          590
let him just go. Why do you order me
and not him to yield? Should I live in a hut
while he lords it over Thebes in the palace?
Should he rule a kingdom, and I a chicken yard?
Shall I be my wife's plaything, her father's servant,
something between a jester and a slave?
It's a long fall from the place I had to this
absurdity! Is this what you want for me?

JOCASTA: If you will seize a kingdom, why choose this one?
There are kingdoms everywhere—go conquer one          600
richer than this, where the crops are abundant, the waters
sweet, and the harbors secure and safe. The world
is yours, and with my blessing you may go
anywhere to impose your will and slake
your thirst for power and grandeur. There's a solution
to all our problems! Select a likely place
and we can reconcile our quarrels, you
and your brother, Thebes and Argos. There can be
peace, I say, and the way is compromise!
Your father-in-law looks to enlarge his holdings?          610
Let him do so. We all can be in league
together, happy and prosperous. Your brother
can join with you, can lend you his support
in money and arms. Such an exile would be
no dishonor nor even discomfort—but glory!
Find some primitive people to whom you may bring
the gifts of civilization, culture, religion,
and all those things in which we take such pride.
Everyone benefits! You could take full credit
and the praise men give to those who establish peace.          620
This is the one way to avoid those sins
the terrible stain of which you cannot want
on our name for as long as men remember us,
which is to say, forever. Go with my prayers

and those of your father too for your success.
Go with your strength augmented, knowing how fickle
Mars can be. Battle is always doubtful,
your careful plans and fondest hopes at risk
as surely as the soldiers in the field.
The prize may be within your grasp and yet                    630
gone, snatched from your hand, and dashed forever
upon the bloody field. You may rely
on guilt but not the gift that guilt may get you.
Assume that all is well, your expectations
satisfied and exceeded—assume a rout.
What honor is there in your city then
for you to preside over? Where's your triumph?
And who will honor you? The price you'll pay
will be too dear. You'll hate the crown you've won.
Give it up. It's not too late. I tell you                     640
you can withdraw, spare your city this
disaster, and spare your mother as bitter tears
as I have ever shed.

POLYNICES:              My cursed brother
    pays no price at all for his betrayal?

JOCASTA: Don't worry on his account. He'll pay. He'll reign—
    and that's his penalty. No one in the house
    of Laius ever sits easy on a throne.
    There'll be disaster. I have no doubt of that.
    Be patient and you'll hear, I promise, news
    to make you smile, or weep, and prompt your thanks         650
    that you are free of the burden.

ETEOCLES:                        But I'm not free.
    I am a king, living or dead.
    (*To* POLYNICES)
                        And you
    are exiled, on my life. I do declare it.

JOCASTA: (*To* ETEOCLES) You'll be a hated king. Is that what you
    want?

ETEOCLES: To rule is to be hated. They go together.
    To rule and be loved is an idle fancy any
    sovereign soon discards. The people's love
    is a drug, pleasant enough at first but it saps
    the courage one needs in order to govern well.
    Their hatred, meanwhile is rather a tonic, I find.                    660

JOCASTA: A hated king never rules for long.

ETEOCLES:                                          We'll see.
    Exile can last a good while, but for kingship,
    I'd say . . .

JOCASTA: You're willing to risk your home, your city?
    Your honor?

ETEOCLES:              Pay any price—with my face on the money.
    (*They freeze into a tableau*)

CHORAGOS: That's it? But what happens? What kind of an ending is
    that? Is this your idea of a play?

SENECA: But you know perfectly well what happens. Eteocles and
    Polynices kill one another. Eteocles is buried with honor, and
    Polynices is left out there on the field until Antigone defies Cre-
    on's order and buries her brother. And is put to death for what
    she's done. But we know all that. It follows inevitably, from the
    moment the two sons turn away from their mother's perfectly
    reasonable and, I think, quite eloquent arguments. That's where
    the tragedy is—that language itself is useless. That the passions,
    though stupid, are powerful and real, and that logic and rhetoric
    and all those things we say we live for are all but irrelevant.

CHORAGOS: Is this your idea of a play?

SENECA: No, probably, not. But it's my idea of the truth. Of reality. Of how we live. As I suggested earlier, the making of perfect plays seems wrong, somehow, when we live in such a shambles. Stupidity and blood cannot be represented by shapely verse dramas with decorous choruses mouthing platitudes.

CHORAGOS: They never did show up, those Phoenician women, did they?

SENECA: No. I'm sorry. Not for my play so much as for the world we live in, which is, I agree, outrageous. The eloquence of the characters seems to me heartbreaking, considering how ineffective it turns out to be. Antigone is eloquent too, even though she has nothing to say in this second scene, but she is there, for us to look at and weep for. We know it is her life they are throwing away. And sometimes, I have the notion, she knows it too.

CHORAGOS: You might have indicated that. It would have been effective.

SENECA: What would there have been for her to say? Or for me to put into her mouth? Screams of agony? Tears at the stupidity of what was happening—tears that would be all the more bitter because these people are her family, the people she loves. The Greeks understood that. And the Romans. I think you understand it, too. Thank you for coming. I apologize for the play, and for the world, and wish you a good night.

## Acknowledgments

Parts of Dana Gioia's Introduction to this volume have appeared in *The New Criterion, Sparrow, The Formalist, Image, Tennessee Quarterly, Hellas, Carolina Quarterly, Spectrum* (Scotland), and *Edge City Review*; and Juno's monologue of his *Hercules Furens* was published by Aralia Press in a chapbook entitled *Juno Plots Her Revenge.*

Portions of Rachel Hadas's translation of *Oedipus* appeared in *Other Worlds Than This*, a collection of her translations published by Rutgers University Press.

Kelly Cherry's Introduction first appeared as "Postmodern Poetry in Ancient Rome: On Translating the *Octavia* of Seneca," in *Classical and Modern Literature.*

A scene from Act V of Stephen Sandy's *Hercules Oetaeus* appeared in a festshrift for Edwin Honig, published by Brown University Press.

The first scene of David R. Slavitt's version of *Phoenissae* appeared as "On Cithaeron," in *Grand Street.*